THE VILLAGE THAT WAS FORMBY

(Incorporating MY FORMBY and FORMBY REMEMBERED)

by
JOAN A. RIMMER

Illustrations by Muriel Sibley

This edition first published in Great Britain in 2007 by
Nirvana Books
Mayfield Court   Victoria Road
Freshfield   Liverpool   L37 7TL

A catalogue record for this book is available
from the British Library.

10 9 8 7 6 5 4 3 2 1

ISBN 978-09549427-7-9

Printed and bound by
T. Snape Ltd. Boltons Court, Preston PR1 3TY

ACKNOWLEDGEMENTS

I am indebted to so many kind people for their help in making this book possible. They are all deserving of acknowledgement but are unfortunately far too numerous to mention individually. Without their assistance I could never have attempted this work, and so to each and everyone one who talked to me, lent me their photographs and other material, and endured my endless questions I thank them from the bottom of my heart. This is their book as much as mine.

INTRODUCTION

MY FORMBY was published in 1989 followed by FORMBY REMEMBERED in 1992. To my surprise and delight both books became immediate local best sellers and have long been out of print. I have, however, continued to receive numerous requests for them which I have always regretted being unable to supply. Throughout these intervening years Formby has undergone yet more enormous and unimagined change, and so in response to those requests this completely new and up-dated edition brings back into print both my previous titles together with a wealth of new material covering many of the more recent events which have further distanced our present town from its original farming roots.

Despite all the changes and my strong opposition to many of them my love of Formby remains and always will, and I count myself truly blessed to have been born and still live in this very special place.

I hope all readers will find interest and enjoyment in sharing these memories and observations of THE VILLAGE THAT WAS FORMBY.

CONTENTS

MY FORMBY

Recollections of Village Life

FOREWORD

In 1987 when my first collection of poems was published I little knew of the enormous interest they would generate, and that such simple verses of everyday events and people would prove so popular. Within weeks 2,000 copies had sped around Formby and across the world. The following year my second publication appeared and the whole nostalgia scene was in full swing. It seemed that everyone had an insatiable yearning for the past – for a way of life that had somehow drifted into oblivion. Progress had swept us all along unawares and the vast changes around us had been a gradual process, slightly bewildering, mildly regrettable, but apathetically accepted as inevitable until suddenly one tiny book of poems seemed to stop us all in our tracks.

We are not unique. There are countless 'Formbys' up and down the land whose small communities have been swallowed up or taken over. For those like myself who remember it all there must be regrets for what we have lost and for our impotence in allowing it all to happen. For newcomers there is a curiosity of how it used to be and an incredulity of such change. For all of us there should be interest and a little concern. It has happened. We cannot go back. But we can look back and we can remember. For every poem I have written there are many stories some of which I would like to share with you in recalling the village I loved so dearly. As a conclusion to the book both volumes of my poems, originally published under the titles FORMBY MEMORIES and MORE FORMBY MEMORIES and now out of print again, have by request been added, together with a further selection, as a relevant part of the Formby story. I hope that a younger generation may also find the book interesting. My thanks go to all the people of Formby with whom I grew up and lived amongst. They made the story. All I have done is to tell it in the way I remember it.

Formby was a magical place when I was a child. Looking back to those wartime days it is difficult to envisage that childhood village when looking at Formby today. This trip down memory lane will recall the characters and places which were the cornerstones of life here in those not too far off days which could be a million years ago.

I do not want to dwell too much on my ancestry but it does seem relevant to use some space in establishing where I fit into the story and give a little of my background. My parents, like their parents etc., were sandgrounders. My mother's family were staunchly Roman Catholic, and it was viewed with horror by them all when my mother committed the mortal sin of marrying my father, an equally devout Protestant, at St Michael's Church, Altcar on 21st October 1929. The rift continued until some six years later when their first and only children, my twin brother and I, were born on 29th April 1935 and we seemed to some extent to heal the breach in the relationship.

Religious intolerance at that time was very intense in Formby and it was only in later years I realised how very courageous my mother had been in defying her mother and how very much she must have cared for my father to do so. A very

St. Michael's Church, Altcar

formidable lady was my grandmother! My grandmother's maiden name was Alice Formby. She came from a farming family and on leaving Our Lady's School became a teacher there until her marriage to Thomas Ashcroft. She had five surviving children and my mother, Annie, being the eldest was expected to bear much of the household responsibilities.

My grandfather died before I was born, but quite early in his married life had suffered a severe accident in which he lost his leg. Times were hard and my grandmother and all the children worked tirelessly to make a living. As the family

My mother

My father

grew up my grandmother became the proprietress of the local fish and chip shop, a venture viewed with great disdain by other branches of the family, where she worked extremely hard, with her two daughters, my mother and my aunt Edith, as almost unpaid slaves. She also showed great enterprise and business acumen by dabbling in property deals and moving from house to house quite frequently, borrowing money to do so – something quite extraordinary in those days for a woman with a disabled husband, a large family and no capital.

My mother's entire life seemed to consist of hard work. On leaving school, unlike most working-class girls who went into service, she worked in the office of MacSymon's grocery store in Formby Village learning the rudiments of book-keeping and accounts. She moved from there to Bobby's, a high class department store in Lord Street, Southport (much later to become Debenham's) starting off as the office junior and quickly climbing the ladder to eventually take charge of the accounts department. Again unlike the norm for those times she continued working after her marriage staying with Bobby's for thirteen happy years and leaving them only two months before the birth of my twin brother and myself. From then onwards she worked indefatigably for my grandmother at the chip shop lifting and carrying great sacks of potatoes, 'eyeing' potatoes by hand in icy buckets of water as well as looking after us all at home. The early death of my father necessitated her finding a job and this was when she joined the counter staff of Rimmer's fruit and vegetable shop (no relation) on the corner of the village, only leaving them to nurse her mother through her final illness. After the death of my grandmother she went back to work again this time at Ewing's cake shop in the Village where she stayed until retiring in her 60's. For the remainder of her life she played an active part in the village community establishing, along with her namesake Councillor Jimmy Rimmer's wife, the weekly whist drives at the

Luncheon Club, and continuing in office with the Women's Gas Federation, of which she was a founder member, until ill health forced her resignation. She was very kind, generous, and wise. She was also my best friend. She died a few days after her 83rd birthday in January 1987.

My father came from Great Altcar, though the family were originally from Formby. I have a family tree dating back to 1640 on my father's side and it gives me pleasure to see that one of his forebears, Dr. James Longton, was the first doctor to practice medicine in Southport. It would appear that somewhere along the line the family slid rapidly down the social scale when probably my great grandfather appeared on the scene. This is only supposition, but from being landowners and gentry there was obviously some fall from grace as my grandfather, Robert Rimmer, who I remember so vividly and was the salt of the earth, could never have been described as gentry! He was a grand old chap – very forthright and down-to-earth, but like so many country people unrefined and uneducated. He was a farm worker and a genius with cattle and crops, always winning with his prize cows at the annual Formby Flower Show.

My grandmother was a quiet, gentle and lovely lady who bore him a daughter and four sons. Polly, the eldest, worked all her life at the Formby Golf Club and was loved and respected by all, from the staff to the members and guests including the then Prince of Wales, later the Duke of Windsor. My brother and I adored her and spent countless happy hours at the Golf Club in a world far removed from our own. The four sons were all fine strapping young men and all tragically and unaccountably died in their 40's and 50's leaving their parents to mourn them. My father, Richard, was 51 when he died, a tragic loss to us and to the many people who loved him. He was a kind, gentle and happy man – a true gentleman in every sense of the word, and to this day I have never heard anyone speak ill of him. My grandfather outlived all his family and died in his 80's and was laid to rest alongside them all in Altcar churchyard.

That then is a potted background to my family. What follows is my life in the most idyllic of settings – the Formby of my childhood.

My earliest recollections are of the outbreak of war when I was just four years of age. My brother, Derek, and I were playing along our side path when my mother rushed out and brought us in telling us that war had started. I think I vaguely expected bombs to fall and guns to fire. Nothing happened at all.

We started school at Holy Trinity in 1940 still unaffected by the war, and those years at that tiny school were probably amongst the happiest of my life. Formby's population was around 7,000 though evacuees were beginning to arrive from Liverpool. We country children were a bit afraid of these streetwise kids with their strange accents who seemed so much tougher than we who had led such sheltered lives, but like children the world over we all mixed in together and life was fun.

I remember clearly the day I started school. My brother and I stood hand in hand inside the classroom door. My mother left us, and my brother immediately fled from the classroom to follow and find her, leaving me next to another small boy, now a successful tradesmen in Formby, whose mother had also just departed leaving him in the classroom. He, obviously very frightened by his new

The Post Office and Holy Trinity School

surroundings, promptly wet the floor. I stood silently in total perplexity at the strange behaviour of these two boys.

We had just three classrooms and three teachers at Holy Trinity. Miss Reily, the headmistress, Miss Culshaw, the infant teacher, and Miss Heaton. Miss Heaton was everything the other two were not. A local girl, young, attractive, sang in the church choir, and played the piano. We would all stand around her piano and sing our hearts out as she accompanied us. The school had a small variety of musical instruments and when we had music lessons I always longed for the tambourine and always got the triangle. I still remember the bitter disappointment of producing a pathetic ping from the instrument when I so desperately wanted to be responsible for a gigantic sound. The boys maybe fared less well with Miss Heaton. She was strict, as were all our teachers, and used the ruler mercilessly on those boys who misbehaved, but she only ever needed to use it once. We all loved her and would do anything to please her and when she married the curate from our church, the Rev. Fred Bussby, it seemed a fairy tale come true.

Miss Culshaw was quiet and patient and seemed rather in awe of Miss Reily. She drove a car which for a woman in those days was quite unusual. She had a difficult job in starting off the basic education of us all. Her class-room had a big fireplace with a roaring fire blazing, a rocking horse in the corner, and charts around the walls with a large number on each followed by the appropriate number of spots to indicate that number. To make a number 5 we were instructed to make the boiler, then the chimney and then the smoke! We were all relentlessly rehearsed in our 'times' tables – something I have never forgotten and in the age of the calculator might seem totally unnecessary but to me, and no doubt all my contemporaries, is a priceless asset. Reading, writing and arithmetic were the essentials.

Miss Reily was the very masculine head of the school, completely unconcerned with her appearance and claiming never to use a mirror. She wore the same hat throughout her entire working life. She was tall and angular with enormous bony hands and feet, and when peering at the classroom clock seemed to develop a grimacing squint. Miss Reily instilled terror into our very souls with her tremendous bellow, but although she was feared she was also respected, and as we grew older held in great affection by many. Her Christian kindness to those children in any way underprivileged was illustrated in many ways and especially in her generosity in having children to stay at her home in Southport for short holidays. She read us enchanting stories and poems. She took us on nature walks

The Village cottages of Mawdsleys and Wainds

where we identified so many different wild flowers, trees, and birds. Great emphasis was laid on neatness and correct spelling, and there was a definite yet unobtrusive religious background to our education with prayers and hymns being held every morning and evening. Our vicar, Canon Dawson, was a familiar figure to us all and every Christmas would come into the school and give each child a silver threepenny bit.

Miss Reily's home was in Southport but during the war years when transport wasn't always reliable she lodged at Raby Bank, a large detached house owned by Mrs. Rennie on the corner of Elbow Lane and Cropton Road (now replaced by a modern house). Her lunch (or rather dinner as we called it), in the days before school meals, was cooked for her by Mrs. Waind, an old lady who lived in one of the nearby cottages in the Village, and at 12 noon two children would be sent to collect the meal. On one occasion, a Pancake Tuesday in fact, as the girls were carrying the dinner to the school a dog jumped up and ate the pancake. In fear and trepidation the empty plate was produced. It seemed such a feeble excuse to say a dog had eaten the pancake, but presumably for that very reason Miss Reily accepted the explanation. In later years and especially towards the end of her teaching career Miss Reily mellowed considerably and the familiar sight of her striding figure accompanied by countless children all vying for the distinction of carrying her case to and from the station was an indication of the feelings of her young charges.

All our teachers were strict disciplinarians and there were probably times when we hated them – or thought we did! We all knew without any doubt the fate which would befall us if we misbehaved, and most of us had the good sense to avoid such punishment. Whether we did so or not their treatment of us left no emotional scars in later years, and in fact our teachers were held in great affection and remembered with gratitude for their care and dedication.

The school itself was a solid red brick building at the end of the Village next to the bank and the post office. The tiny cloakroom was immediately inside the entrance with the largest classroom beyond the cloakroom. A partition divided that classroom from the smaller one at the far end of the school from which we entered the playground. The infants' classroom was on the right of the school. The playground was minute with all the toilets situated across the yard, and come rain, hail or snow the only way to reach them was by running through the puddles

The Village

to the freezing compartments at the other side. We never lingered long. The playground was so tiny that when the weather was suitable we were all taken in a long crocodile to Duke Street Park for games, or football in the case of the boys. If the weather was bad we all filed into the parish hall for country dancing.

Being at school during the war meant carrying our gas masks with us every day. Mine was an ordinary model in a cardboard box which was slung across my shoulder, and how I envied those fortunate children who had Mickey Mouse gas masks. We were all expected to wear our gas masks on the days we were taken to the air raid shelter behind the Beauford Hall as an emergency exercise, but as the horrible contraption almost caused me to suffocate I never did actually put mine properly on my face.

There was a little passage way through to the school entrance alongside the Village shops. Walking home through the Village we first passed McLardy's outfitters where Lizzie Massam was the assistant and where her invalid sister could often be seen in her bath chair outside the door watching the comings and goings of the customers.

Lovelady's cake shop was next door and the smell of freshly baked bread from the bake-house wafted across our tiny playground. It was a real treat when we could afford a ha'penny to buy a crusty cob to eat on the way home. The window's of Lovelady's were covered with big brown blinds on Wednesday afternoons which was half day closing, and we children would all take turns to stand half way in the doorway raising one arm and leg to see our reflection in the window as though both arms and legs were being raised – a trick enjoyed by comedian Harry Worth on a very much later T.V programme.

Next to Lovelady's were the two cottages of Ben Mawdsley and his sister Sally Postlethwaite and her family, and their neighbours, the Wainds. The huge pear tree in Mawdsley's garden was always laden with fruit, and flowers grew profusely. Golding's the cobblers came next, and then Wright's fruit and vegetable shop. Charlie Sole had a tiny shop where he sold and repaired clocks and watches, and Clinch's the cleaners was alongside with a public clock above their shop and where Rose Gallagher was in charge of our sartorial cleanliness.

Irwin's the grocers came next with Fred Stevens on the bacon slicer and Peter Thomas on the delivery van, then Clague's the chemists next to Inchboard's haberdashery and Parker's haberdashery and hairdressers. These shops were

Mr. Clague and Mr. Corless outside their pharmacy (now McDougall's)

protected by iron verandahs giving shelter on rainy days, and were ideal meeting places for our mothers to chat. Bill Swift's bike shop was next, across the entry, with the most jumbled mess of rusty articles covered in dust. The boys cat-called at old Bill who often lay in wait with a tin-can full of water, which we strongly suspected was his own, and pitched the lot over the nearest child.

Halstead's butchers was next door and then Ernie Bill's saddlery (he later moved down the Village next to the school). With so many farms in the village Mr. Bills had a thriving saddlery business and the wonderful smell of leather pervaded the shop as you entered. Apart from the obvious work on saddles and bridles he dealt in any type of leather work. As we grew older and became the proud possessors of school satchels they invariably needed repairing at the end of term and at the start of the long summer holidays. We always took them to Mr. Bills immediately we broke up school and always without fail at the end of the holidays we would still be pestering him for the return of the satchels. We never got them back until the day before returning to school which in Mr. Bills' opinion was just what we needed and quite soon enough! Mr. Bills also had the important job of carrying out any repairs to the huge Union Jack flag which was displayed on the Council Offices flag pole.

The Food Office was next (on the site of the present Gas Showrooms) set back in a garden, with Freddy Norburn in charge, and where our mothers queued up for our ration books. Everything from food to clothing was rationed, but despite the meagre rations we were very fortunate to be living in the country where most people grew their own vegetables, kept poultry, and knew how to acquire the odd hare or pheasant. We were particularly lucky having grandparents living in the farming community of Altcar and therefore there was no noticeable shortage of fresh vegetables, fruit, eggs and when a pig was killed (by licence of course!), pork, bacon and the most delicious black puddings in the world. My grandmother was renowned for her home-made black puddings, and whenever a pig was killed the blood and fat were brought to her. The recipe unfortunately died with her, but they were without doubt, along with her potato cakes, the most delectable ever made. We would also bring home eggs to be put in a bucket of waterglass to preserve them. Taking the eggs out of the bucket involved groping about in the cold, revolting, gluey mess, and it was enough to put anyone off eggs for ever.

Dalley's grocers were next to the Food Office, then an electrical and radio shop, followed by Charlie Stevens, the chemist, who made a miraculous chilblain stick, then the toy shop and Clark's cake shop at the end just before Martin's Bank. There were always queues at Clark's for their delicious confectionery and home-made bread which cost 4½d for a large loaf and required bread units (B.U.'s).

Behind this row of shops the police horses were stabled, the stables later becoming the garage of Mr. Warr, with the dancing class above. That then was the school side of the Village.

Directly opposite the school was a large house called The Elms, which later was bought by a Mrs. Vandervord who changed the name to The Priory and for a time became a private hotel. The house was surrounded by huge elm trees and a plethora of plants grew in the spacious gardens. For many years a parrot in a cage hung outside the door and was notorious for its wolf whistles which could on

Mr. Warr's garage

Previously called The Elms and now a block of shops housing the new Post Office in Brows Lane

occasions be a cause of embarrassment. We all took delight in whistling to the bird and waiting for its penetrating reply.

Beyond The Priory and opposite the post office was a small shop belonging to Ashcroft's the painter and decorator which later became Delahunty's. When Delahunty's extended their shop there was a tree which grew right across the entrance and which customers had to dodge round to enter the shop.

Crossing the road from the school was the Bon Bon sweet shop on the corner with Greenhalgh's fent shop along the side of Elbow Lane. Mr. Greenhalgh was often seen pedalling around Formby with his wares in a type of side car attached to his bicycle. The proprietor of the Bon Bon was Mr. Gilbert, a character reminiscent of Uriah Heep always wringing his hands and asking "Anything else?" Mr. Gilbert was never keen on giving change and always used his persuasive wiles in trying to coax his customers into spending every penny they had. Anyone foolish enough, or well-heeled enough, to tender a pound note for a penny box of matches would be asked "Anything else for the odd 19/11d?" Many of the young lads of the village would often go to the Bon Bon at night time after the shop had closed for cigarettes. They would rattle on the door, and down would come Mr. Gilbert who would never open the door, but neither would he refuse a sale. He would ask through the letter-box what they wanted and they would shout back their order. He always insisted on the money being dropped through the letter-box before parting with the cigarettes, and invariably he would push through an inferior brand – usually Black Cat, Robin, or Turf – and as he already had the money there was nothing anyone could do about it.

Charters' the butchers, Johnson's the cleaners, and Rawsthorne's upholsterers were next, followed by Elliott's with their open front to the shop and a blazing coal fire very often fighting a losing battle against the elements and being extremely cold and draughty where John and Janie Berry and May Holden served the fish, fruit and vegetables.

Sanderson's, who owned the farm and slaughter-house in Duke Street near to the park, had the ice-cream parlour next door to Elliott's, and then came old Mrs. Smith's sweet shop. This shop was rather dingy and despite it probably being the most popular place in the Village for children we always had to be on our best behaviour. Mrs. Smith had a very brusque manner and would always put us in our place. Anyone entering her shop eating a biscuit would be told in no uncertain

Duke Street: the Doctor's surgery was on the left; further on the left was
Sanderson's farm and slaughter house

Mrs. Smith's sweet shop, with Evans' cottage set back

terms to go and buy their sweets from where they'd got their biscuit. In common with many old people at that time she had a deep mistrust of banks and was reputed to have money hidden away in the fabric of the walls of her shop. She certainly always seemed to be able to lay her hands on ready cash and on chocolate bars and sweets when there was a dearth everywhere else. Her shop later became modernised with an attractive bow window when Mrs. Gerrard became the proprietress.

Evans little cottage stood alongside Mrs. Smith's and was set back with a long garden full of various types of flowers. Bennett's newsagents, with a gents' outfitters in one half of the shop run by Stanley Taylor, started the next run of shops where I queued for almost an hour one November the 5th to buy a ha'penny banger. On their outside wall was a huge blue and white thermometer advertising Stephen's ink.

Derbyshire's sweets and tobacconists were next, then Tilly Woodfin's cake shop with an ornate wedding cake always displayed beneath a large glass dome. MacSymon's the grocers came next and then Charlie Kershaw with his second-hand furniture shop. Charlie Kershaw used a handcart to transport his second-hand furniture and was a familiar sight around the roads of Formby. His was a thriving business making it possible for many families to furnish their homes, however sparsely, with the basic essentials of chairs, tables, and beds. Hire purchase was still a thing of the future and even when it was first introduced was viewed with great scepticism by many who had been brought up to buy only what they could afford. As many could barely afford to live Charlie Kershaw was a constant source of salvation. Another second-hand dealer was Mr. Winstanley who also flourished from other people's cast-offs.

The Chandler's, Formby Village

Ewing's cakes and bakery shop, with Brenda Emblen
(daughter of the owner) with her children

Mrs. Ewing in the family shop, 1962

Tommy Makin's barbers

MacSymon's (later Ruff's) was a very superior and high-class grocery store. The tantalising aroma of freshly-ground coffee greeted each customer, and the huge bacon-slicer set on the polished wooden counter was a fascination to watch in action. The staff of all our shops remained static with many starting and finishing their working lives with the same firm. This meant that regular customers knew the staffs very well indeed and received real personal service with the shop assistants almost knowing the customers' needs before asking for them. Harry Mawdsley, Joe Norris, Bill Norris, and Joan Rimmer (yet another one!) were just some of the long standing employees who remained with the firm until retirement, and no doubt their successors would have done so too had the firm and they survived.

Next door was Norman's cake shop (later to become Ewing's and where my mother worked for the latter part of her working life until her retirement), followed by Williams Deacons Bank, with Hurst's chandlers and hardware next door. Then came Tommy Makin the barber, Alderson's butchers, and the famous Rimmer's on the corner.

Rimmer's windows were a delight to behold. Jimmy Rimmer, our local councillor who held office as the chairman of the council eleven times, was responsible for the fruit and vegetables, and the windows were his pride and joy. During the war years produce was scarce and the first banana I ever saw was

The famous Rimmer's (pre-war) – now the T.S.B.

when I was probably ten years of age and it was being eaten by a school friend, Ken Pinkstone, who carefully peeled and devoured it whilst we all stood staring in wonderment.

It was after the war that the windows of Rimmer's became the splendid displays they were. They were most beautifully arranged in perfectly balanced pyramids of apples, oranges, pears, potatoes, tomatoes, cauliflowers, onions, and every other fruit and vegetable imaginable. It was a positive art show, and the windows were never disturbed whilst the shop was open – all the produce for sale being taken from behind the displays. In the middle of the shop towards the back

The Village

was the office with a colourful array of flowers and plants neatly arranged around it and where Miss Shan and Elsie Bridge carried out the work of invoicing and accounts. The fish and poultry department was on the opposite side to the fruit and vegetables with Bobby Rimmer, another of the family partners, in charge.

Once a week Bobby would travel to the family's other shop at Ormskirk with the lorry loaded up with boxes of fish and sacks of potatoes, and as very young children we would enjoy the thrill of travelling, along with his own children, on the back of the lorry, all of us rolling around as the old vehicle swung round the twisting roads through Altcar and Downholland on its journey to Ormskirk amid screams of delight from us all.

Rimmer's was an old established family business which like most businesses at that time provided a free delivery service to their customers. Every Wednesday, during the time my mother was employed there in the 1950's, it was her job to cycle around the entire Formby area to collect the lists of orders from their customers. She would set off for the Freshfield end and work her way back to the south of the village. This would take her the whole day, and in the winter months when the weather was often very bad with heavy snowfalls she would carry out the work on foot. This would then take two days to get round, but it never occurred to her, or indeed would it have to anyone else, that she was doing anything unusual. The orders were then made up for the customers and delivered by an errand boy on a bicycle, or if too large by the van driven by Nellie Rimmer, another of the family partners.

Nellie was quite a character, very over-weight, and the butt of endless jokes from her brothers in the business. Whenever Nellie took her holidays her brother, Jim, would always inform the customers that she was off to Woodward's weigh-bridge to make sure the transport could carry her. He also insisted that she was paid a weekly wage by Raleigh for proving the strength of their cycles. On one occasion she was riding her bicycle towards the shop with a large box balanced across the handle-bars. No doubt because of her size and the cumbersome load she was carrying she was finding difficulty in getting off the bicycle. She went round the round-about for the first time shouting to Jim to help her with the box. The unfortunate woman was left to cycle round and round the island whilst Jim stood alongside shouting, "Just one more time, Nell" to the amusement of all the passers by. After five circular tours he went to her rescue.

Throughout my mother's employment at Rimmer's I know what a happy shop it was. The work was hard, the hours were long, and the pay was low, but the general congeniality was quite superb, and no doubt very similar to that of all the other Village shops at that time.

One of Rimmer's regular customers was the very precocious young son of a respected local family. The staff were all mature women and dreaded the appearance of this child who treated them as positive serfs. One day he asked my mother for a cucumber which she selected and was about to place in his basket, when he sneered "Not that one – a decent sized one" and pointed to a large green marrow. Before my mother could speak Marcia Ashton leapt forward, snatched the cucumber from my mother and placed the great marrow in his basket. He paid for his goods and marched smugly out of the shop. The marrow was never returned, but he was decidedly subdued on his next visit to the shop.

Another regular shopper was Miss Ainsworth who drove around the village in her motorised wheelchair and would stop outside the shops and batter furiously with her walking stick on the plate glass windows for attention. How the windows survived her onslaught was nothing short of a miracle, and the sheer ferocity of her attacks never failed to have the desired effect of bringing the shop assistant racing outside to give her instant service.

All the shops closed every day for lunch between 1 p.m. and 2 p.m. One interesting incident occurred when Jimmy Rimmer had remained at the shop during the lunch hour and whilst the shop was closed. He was busy in the back yard stacking orange and banana boxes when a young man appeared and asked whether there were any cafes in the area. "No" replied Jim "but there's Mrs. Trevitt's chip shop round the corner and if you're going you can get some for me". With that the young man disappeared returning a few minutes later with two parcels of chips and fish. They both sat on a banana box talking and eating, and eventually the young man rose to leave explaining that he was addressing a meeting of the Ladies Co-operative Guild which met above Alderson's butchers next door. When Jim later saw Mrs Blackley, the secretary of the Guild, he (being a prominent Conservative councillor) joked with her that they must be desperate having a "young scruff like that as a speaker". "Mr Rimmer", she haughtily replied, "that young man will one day be Prime Minister of this country". "If he's ever Prime Minister, then I'll be King of England" Jim retorted. Jimmy Rimmer was never King of England but Harold Wilson did become Prime Minister, and it was always with great pleasure that Jim remembered his encounter on the banana box.

Turning into Three Tuns Lane was still regarded as 'the Village' with Winstanley's second hand shop, then Miss Holden's haberdashery, Ackers the cobblers, and Soapy Smith's chandlery.

At the far end of Three Tuns Lane, beyond the Queens Cinema, the Conservative Club, and Mawdsley and Tyrer's decorators, was the second shop of Alderson's butchers, with Alice Mercer's sweet shop next door where she sold the most delicious home-made ice-cream but only wafers – no cornets available! and where she also stocked anything allied to the Catholic Church.

Next door was the cake shop of Mrs. Parr. Mrs Parr was a very small and bustling lady whose husband owned the garage next to the Police Station. Her shop was quite spacious but was completely bare, with totally empty shelves and counter adorned with paper doylies, and a huge mirror on the wall. The bake-house was behind the shop and a good fifty yards away and Mrs. Parr must have walked miles in the course of a day as every item asked for had to be brought from the bake-house. To add to all this trailing about she never waited, or asked , for a complete list of each customer's order but would take off at a gallop for a loaf, bring it back, then race back again for a cake, and so it went on. All this quite unnecessary exercise must have been a factor in her longevity as Mrs. Parr lived well into her 90's still making wedding and celebration cakes almost to the end.

Although these shops were not strictly considered to be part of the Village, they were all close enough to be very busy businesses. Chapel Lane (The Village) officially stopped at the round-about, but we still thought of the beginning of School Lane as part of the Village with Slater's grocers on the corner of Halsall Lane run by two brothers, Wilf and Neville. Theirs was a similar shop to MacSymon's, with a long scrubbed white-wood counter and the traditional big bacon slicer, and the same aroma of coffee filling the air, and sacks full of produce on the floor. Annie Brooks was their main assistant until the business closed and she moved across to MacSymon's. One regular customer, renowned for her penny pinching ways, used to come in every Friday morning carrying a telegram form picked up from the Post Office on which her weekly order had been written – very much cheaper than writing her order on her own notepaper!

Slater's grocers and the Library

Next door was the Library in a tiny shop with Mrs. Derbyshire in charge of a very limited stock of books. She was a widow and had originally been a dressmaker before ruling us with a rod of iron in the Library inspecting our hands before allowing us anywhere near a book. Although the children's section consisted of only a few shelves of books the selection available was a treasure trove. Long before the advent of television the only home entertainment was the wireless with such wonderful programmes as Dick Barton Special Agent which we eagerly listened to every weekday at 6.45 p.m. always ending on a cliff-hanger. There was also Happidrome and Monday Night at Eight with some wonderful characters known as Ramsbottom, Enoch, and Me, and a slot in the programme called Penny on the Drum. We were entertained by the inimitable Tommy Handley and his ITMA show embracing such characters as Colonel Chinstrap, Fumf, Mrs. Mop and all the rest. Books and reading, therefore, were our main recreation, and free access to what could never otherwise have been available was a privilege greatly appreciated. Even the forbidding Mrs. Derbyshire didn't deter us from the literature which so enriched our leisure hours. Derbyshire's sweet shop also ran a small private library for which each borrower paid a lending fee. Quite a coincidence that two Derbyshire's should be concerned with our reading matter.

Next door to the Library was Needham's electrical shop where my grandparents took their accumulator to be charged for their wireless set. Living in Altcar, even as late as the 1950's, they did not enjoy the amenities of electricity or gas and relied solely on oil lamps for light, and coal for heating and cooking, and in fact when Altcar became electrified my grandparents were the last to be connected and resisted the change until the bitter end not wanting to be involved with such a new-fangled, dangerous, and utterly unnecessary invention.

As well as being a bustling commercial centre during the day the Village was also residential with many of the shop owners or their employees living above the shops, and therefore even at nights and week-ends when the shops were closed there was always plenty of activity.

This then was our Village, and these were the family businesses which served the community and which we passed every day coming and going to school. Not a super-market or building society in sight and only two estate agents, one run by Mr. Pickstone, and the other by Noel Evans, with Harry McNamee, tucked away on the corner of Elbow Lane.

On both sides of the Village grew huge horse chestnut trees giving the whole tree lined thoroughfare an air of grandeur, and the road surface itself was completely uncluttered by the total absence of today's hideous but necessary yellow lines.

In addition to all these Village shops Formby had numerous small general shops scattered throughout the area, many in close proximity to one another. Mrs. Mitton was one shopkeeper who had actually lived in Southport before emigrating to Australia in 1904. To travel 12,000 miles and take half a year to get there only to find a barren wasteland must have been soul destroying. To immediately turn round and come back again seems to add the comic touch. However, without that arduous and futile journey Formby would have been the poorer. Her shop was as dark as a dungeon and very small but was full of all manner of goods. The lane in which she lived was later named after her but spelt differently. She lived her final years in a flat in Chindit Close and died at the grand old age of 104 in the early 1960's.

Apart from Mrs. Mitton, my grandfather's sister, Jessie, had a similar type of shop in Cummins Avenue. She had been employed at the Formby Golf Club for many years and late in life married the golf steward, Mr. Ferris, moving with him to the shop. She was a refined, gentle lady, and the complete antithesis of her brother, my grandfather. Like Mrs. Mitton, and indeed the majority of these shopkeepers, she also lived to a great age remaining active almost to the very end of her 96th year.

Just across the road in Massams Lane was another general shop belonging to Hepworth's (previously Aldred's).

Devon Cottage, Cummins Avenue (next door to Mrs. Ferris' shop)

Mrs. Mercer was another old lady who had another such shop at Cross Green, and yet another was Butterworth's next door to the Royal Hotel. On the corner of Marina Road was Creek's general shop, and over the Eccles crossing railway line was Tickle's and Shadbolt's.

Opposite the Police Station–Rothwell's Stores–Mayoral procession:
Councillors Jimmy Rimmer, Ernest Duke, Mr. John Breese, followed by
Southport's Mayor Alderman Townend (in the top hat)

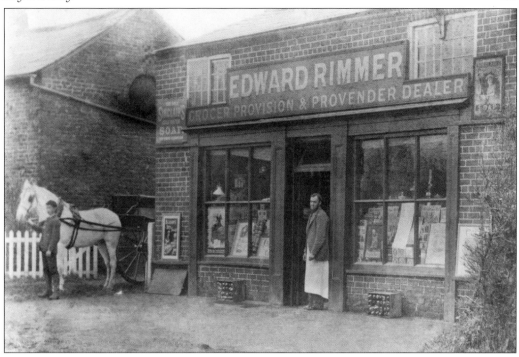

On the north side of Old Town Lane (later the Electricity Offices and now a block of flats)

Nearer to our home on the corner of Church Road and Kenyons Lane was Rothwell's with Bob Hogg, Brenda Mawdsley, Tom Ward and Jimmy Seaford all serving behind the counter, not to mention Mr. Rothwell himself and his sister Elsie, quite a squash in a small shop, but large staffs were often essential for the personal service they provided.

Not too far round the corner in Watchyard Lane, opposite to Whitehouse Lane, was yet another shop owned by a Rimmer family. Close to our chip shop at the Freshfield end of Church Road was Bradley's who also had their own bake-house and sold the most mouth-watering pies and iced buns. Bradley's also owned the nearby hairdresser's shop run by Nan Rimmer and ably assisted by the jovial May Hughes.

Only a few doors away Cranshaw's also had a small general shop, and yet another just across the road was Boardman & Tetlow's selling exactly the same type of goods as all the rest, with Frank Wright next door supplying sweets and tobacco plus no end of household goods. Frank had only one arm but with perfect dexterity could lift down from the shelf above the large sweet jars, unscrew the lids, and expertly tip the required amounts into the small paper bags. Further again towards Freshfield was Mrs. Cairns on the corner of New Road, with Knight's opposite the Grapes, then Bell's in Southport Road. In Gores Lane was the very superior family grocery business of Dean's where they had at one time advertised "carriage trade".

It could be wondered how, in such a small community, so very many such similar businesses, not to mention all the independent small bakers and butchers, were able to survive and remain in business alongside the two Co-op shops and all the Village shops. The fact is that they did, and seemed to thrive, with almost all of them offering a free delivery service.

Returning to the area of the Village we had the Queens Cinema just along the road in Three Tuns Lane where we would queue up on a Saturday with our sixpence to see a cowboy or comedy film – usually Hopalong Cassidy, Old Mother Riley, George Formby or Frank Randle.

In those pre-television days we had two cinemas in Formby with the films being changed twice a week and with two performances each evening and Saturday matinees, and at both there always seemed to be queues.

The Queens was the local flea pit and if the film didn't break down we didn't feel we'd had our money's worth. This was the invitation for all the chanting, stamping of feet, and shooting of bits of paper. It was the highlight of every performance and we were rarely disappointed. Sally Houghton and May Aindow, the usherettes, bustled about beaming their torches on the trouble-makers, and a man with a wooden leg hopped about doing I'm not sure what. If the fault in the film projection could be remedied we all then settled down to watch the film. If it couldn't we were all given free tickets for another performance – something we quite relished if the break-down came well on through the film. At the back downstairs were double seats (cuddle seats!) for the courting couples, and on reflection the whole building must have been very small but at the time seemed quite palatial. The upstairs balcony seats were more expensive at 1/3d than the 6d or 9d we paid downstairs, and always at the top of the stairs was a very large young woman seated on a stool collecting our tickets. She was the daughter of Mrs. Meadows and lived in one of the cottages just a few doors along from the Queens.

Amongst the regular patrons of the upstairs seats were a Capt. and Mrs. Hodge who lived in Duke Street. Capt. Hodge only had one leg and was presumably a casualty of the first world war. The films in those days were categorised as 'U' or 'A' (Universal or Adult). Even the adult films by today's standards were quite innocuous and children were admitted to these films if accompanied by an adult. For one first house performance a group of us had gone to the pictures unaware that the film had been changed and was an 'A' film. We were obviously disappointed and after much discussion decided to tag along beside Capt. and Mrs. Hodge in the ridiculous hope that Sally Houghton would believe us to be part of their family. The fact that she knew us all seemed not to enter our heads. We stuck close on the heels of our 'Auntie and Uncle' and confidently asked for our tickets. We must have looked particularly pathetic, innocent or enterprising because to our surprise these two respected elders agreed that we were with them and we all trooped into the upstairs seats when we had only paid for downstairs.

Across the entrance of the cinema were big metal gates which concertina-ed together to either open or close the building. Down the passage way beside the next door Conservative Club all the bikes were piled, along with any prams or push-chairs which older children in charge of their younger siblings had dumped, as the 'pictures' was an easy way of keeping their charges amused and enjoying themselves at the same time.

Bubbles Dickinson's cottage, Church Road/Piercefield Road corner

On the wall nearest to the Village stood the large bill boards holding the posters advertising the films being shown and the forthcoming attractions. As a very special treat some of the cinema patrons would walk across to Mrs. Trevitt's chip shop a little further along Three Tuns Lane on the opposite side, but we always regarded her chips as very inferior to my grandmother's and never darkened the door! On the outside wall of Mrs. Trevitt's shop was a plaque advertising the Cycling Club which called on their excursions from Liverpool.

The Embassy, our other picture house, was quite something else. Originally a roller skating rink, it was bigger, much more plush and sparkling clean. No necessity for the Flit spray in the Embassy! And it was a rare event, almost unheard of, for the film to break down. The films, too, were of a superior quality both in content and condition. Glorious technicolour was shown as opposed to the black and white of the Queens. The box office was situated just inside the entrance to the left, where Stephanie Hilton, looking almost like the film stars we were paying to see, sold us our tickets, and the stairs ran up to the right. The toilets and washroom were at the top of the stairs in the centre, and the main entrance to the auditorium was directly opposite the staircase. This was regarded as the downstairs seats despite having had to climb the stairs to reach them. The back rows were always reserved for the courting couples, and it was probably in the protective darkness of the Embo where half the juvenile population first started smoking. A brass rail with a curtain suspended from it divided the front stalls from the rest which were always packed with youngsters. The seats were so close to the screen that it was a most uncomfortable position to be in, but as they were the cheapest seats in the house they were also the most popular.

In addition to the plebs, the higher echelons of our society frequented the Embassy, arriving by car and taxi – a very elitist form of transport in those days.

Jack Mawdsley, the commissionaire, was always in attendance, resplendent in his gold braid trimmed uniform, touching his forelock with suitable humility and deference, and after receiving his tip silently cursing his benefactors to the ends of the earth. The moment the lights went out and the performance began Jack would beat a hasty retreat across to the Grapes only returning in time for the interval as though he'd never been away. During the day Jack was a bookie's runner in the days when gambling was illegal.

The queues were endless every night, and again the bicycle shed at the side of Ivy Cottage was crammed full and not a bicycle lock to be seen. Our two cinemas were poles apart, but one thing uniform to both was the respect shown at the end of every show for our King. With one accord everyone stood silently for the national anthem.

After the Embo the chip shop treat was at Ashcroft's – our shop – which was quite definitely supreme! The shop was situated in Moorhouse Buildings on Church Road and at one time had been the home of the Formby Council Offices until the building of the present Council Offices in 1927 in Freshfield Road. Also in the same block behind and above our shop on the corner of Old Mill Lane was the British Legion Headquarters where the Harden family lived. During the austerity of the war years when food rationing was in force the chip shop was a haven and provided the sustenance for many a family. The chips during the war cost just 1d a bag and the fish 2d or 3d depending on whether it was a tailpiece or not. The cooking range was fired by coal and my mother, aunt and grandmother – all very slim ladies – developed arm muscles like the village blacksmith with the heavy work they did; shovelling coal into the furnace, humping huge sacks full of potatoes, carrying heavy buckets of peeled potatoes, and heaving great steaming

THE VILLAGE, FRESHFIELD.   223991.

Church Road: Wilson's Garage on the right; Ashcroft's chip shop is far left

The Gild Hall Band—Jack Cooper, Bernard Norris and Norman Brooks

baskets full of chips from one frying compartment to another. As well as the usual chips and fish they sold 'fingers' which were chips coated in batter, and bags of 'crispies' which were the batter bits which had fallen from the fish in the cooking. All absolutely scrumptious but in today's health conscious society potentially lethal in cholesterol.

Tripe, cowheel and pig's trotters were also very popular and these were delivered from James Mitty's, a wholesaler in Liverpool. A regular customer for tripe was Arthur Evison who ate it by the pound – never cooked and swimming in vinegar!

The fish was supplied by Ross's and usually came from Fred Sandys at the Freshfield shop opposite the Grapes Hotel. If ever there was a shortage then Mr. Price from their other shop at Cross Green would always come to the rescue.

Webbs of Southport supplied the crates of mineral water, and a wonderful character called Arthur Bulmer was the delivery man. He was one of the jolliest of men and after leaving our shop would deliver to the Gild Hall just across the road, and always had a lengthy session playing with Susan, the young grand-daughter of Mrs. Howard, the caretaker of the hall who lived on the premises. Arthur married Susan almost every week, walking the length of the Gild Hall with Susan adorned in a net curtain and Arthur singing "the hen's last march to the midden".

Chips and fish were always wrapped in newspaper and customers were encouraged to bring their discarded papers to the shop and in return often received a free bag of chips. The shop itself had none of the refinements of today's fish and chip emporiums. It was very basic with a bench along the wall where the customers could sit down if there was a delay in serving, and quite a high counter which children often needed to stand on tip toe to see above it.

The Auxiliary Fire Service (Jack Ackers is 2nd left)

The airmen from Woodvale and soldiers from Harrington Barracks all poured in at nights, and many of these young men met their future wives in the romantic surroundings of the chippy. My aunt Edith was one, her future husband being a commando back from Dunkirk.

Our house had an ever open door for the families of these young service men, whose parents, worried about the attachments made by their sons to these unknown Formby girls, often came and stayed to ask my mother's and grandmother's opinion of their future daughters-in-law and meet their families. My grandmother, whose own sons were away fighting in the war, showed great kindness to many of these young service men and often provided meals for them at her home in Graburn Road. It was always astonishing how in war time with food rationing and severe shortages she could produce a positive feast. She had a store cupboard which was permanently locked, but on the odd occasion when we caught a glimpse of the open door were truly amazed at the supply of tins crammed in from floor to ceiling. She had obviously been hoarding the contents in preparation for just such a time of emergency and generously shared what she had with the boys from the camp. Years after the war had ended we found huge bags of pepper which would have been more than sufficient for the entire population of Formby. My brother and I loved these brave men who were winning the war for us and I am still in touch with some of their families today.

The King's Own Regiment and the Enniskillen Fusiliers were billeted here and their parades through the village were thrilling. The bands and marching men brought us children out in droves. We marched along with them in excitement, saluting when they did and clanging our heels together as they did. One young boy was so intent on copying our heroes he walked slap bang into a tree outside Mrs. Smith's sweet shop in the Village stunning himself almost unconscious. Out rushed Mrs. Smith, dusted him down, gave him a sweet, and though still dazed he was back on his feet and marching with the troops. The greatest thrill of all was watching the massive tanks rumbling along the roads and barely managing to manoeuvre the corners.

All this unaccustomed activity in Formby was exhilarating and 'the war' was almost just a phrase to us. We noticed, of course, that all our iron railings had disappeared including those which had surrounded the park and along the railway station bridge, as well as any householders' iron gates. These had been commandeered for the war effort, and posters were widely displayed warning us all that "Careless talk costs lives", "Walls have ears", and that we should "Dig for victory". Mr. Chad also peered down from behind his wall, caricatured by his long nose and fingers, and reminding us of the severe shortages by proclaiming from the hoardings "Wot no sugar", "Wot no coal", etc. Blackout regulations were in force throughout the war and there were, of course, no streetlights. Not a chink of light had to be seen through a window curtain, and any offenders were heavily fined. As children we were never allowed out during the hours of darkness on our own. The blackout was exactly that, and was, even to the toughest of adults, a frightening experience. My mother came home from the chip shop very late one night and during an air raid. The short journey from the shop to our house on her bicycle left her petrified. She reached our house and with utter relief put the key in the door and nearly died of fright when a huge dog leapt out. The poor creature must have been as terrified as she was and had cowered inside the open front porch in an attempt to escape the howl of the sirens.

Motor cars were very few and far between, but what cars there were lay idle through lack of petrol (red petrol was sold on the black market!). Riding bicycles in the dark meant covering the lights with heavy material to dim them. Air raid wardens (the A.R.P.) patrolled the area making sure the blackout regulations were enforced and thus giving no hint to any enemy aircraft above. The A.R.P. were voluntary recruits from the community and included women of all ages from teenagers to middle-aged, and those men not enlisted for war service which meant mainly older and retired men. Their headquarters were at Roselands and they also had an office behind the Food Office where they were under the supervision of George Squires and one of our local policemen, Fred Beswick.

The wail of the air raid sirens both terrified and excited us. Air raid shelters were allocated for different areas, but we usually hid under the stairs waiting for the plaintive moan of the all clear siren. Sometimes we could see the blackness of the night sky pierced by the beam of a searchlight. The Home Guard practiced their manoeuvres in a field on the corner of Freshfield Road and Marsh Brows alongside the cottage of Mrs. Hale who kept goats.

Although Liverpool had suffered devastation during the May blitz of 1941 we were almost unaffected here in Formby. The odd bombs did fall. Incendiaries had set alight the pinewoods around the golf course no doubt convincing the enemy that Liverpool and its docks had been flattened by the inferno which followed. Carrs Crescent received a bomb, another fell in a field in Bull Cop, and four bombs dropping in an almost diagonal line – the first landed in the garden of Clague's chemist in the Village where Tom Corless, the dispensing chemist, lived above the shop with his family. For weeks they had all been trying to uproot the remains of a massive tree stump from the garden without success. The blast from the bomb blew it out from the ground like a tooth extraction. The next bomb hit the chimney sweep Jimmy Meadow's cottage on the corner of Old Mill Lane and Gores Lane. Undeterred he and his family remained living in the house protected only by a tarpaulin sheet for the remainder of the war. Graburn Road got another bomb, and the final one hit the area near the by-pass where the present Freshfield roundabout petrol station is situated. Shrapnel was everywhere and we roamed the fields collecting it all.

The Freshfield Roundabout Garage which was bombed

A plane came down in Duke Street park and I well remember climbing on it to see inside the cockpit. I slipped and fell tearing a nasty gash in my leg. Amid screams of pain I was carried to a house in Phillips Lane where iodine was poured over the wound. The initial screams were as nothing compared to the howls of agony as the iodine penetrated the wound.

The May blitz had left Liverpool in ruins. Whole streets had been blown apart and those families not killed were left homeless. The unrelentless onslaught night after night drove many eventually to leave their city for the tranquil safety of the countryside – only a comparatively short distance away but a whole world away from the nightmares of the raids. Formby gave shelter to many. Our home again had an open door, and I can recall coming downstairs one morning to find people sleeping all over the floors in our small semi-detached house. I had been carried half asleep that previous night into my brother's bed whilst my parents had given theirs and mine to these refugees from the blitz. Looking back it is difficult to remember just how many were in our house but it seemed like dozens. This was without doubt the turning point for Formby's village life. The exodus from Liverpool had begun. Many who had originally only sought a temporary reprieve from the horrors of the war found they liked the quiet country place they had found and decided to stay. Their friends and relatives visited them, also liked what they saw, and so it went on. Formby began to grow. And to change.

* * * *

Formby was a paradise of fields, ditches, trees, wild flowers, wild life, and of course the shore. There were vast open spaces and lots of country lanes for walking. We collected wild flowers which we pressed, and cabbage white butterflies which we pinned on cards and entered in the Flower Show.

The ditches were a constant source of pleasure to us and annoyance to our mothers when we always arrived home wringing wet. Time stood still when we were playing in the ditches, either fishing for tiddlers, sticklebacks, jack sharps, frogspawn, tadpoles or even just messing about in the muddy water, reeds and marsh marigolds. Certain parts though, where the water appeared stagnant, were covered in a green slime which we avoided like the plague having been warned of the dire fate awaiting us if we ventured anywhere near this natural phenomenon christened Jinny Greenteeth. We would immediately be swallowed up and lost forever.

The ditches played an important part in Formby's drainage system and ran all over the Formby area. Being very low lying there were parts of Formby permanently under water and when much of the building boom began in the 1960's many of the ditches were simply

Three different families but all Rimmers—
Anne, Joan, Margaret, Derek, Billy and
Geraldine in the pram

filled in and large areas of what had hitherto been swamp land became the estates of today. Some of these ditches were piped, but the old Formby people, watching the growth of the place, all commented on the fact that there would be problems with flooding in later years – a prophecy come true.

Most children usually stayed around their own areas to play, apart from during the school holidays when we could wander just anywhere, and as there were so many fields we had total freedom and safety.

Priesthouse Lane, where I was born and in fact still live, was formerly named Chapelhouse Lane. The name was changed in the 1930's because of it's similarity with Chapel Lane. At that time there were only seven houses, all on the south side of the lane – two modern pairs of semis, the thatched cottage, the Priest House and the farm. For so few houses there were an awful lot of children – fourteen of is in just four houses and ten of those named Rimmer! We were not related to any of our neighbours but we all called one another's parents auntie and uncle.

Apart from the Sutton family, whose children had grown up, we were the only Protestants down the lane, therefore all our friends attended the Roman Catholic school of Our Lady's. We all got on well together despite calling one another the Proddy dogs and the Catty dogs, and I got to know probably a little more than most non-Catholics about their church and religion (a subject never mentioned at home because of my mixed pedigree) which at that time was very different than in the present ecumenical times. Father Scott and Father Anderton were frequent visitors to their homes and just as I talked to my friends about my teachers so they talked to me about theirs. It seemed strange to me that nuns were teaching them, and they appeared to be equally as terrified of Mother Perpetua

Father Scott and Father Anderton

and Sister Theofane, otherwise known as Ma Pep and Sister Fierce Face, as we were of our Miss Reily.

Fields were situated back and front of the lane which was lined with trees meeting in the middle to form an arborial tunnel which was very dark and spooky. When going to my cousins in Flaxfield Road I never ever walked, but ran like the wind through the trees afraid of the darkness even though the sun would be blazing above. A ditch ran the length of the lane opposite the houses and the unmade dirt-track road surface was a myriad of puddles on wet days.

Across the ditch was the field patterned with buttercups and daisies where the cows grazed. Blackberry bushes grew everywhere and we picked them by the tea-canful always using an old walking stick to hook around the bunches of fruit to protect us from the prickles of the brambles. Once the cows had gone back to the farm the field was our playground – jumping the ditches, climbing the trees, hiding in the brambles, making dens. And then once a year Wallis's Fair would arrive. Usually held in the Bay Horse field, but sometimes in our field, it was the pinnacle of our delight. "Meet me in St. Louis, Louis, meet me at the fair". Every night the music blared forth. Formby was such a quiet sleepy place this cacophony

Bay Horse

of sound and bright lights was a wonderment of excitement to us all. The bobby horses were our favourite and how we were never seriously injured was nothing short of a miracle. Instead of sitting properly on the horses some of us would jam our outstretched legs on either side of the metal railings around the circular ride, and as the whole thing went faster and faster we would show off shamelessly, balanced precariously by just our feet and completely oblivious of how very dangerous it was. Nobody every chastised us and nobody to my knowledge ever got hurt. We wandered round the sideshows, eking out our few coppers and hoping by knocking down a pile of tins with a mop, or rolling a penny into a clear square we would win a longed for prize. We all envied the nomadic life of Valerie Wallis, the young daughter of the owners of the fair, and marvelled that any child should be able to live in a caravan and travel from place to place in such a different environment from our own.

The contrast of the Fair and the Bay Horse could not have been greater. The Fair was so vibrant and exciting. The pub so dilapidated and quiet. Lil Alcock and her sister, May, were the licensees of the Bay Horse which was so run down it was only frequented by those locals who were none too fussy regarding the salubrity of their surroundings. Until, that is, the arrival of the U.S. troops to Burtonwood and then to Hill House, Altcar. They must have viewed with astonishment this pokey little pub and they poured in. These were the first coloured people we children had ever seen and many of us genuinely thought they had dirty faces. Although we were much too young in those pre-sex education days to understand anything whatsoever about the facts of life we could not fail to notice the increase in female clientele once the G.I.'s arrived. It was all so exciting to have such activity around us and it was wonderful to ask these strange looking soldiers "Got any gum, chum?" and to always receive a packet of chewing gum. Everything, of course, was rationed and sweets were something we only got on rare occasions with our 'personal points' coupons.

Priesthouse Lane Cottage in 1930

Immediately next door to us was the old thatched cottage in which lived an old lady, Miss Rawcliffe. Originally from Preston, she had been a buyer at Broadbent's of Southport and was reputed to have been a real stickler in her job and rather eccentric, sometimes sitting behind the counter at Broadbent's with her feet in a bowl of water. My brother and I plus all the other children from the lane played endless tricks on Miss Rawcliffe and would have been mortified had she ever caught us.

My mother's wash house was along our side path and against the privet hedge between our house and the cottage. It was a very cold and draughty tin construction housing an old gas boiler, a mangle, dolly tub, dolly pegs, and a washboard. There was no water laid on, and in any case the tap water was so very hard that my mother used rain water which she carried from the huge rain barrel at the back of the house making washing days sheer drudgery. An extension gas pipe ran across from the house to the top of the wash house on which my brother and I would swing back and forth totally unconcerned that we could have fractured the pipe with perilous results. The scrubbing of the clothes on the washboard, dabbing of the blue bag in the rinsing water, and mixing of the starch were all normal routines of washday and all back-breaking tasks which in the winter were particularly onerous, and today in the age of the automatic washing machine and launderette almost beyond belief. My brother and I often climbed on top of the rickety roof and, hidden behind the tall hedge, would dip our paint brushes in jars of water which we then flicked over the top of the hedge when Miss Rawcliffe emerged causing her to think it was raining and to shuffle back indoors – a very stupid prank which gave us great childish satisfaction and something for which we would have suffered had our mother ever found out.

It was Miss Rawcliffe who named the cottage Stoneyhurst and who had the date shield placed on the cottage soon after she had bought it in the 1930's. She did no research into its history but merely decided that 1613 sounded a suitable date and that was that! In fact she was probably about 100 years too early in her assessment of its age. She kept a pet cockerel in the cottage which went everywhere with her – even on the bus tucked inside her coat. In the end the bird turned on her and pecked her through the nose. As she grew older she became even more eccentric. Every Sunday lunchtime it had been my mother's custom to send either me or my brother round to her cottage with a roast dinner for her. This went on for a good number of years until she suddenly said she didn't want us to go round any more. She would still like the dinner, but it must be pushed inside the privet hedge outside the back door between our two houses and she would collect it from there. The following day the empty plate appeared back in the hedge.

Towards the end of her life the cottage became very neglected and dilapidated with the gardens so overgrown it was difficult to see the existence of a cottage at all. She died in 1958 and the next tenants were Mr. and Mrs. Jarvis who worked miracles in transforming what was a tumbledown ruin into a very picturesque home, but sadly a wattle and daub cottage of such an age fell to the ravages of time and in 1981 it was condemned. Although by now a listed building its condition was such that it was beyond saving and reluctantly it was demolished and replaced by a replica with the only original piece being the cruck.

We lived in close proximity to several farms, and quite near to the brook. The nearest farm was that of Teddy Mawdsley who lived in the Priest House which was next door but one away from the cottage. His pig sties were adjacent to the houses and the smell of the country was rife.

The Priest House was a very drab and unpretentious building erected in 1712 by the Squire, Richard Formby, as a home for the resident Roman Catholic priest. A plaque on the front of the house bore the inscription RFM 1712 which were the initials of Richard and Mary Formby who later became Protestants, and with the change in the established religion the house became redundant.

Many legends surround the house – of how Mass was held in secret there during the reign of William and Mary, and of the underground tunnel leading from the house to Watchyard Lane where a 'look-out' would watch the yard of the nearby church in School Lane to warn those worshipping in the house. The name Watchyard Lane was even said to be derived from this, but some of these stories have been questioned in more recent years and doubt has been cast on their authenticity. Nevertheless this is the stuff of legends and the stories have survived through the ages and could possibly have some substance. When the house later became a farm and was occupied by Teddy Mawdsley he stabled the horses which were used to tow the life-boat from its shelter in Birkey Lane to the shore.

We were fortunately on the main drain sewerage system and enjoyed the luxury of an indoor flush toilet, but the Priest House, in common with many houses, had no such amenity. Every week the marmalade cart (otherwise known as the lavender cart, the chariot or the plain and simple muck cart) would come to collect the effluent from the outside lavatory buckets. At first the filthy metal cart with buckled wheels was drawn by a flea-bitten old grey horse. As the buckets were tipped in the metal trap door clanged down and the smell was atrocious. Later it was drawn by a motorised wagon, but still its unsavoury load dripped along the route it took, the obnoxious stench clinging to the air as it trailed around the roads of Formby. A great number of households depended on the marmalade cart well into the 1950's.

Several different workmen had the misfortune to work on the cart. One was always in attendance. Nicknamed Hagan, his real name was Eddy Ruane. He had a bulbous purple nose, which obviously didn't function as efficiently as other people's or he could never have survived the years he did on the marmalade cart. He always sat on the back of the cart, and one story goes that Hagan's coat fell into the cart and he desperately grappled to retrieve it from the revolting contents of human waste. The other men yelled at him to leave it alone. "It's only a coat, Hagan, you can get another and it's ruined anyway". "It's not just the coat" he replied, "me baggin's in the pocket", (baggin being the local colloquialism for sandwiches).

The Priest House eventually came to an ignominious end in the mid-fifties after having been home to a large family of evacuees from Liverpool, the Hannaways and Morrises, throughout the second world war years. The house never enjoyed the facility of electricity, and almost every morning at a very early hour and in pitch darkness the young daughter from the house would be sent to either our house or another neighbour's for a penny change for the gas meter. Very often the only lighting was by candles which gave the house an even more eerie appearance as they flickered in the windows. Though very neglected and vandalised it was nevertheless a sturdy building of such solid construction that the bulldozers were unable to demolish it and explosives had to be used. A carved altar cupboard, presumably for keeping the sacred religious vessels used in the celebration of Mass, was found during the demolition and was removed to the Roman Catholic Church rectory where it still remains. The date plaque is now in the possession of the Formby Society having been retrieved by Mrs. Sutton from the next door farm. The house numbered 17 now stands on the site and one family of occupants were convinced they saw on many occasions, both inside and outside their home, a ghost wearing a large hat and cloak and being in no way alarming or menacing. In fact they became very fond of the apparition!

Mrs. Sutton's farm was just next door, correctly named Chapel House Farm. This was very small and had been built in the 1700's. The farm consisted of just a

The back of Chapel House Farm

few cows and poultry, but the gardens were always full of flowers, and on the occasions when we needed to take flowers to church, and especially on Mothering Sunday, all the local children made their way to Mrs. Sutton's and collected bunches of all varieties of flowers for which they paid just a few coppers. In the spring the wild daffodils were a picture.

Just at the end of the road, on the corner of Kenyons Lane and Watchyard Lane was yet another farm belonging to Ag Shaw (whose real name was actually Rimmer). Again this was very small but she kept a few cows and pigs and had an excellent orchard at the back. Her cows often strayed into our gardens from the opposite field wreaking havoc with our mothers' washing lines and scattering once clean washing all over the place.

Ag Shaw was quite a character, always wearing a long black dress. She had a large mole on her face sprouting the odd whiskers and was the most hard working woman imaginable. Five roads all met at her corner – Kenyons Lane, Watchyard Lane, Bull Cop, Flaxfield Road and Priesthouse Lane. On the corner of Priesthouse Lane was the old pinfold in which stray cattle were rounded up. The pinfold had long since ceased to be used for it's original purpose and was more a playground for the local youth of the area. It was constructed of large stones and divided into three compartments by wooden staves, with a door opening towards Kenyons Lane. The boys from Our Lady's School would often congregate to have a rare old fight inside the pinfold with all their pals looking on and roaring encouragement. When things began to get heated Ag Shaw would blow furiously into an old police whistle and the boys, believing it to be the strong arm of the law, would scatter like flies in all directions.

Along Kenyons Lane, and next door to Ag Shaw's farm, lived Humphrey Dickinson and his sister Marjorie, a very quaint couple who kept bantams. Everybody at that time seemed to have some kind of poultry. We had hens ourselves, and the foul smell of Karswood poultry spice, along with the boiled potato peelings, pervaded the house at feeding times.

The Water Board office was just along the lane where Jack Ackers lived with his sister in the adjoining house. Jack was a real character, a very happy man who walked with a slight limp, always sported a gold watch and chain across his chest, and had endless tales to tell. Whatever the disaster or

Ag Shaw by her farm gate in Kenyons Lane

emergency his only speed was almost stationary. A burst water main could be spurting water 16 feet high or someone's house could be knee deep in water, but Jack would still have to cogitate on the situation, consulting his book and licking the end of his pencil, before taking any action. He was a very familiar figure all around Formby with his Water Board rods strapped to the cross-bar of his bicycle, and whenever he tested the water hydrants and flushed the road he attracted hoards of children as a very inquisitive audience.

Across the road in the two old cottages lived Miss Petrie, who strode around the district always brandishing a walking stick, and next door Miss Formby, who had been a teacher at Our Lady's School and was more often referred to as Miss Annie.

That so many such truly remarkable characters should reside in one very tiny lane was quite extraordinary, but Formby was indeed rich in characters, and not only our own locals but also tradespeople and others who visited the district. People like the onion man who came each summer from France wearing his beret and with strings of onions festooned around his bicycle and his neck. The pot man who called at the houses with a huge basket balanced on his head containing a variety of pots which he sold door to door. There was also the knife grinder whose treadle grinder sharpened our knives and scissors, and, of course, the rag and bone man whose horse and cart clopped along the roads collecting any old cast-offs for which he paid a few coppers or exchanged for a goldfish or a balloon. Our gardens benefited from these horse drawn carts, and there was never a shortage of manure which we would shovel up from the roads and use to fertilise our crops.

Bull Cop opposite Lowe's Farm (now Gardner Road estate)

Turning into Bull Cop we passed acres of fields and reached Lowe's farm, or more correctly Devon Farm, the home of Jimmy Lowe, the asparagus king, although this was not the farm where the asparagus was grown. Lowe's farm was a paradise for us. Jimmy Lowe had four daughters all living alongside the farmhouse and his several grandchildren were our playmates. In fact, it seemed half Formby congregated down at Lowe's farm. Climbing over bales of hay in the big Dutch barn and hiding from one another was a pastime of which we never tired. 'Helping' in the shippon by strewing fresh straw, watching the hand milking of the cows and filling the milk churns, with a special treat for us to open our mouths and Bert Lawton, the milkman, would aim the warm milk directly from the teat into them. The delicious warm taste of the milk was sheer nectar. We brushed the horses and cleaned their harnesses, fed the cows and calves, and on reflection must have been perfect pests to the workmen, but we were never made unwelcome. We knew what was not allowed and would never have risked doing anything to jeopardise our chances of coming to the farm.

The milk round was our highlight. Early every Saturday morning at least half a dozen children would be badgering to get on the float for the milk deliveries. Dolly, the poor old horse, dragged round not only the milk churns and the milkman, but also the extra load of at least four or five children. The float was very small and we clung on, some on the back step, with the float almost touching the ground as it trundled along. Bert Lawton was very fair in deciding who went on board and gave us all deliveries to make. We knew our favourites where there would always be an apple or a penny, and if we were fortunate enough to deliver to Polly Ball in Flaxfield Road we got both! The milk round must have been the fastest passage of time in the whole week.

During the week two deliveries were made – one in the morning and one in the afternoon, but milk was not delivered on Sundays and the customers had to go to the farm to collect it. There were no such things as fridges and in the summer months keeping the milk fresh for just one day was a difficulty. It would therefore have been impossible to have ordered sufficient for two days to cover the weekend. Milk which came straight from the cow and was untreated in any way had a much lesser time of remaining fresh than today's milk which has gone through so many processes. It was our ritual therefore that early every Sunday morning my father, brother, dog and I would walk down to the farm carrying a huge enamel jug for the milk to be ladled into it. It never seemed a chore and was something we always looked forward to no matter what the weather.

When October half-term holiday came round it was always known as the potato-picking holidays when a big majority of the Formby children went potato picking. I never went, but my brother never missed and most of our friends also took part. All the local farms employed as many children as possible, being very cheap labour, and there was no shortage of recruits. The Altcar farmers also welcomed the Formby children and some of the farmers sent a lorry down to pick up and transport the children to the farm though many pedalled off on their bicycles. One Altcar farmer would only employ girls as he considered them (quite rightly of course!) to be more reliable and hard-working than the boys and they also did not spend half their time pelting one another with potatoes.

Bull Cop lead down to the brook, past the timber yard, where the boys would swim and where they made diving boards from old planks or tree branches. The trees were marvellous for climbing and very often a rope was attached to a high branch and we would all take turns in swinging back and forth.

The by-pass was very close to the brook and on Sunday mornings our friends who were lucky enough to have roller skates spent hour upon hour skating up and down the stretch of by-pass between Moss Side and Woodwards in complete safety with no sign of traffic. Our skating rink was York Road where there was never any appearance of traffic at any time and where we performed all manner of twirls, leaps and acrobatic manoeuvres.

All the seasons were a delight. The frogspawn in spring, the tiddlers in summer, the blackberries in autumn, and the ice in winter. The swamp was at the end of Bull Cop. Before the winter arrived we didn't bother too much about the swamp, but once the freezing temperatures came it was our playground. Up and down the ice we all skidded making long slides which sent us shooting off at frantic speeds, often completing the slides on our backsides. The water beneath was so shallow we could never have come to any harm had the ice broken and the worst fate would have been wet feet.

Every season of the year was an adventure when growing up in Formby, there was so much to explore and discover and so much to enjoy, The winters were much harsher than our present winters and there was no such luxury as central heating. Our homes were heated by open coal fires which were stacked so high the warmth penetrated the fabric of the building and kept our houses very cosy - the heat rising through the chimney to keep the upper rooms warm. Even the trauma of being ill in bed diminished with the comforting sight of a coal fire in the bedroom grate. Nevertheless in very frosty weather it was quite usual to awaken to feathery-ferned lace patterns of ice coating the inside of the window panes.

During the war everything was in short supply and at one time there was an acute shortage of coal and we supplemented our fuel with logs and coke. The coke was also rationed and my brother and I used to go on our bicycles to the Gas Works in Watchyard Lane for a sack of coke. We would then struggle home along with dozens of others pushing our unwieldy load to eke out the coal supply. We also collected coal and wood from the shore which had been washed in with the tide. Every single house had an open coal fire and disposing of the ashes every morning must have been something of a nuisance in many households. Down our road we had no such problem. The road was unmade and full of pot-holes and our ashes were simply tipped on the road.

All these coal fires necessitated the services of a chimney sweep and though many families undertook the task themselves the majority engaged the professional for the job, and in most cases this was the well known and popular Jimmy Meadow, a jolly round man who could probably have passed unrecognised without his soot covered exterior, his bike, and his brushes. The chimney sweep's visits were invariably very early in a morning, usually before 7 a.m., with the entire room being enveloped in sheets to protect the furniture from the film of soot which unavoidably seeped into the room, followed by the pleasure of being sent outside to ascertain the emergence of the brush from the chimney pot. A successor to Jimmy was Tommy Birchall, a comedian whose entertainment value surpassed even his chimney sweeping skills.

One year the winter was particularly severe and walking to our grandparents in Altcar was almost akin to travelling through the Alps. Huge banks of snow had been displaced on either side of the road by a snow plough creating what seemed almost a tunnel through which to walk. The weather was so bad that we were actually sent home from school one day because of the intense cold – the only occasion I can recall this ever happening throughout all my schooling. Instead of going home as we should have done a group of us went to Lowe's farm tramping through the deep snow and revelling in every footstep. I climbed a heavily snow laden tree and not surprisingly fell from quite a height into the frozen ditch below. As I lay whimpering in the ditch convinced that I was dying with a broken back I imagined the loving reception that would greet me if ever I survived, was discovered, and carried home to the warmth of our roaring fire. Nobody bothered or came to my rescue, and eventually I managed to scramble out of the ditch, by this time crying my eyes out from the shock and pain. Miserably, I limped home soaking wet, freezing cold, and aching in every bone, to be set upon by my irate mother for not coming straight home from school, for climbing trees, and for getting wet through. Mothers could, on occasions, be every bit as cruel as teachers.

We had three huge beech trees directly in front of our house. There were so many trees in the lane that the front rooms of our house were permanently in semi-darkness. My father decided that the three trees must go and he and his brother, Miles, tackled the job themselves. My mother was not only a little concerned that one wrong move and our house could have been demolished with the tremendous weight of the trees. However, their skills as woodmen were superb and each tree fell across the ditch and into the field in front, their length stretching almost to the blackberry bushes behind the back of the gardens of the Kenyons Lane houses. People came from everywhere to collect the firewood and our fires were well stoked for ages.

With our roads being unmade they were like mud-baths during the winter. We were comparatively close to the main road so trudging through the mud for such a short distance wasn't too tiresome – we carefully picked our way hopping from one slightly less muddy patch to another until we reached the end, but our friends in Bull Cop were not so fortunate. They always set off from home wearing their wellingtons and carrying a pair of shoes. They would then call at Ag Shaw's farm and leave their wellies in her porch, change into their shoes, and continue on more properly shod for school or wherever. On the way home, they would again call at her farm to change back into the wellies before carrying on home.

The presence of so many small farms in Formby kept the blacksmith's forge in Liverpool Road very busy replacing the shoes of the horses of the village. Mr. Welch, the blacksmith, was only a small man but must have been as strong as an ox and it was a never ending wonder that the red hot horseshoes could be placed on the hooves of the animals and nails driven in without causing them harm. Cyril Seddon was another farrier who travelled around the farms as well as working at the forge in Jimmy Dickinson's yard in Church Road.

Opposite the Liverpool Road smithy was Stott's cottage with a monkey puzzle tree in the front garden, and just further along was Pierces Farm, the home of Tom and Gladys Rimmer. This was where some of the Waterloo Cup greyhounds stayed when they came to Altcar for the hare coursing, and the familiar sight of the carriages coming and going from the Blundell Arms to the coursing brought an elegant air to our village every February. The coursing was an event looked

Stott's cottage, Liverpool Road

forward to by many as a very popular sport, and sweepstakes were held in much the same way as for the Grand National. Public conscience has now reduced the popularity of the sport which is regarded on the one hand as essential to the correct balance of the environment and on the other as an act of barbarism. Pierces Farm was not in my time a real working farm, the only livestock being poultry, but it was a most attractive place with well stocked gardens and a heavily laden vine in the greenhouse conservatory which was set along the front of the house.

Much nearer to our home was the small farm of Eph Walker, just around the corner in Church Road. His big Dutch barn was across the road in Altcar Road and when the threshing machine arrived it attracted droves of children to watch the work being done. Walker's were also very popular every Bonfire Night when they held a mammoth bonfire at their farm which, just like the threshing machine, attracted crowds of onlookers. Walker's delivered their produce by horse and cart around the village, and it was a terrible tragedy when their horse perished in a fire at Lowe's Farm whilst being stabled there.

Directly opposite our shop in Church Road was Bill Hunter's farm, on the corner of Cable Street, where he lived with his very large family of ten children. His dairy was at the side of the farm but his fields were some distance away at Mittens Lane which meant his cows being herded along the roads every morning and evening. Jossie Rimmer was another farmer whose farm was on the corner of Whitehouse Lane and Church Road, but also used the fields at Mittens Lane. His

The iron range, Whitehouse Farm (opposite the Police Station)

cows often held up the Liverpool to Southport bus as they ambled along Church Road, and just like the horse drawn carts which used our roads and deposited their manure as they went so did the cows, making it quite a normal sight for householders to come into the road and shovel up this excellent fertilizer for their gardens.

There were countless other small farms in Formby including the three in Deansgate Lane of Dean's, Bond's and Foster's, the farms of Tommy and Teddy Sutton, the pig farms of Snowdon's, Baldwin's, and Brooks', as well as Sutton's, Mawdsley's, Houghton's, Aughton's and several others.

The second farm of Jimmy Lowe was called Pine Tree and was located behind the pine woods and sandhills and quite a distance from the sea at Freshfield. This was the farm which firmly placed Formby's name on the map with their luxury crops of asparagus being savoured by the aristocracy throughout the land. The season was very short, only lasting six weeks, therefore the work schedule was very intense. The asparagus was a very expensive delicacy and out of the reach of most local people, but those special favourites of the Lowe family always looked

Jimmy Lowe, the asparagus king

forward to the odd bunch of sprue (the thinner stalks) neatly tied in raffia as a very welcome gift. The asparagus was taken in hampers down to Freshfield Station to be transported all over the country, it was also sent by post from the Formby post office and again the counter staff very often received a bunch of this rare crop.

Not too far from Pine Tree Farm was Pine Tree Café. This had originally belonged to the Wright family, but had been taken over by Capt. Hutchinson just after the second world war, and like the Boat House at Formby, provided drinks and refreshments for the day trippers to Freshfield shore. There was no water laid on at the Café, and Capt. Hutchinson used to bring down from his home in Montagu Road two huge galvanised barrels full of water which had to be used for

Pine Tree Cafe bicycle park with Capt. Hutchinson's Rolls Royce and one of
the Nissen huts used as a holiday home

Pine Tree Cafe, Freshfield Shore.

everything from making tea to washing up. These barrels were transported to the Café in the back of his Rolls Royce complete with curtains at the windows. So much for today's rigid hygiene rules and regulations! Pine Tree Café eventually collapsed into the encroaching sea and today there is no sign of either the Café or the Farm or even the sandhills such has been the coastal erosion.

Being children during the war we were all aware of the shortages and were therefore conditioned to expect little, which must have been something of a relief to our parents who were in no position to have given us a great deal anyway. Despite this I cannot ever say we felt deprived, and when birthdays and Christmas came around we always received presents which delighted us although those same gifts compared with the sophisticated playthings of today would undoubtedly be greeted with derision by today's children.

My mother was the most marvellous manager of money, and on my father's meagre wages bought us simple food which was amply supplemented by the produce of our garden, and made nutritious meals from practically nothing. The oven turned out delicious cakes and puddings for a fraction of the cost of those in the shops, and in our early years she made clothes for us by sewing and knitting. Our home had none of the trappings of today's considered necessities such as fitted carpets and the like, but the polished lino with comfortable rugs and mats laid upon it were the norm in most homes and perfectly adequate for our needs. To say I would like to return to those standards would be quite untrue, but to imply we lived in abject poverty would be equally untrue. It was simply a way of life and we as children were content. No doubt our parents did have real money worries, but they lived within their means and were survivors.

We never went away for holidays and never had any desire to do so. Formby had all we could possibly want for recreation, and our day trips to Southport or occasionally New Brighton more than satisfied us. And, of course, we had the shore – never called the beach! The summers did seem to be very much warmer than our present ones and most of our school holidays, when we were not at the farm, were spent at the shore. The sandhills with the starr grass gave endless hours of pleasure, and with a pile of sandwiches we would be gone for the whole day. To save carrying a heavy bottle full of pop we always searched the shore for empty bottles to reclaim the money deposited on them from the Boat House shop, and then would buy our drinks with the money. During our childhood the Boat House was no longer used for the lifeboat but as a residence for the Norris family – all deeply tanned from their fresh air existence. The Norrises ran the shop and café providing drinks and snacks for the many locals and visitors who crowded the shore. Going into the Boat House from the hot sunshine of the shore was a sharp contrast, it being quite cold and dark with a stone floor covered in the sand blown in from outside.

The shore was littered with wrecks and these we climbed in and out of playing hide and seek both on the wrecks and in the sandhills. All along the shore, during the war, look-out shelters surrounded by barbed wire had been erected and these remained years later creating yet more adventure playgrounds for us all. The sea was much cleaner and this was where I learned to swim and not at the Victoria Baths in Southport where we were taken each week from school on the train.

The huge enclosure outside the Boat House where we left our bikes was literally crammed with hundreds of machines and no thought of them being locked. It was incredible how in such a jumble of bikes we never had any problems in locating our own. The coastguard station was just behind the Boat House set in the sandhills.

Smallholding in Phillips Lane

Dewberries, with their purplish bloom to the fruit, grew in profusion all around the shore area, as well as around the golf course, and we picked them by the load for pies and puddings, going home with our hands and faces stained purple from the luscious, juicy fruit.

On the way to the shore we travelled on our bikes, trikes, or just our feet over the railway bridge and down Kirklake Road. On the north side of the road were very few houses. Just at the bottom of the bridge were the white cottages of Gerry Walker with his scrap yard, and next door Kitty Kavanagh and her sister Margaret. They were a quaint couple and Margaret worked as domestic help at the Roman Catholic rectory. Their cottage, which they had moved to from Phillips Lane, was set back from the road behind a field covered in spring with wild daffodils.

Further along was Huddle Hall, and then the old cottage of Joe Eccles, the postman, who was always fond of some liquid refreshment on his postal rounds, but would never enter licensed premises wearing his post office cap. It always seemed quite permissible once the cap was secreted inside his jacket.

The St. Luke's parish hall came next and then there was nothing else on that side of the road until we reached Kirklake Bank, the home of Miles Formby and his family. Opposite to Kirklake Bank had been fields of tulips grown from bulbs sent here from Holland, and then at the end was St. Luke's Church where the football fanatical vicar, Norman Cowden, officiated, always showing great reluctance to conducting wedding ceremonies on the Saturdays when Everton played at home.

Going further south we passed one or two isolated houses, eventually reaching Stella Maris and Valley House. Stella Maris had been a home for destitute children before being requisitioned during the war for the airmen. Our school friends, Harold and Annette James, lived in Valley House – an enormous detached mansion almost on the shore itself. The birthday parties we attended for Harold were in January, and sliding down snow covered sandhills was almost, if not more so, as pleasurable as the time spent on them in the summer. The views from this sedate old house were superb with sweeping panoramas of the Welsh hills and the wildness of nature all around.

Not too far from here set in the sandhills was Tasker's old shack. He was well known to all of Formby as the hermit having left his home in Liverpool to live the simple life of his choice with only his dogs, cats and sea birds for company. His first home in Formby had been an old caravan in the farm yard of Harry Snowdon at Moss Side, where he cleaned out the pigs, before moving in the mid 1930's to the shore where he built his hut from the odd bits of wood he collected from the flotsam of the shore. His only material possessions were his wireless, his books, his stove, and his oil lamp, and in this simple life he found the contentment which eludes so many. He always welcomed visitors, and only left his surroundings when it was necessary to replenish his frugal stock of food. He was never seen without his sack over his shoulder and his faithful dogs at his side. The local shopkeepers showed benevolent kindness to him enabling him to live his life the way he did, and he survived the elements for many years and died in 1965.

It has been illustrated that Formby was rich in characters, and none more so than Joan Holden who was a household name to everyone, although her correct name was Mrs. Dickinson. She owned two shops – one inherited from her aunt, Miss Holden in Three Tuns Lane, and the other previously Rothwell's outfitters on the corner of York Road and Three Tuns Lane, which became known as "The Junk Shop", "The Tatty Shop", or "The Harrods of Formby". During the war the end portion of this shop nearest York Road had been the Coal Office where Mr. Page was in charge of the coal rations.

Her York Road shop was a veritable Aladdin's cave and the most amazing place ever seen. The windows looked as though they were about to burst with the enormous load of materials and clothing which were piled against them. She and her staff always went to untold trouble to satisfy the needs of every customer, bringing down mountains of stock and never putting anything back. The shop ended up having a tiny walk-way through the middle with mountainous piles of everything along the sides, and despite always being in the most chaotic muddle the staff could always put their hands on whatever they wanted. Whenever buying material Eileen, Maisie, Josie, and Nora would always fling a few extra feet along the yardstick as "it was best to have good hems". The good hems often resulted in sufficient curtains for every window in the house. Joan Holden herself would have been horrified at such generosity.

There was nothing you could ask for and not be able to buy. If it wasn't there at that precise moment it would be obtained for the next day or so – and everything, but everything, was "on appro". In addition to the shop bursting at the seams with stock Joan's car was exactly the same, having barely room for her to squeeze herself into the driving seat, and her house and garage were likewise. There were commodities in her shop which had been there for donkey's years hidden beneath piles of pre-war articles never seen in any other establishment, and totally unfamiliar to many of the younger mothers who shopped there. Years after decimalization she was still charging old currency with most items priced 19/11d, 29/11d or 39/11d.

She also owned property all over Formby and any empty and derelict-looking house would invariably belong to Joan and would most probably be housing even more of her stock. She was one of our real characters and probably one of the most popular. She was a shrewd business woman, deeply religious, who sought solace in her work to overcome the personal tragedy of losing a longed for baby and then her beloved husband. Her shop suffered several attacks by vandals, and shortly before her death in 1980 it was set on fire by lighted fish and chip paper being thrown through the letter box. She suffered a stroke following this experience from which she never recovered. She made a great success of her work becoming a wealthy woman and leaving behind her a legend and a huge gap in the lives of the Formby people.

* * * *

Formby was a very law abiding community with far more policemen than appeared necessary, all living in houses belonging to the Lancashire County Council and situated alongside the Police Station.

In the 1940's and 50's a policeman held a position of respect and high regard in the community, and although a lowly paid profession the integrity of its members was beyond question, and a 'bent copper' in those days was almost unheard of. Every man, woman and child in Formby knew every policeman by name and they in turn knew all of us. We trusted them implicitly. Every night they could be seen trying all the shop doors in the Village and then going on to those shops situated in other parts of the area. There were several occasions when my parents, coming home very late at night from their shop, had forgotten to lock up. Always the next morning they would find a note scribbled on the counter telling them not to forget again. The village, therefore was shaken to its roots as was the local force itself by events from which some police officers never fully recovered.

Crime was almost non-existent in Formby until a series of burglaries mystified and worried the entire village. Formby was a very class-divided society during and immediately following the war. We had the working-class and we had the gentry. Most of the big houses, particularly in the Freshfield area, had servants of one kind or another, and it was mainly, but not only, these properties which were suffering the break-ins. As well as money and valuables even food was disappearing, and when a side of bacon disappeared from the modest home of Stan Lowe in Cable Street we all felt vulnerable. We were now at peace. The war had been won, and probably for the first time we were all afraid. Any residents leaving their homes for even just a few days informed the police, but still the burglaries continued. Then one night P.C. Brooks signed on for duty relieving his neighbouring constable. An hour later he received a telephone call. Intruders were suspected in Bell's grocery shop in Southport Road. Together with a fellow officer he raced round. In total darkness they saw the shop had been entered. They stealthily worked their way round until they were sure the culprits were cornered. They burst in throwing themselves on the two intruders who were clutching their nocturnal haul. The lights were switched on and the shocked face of P.C. Brooks was staring into the face of the man he had just relieved from duty. His partner in crime was an equally respected local shopkeeper. This may seem mundane and of little consequence today. In 1946 it was the biggest scandal anyone could recall. The policemen and their families were shattered. The public in a state of shock and disbelief. The offending policeman's family immediately left the district, and the remaining policemen's wives would not venture out so deeply were they shocked. The offenders were brought to court, found guilty, and imprisoned. The event was talked about for years and will probably never be forgotten by those who were around at the time. This totally isolated incident is not intended to embarrass or detract from the policeman's standing in our community, but rather to illustrate the changing society in which we now live.

* * * *

There were two real highlights in Formby's year – the Gala and the Flower Show.

A Rose Queen seems to typify village life and Formby was no exception with the whole village turning out to participate in the traditional ceremony of the crowning and accompanying events. The Rose Queen procession heralded the start of the annual August Bank Holiday Gala with the lavishly decorated lorries from the local garages of Woodwards and Stevens & Hooks following the Formby Silver Band from the War Memorial to the King George V playing fields behind

The Gala: Queen Mary Mawdsley;
Cushion bearer Christopher Rimmer; Dancer Pat Dockery

The Gala: Judging the fancy dress. Left to right: Councillors Jack Dean, Bill Alderson, Mrs. and Councillor Jimmy Rimmer, and Pat Tickle

the Gild Hall. The crowning ceremony was usually performed by the Chairman of the council, and then the queen's entourage took part in dancing on the platform for the crowd's entertainment.

The fancy dress parade was always a delight and showed great ingenuity on the part of all the competitors and their families. The sports and races followed with practically all the children of the village taking part in a wide variety of sporting and novelty races including egg and spoon, sack, potato, and three-legged races. There were always several heats in each race followed by the finals, then the parents and even grandparents participated in the adult races, again including novelty races such as thread the needle, slow bike, and ham cutting.

The highlight was the Formby Mile which was run round four laps of the outer circle of the field. This was a prestigious event taken very seriously by the athletic men of the village and the annual cup was a highly prized possession. The familiar names of Peter Bradshaw, Oscar Burgess, Harry Mawdsley, and Harry Jackson battling it out every year delighted the cheering and encouraging crowds. One year on a lighter note Joe Moss appeared resplendent in a pair of ladies corsets just to add to the jovial atmosphere and take the edge off the serious competition, but

---

A.M.D.G.

Church of Our Lady of Compassion, FORMBY

878

45TH ANNUAL

Gala and Sports

to be held on

Monday, August 5th, 1957,

in the

Gild Hall & Adjoining Grounds.

Programme - - Sixpence.

Admission to Field - - Adults, 1/-   Children, 3d.

Admission to Whist Drive, 1/6.   Dance, 3/-

LISTEN TO LOUD-SPEAKER FOR SPECIAL ANNOUNCEMENTS

Printed by the Hulme Printing Co. Southport

The Gala: Myself and my twin brother, Derek, August 1939, the last Gala before the Second World War.

unsurprisingly failed to complete the course. There was one occasion when a miscalculation owing to the handicap of some of the competitors resulted in the cup being claimed by someone who had run one lap short. It took all the diplomacy of the parish priest to prevent an all out war erupting.

The Ladies race always proved popular with Nellie Rimmer regularly competing under the pseudonym of Little Nell – always running bare foot and with a very lengthy start, appearing to be almost at the finishing post before running a step, and always being overtaken by every other runner and finishing last each time. Little Mrs. Airey, built like a whippet and with the stamina of a horse, was another successful and regular competitor running alongside girls only a quarter her age. Almost every year in this race there was one particular lady who was notorious for causing trouble by claiming to have won despite the evidence of the stewards at the finishing tape. She could be relied upon to storm on to the platform as the prizes were being distributed and demand her rightful dues, making something of a mockery of the priest's customary speech about a good loser being more admirable than a good winner, as the complainant was being manhandled off the stage.

The variety of side shows had the crowds flocking and the Gala was a real money spinner for the Church of Our Lady of Compassion. It was a day of enjoyment for the whole village and the end of an era when it finally ceased to be held.

A step up from the Gala was the Flower Show which was THE event of Formby's year. It was awaited with great anticipation and was the place where everybody met and where past residents returned each year. Always held on the second Saturday in July it was for many years renowned for its good weather and excellent high standard. The farming classes were the main attraction with cattle, pigs, sheep, and horses competing for prizes, and all the local farmers decorating their animals, washing, brushing, and grooming them, with the manes of the shire and heavy horses beautifully plaited and beribboned and shining brasses adorning these majestic animals.

The horse jumping in the main arena with such famous names as Sir Harry Llewellyn and Foxhunter drew the crowds, and the Flower Show was quite rightly hailed as the finest one day show in the country. The surrounding exhibition marquees stood comparison with any anywhere, and the vegetable and flower tents were a picture, crowded with tastefully displayed exhibits from national as well as local firms. The childrens' tent was a particular favourite and reflected well the excellence of the village schools and the dedication of the teachers in encouraging such talent. Every school competed to out-class their neighbouring schools and the pendulum swung each year from one school to another in the number of prizes awarded to each. Classes were held in every conceivable subject from hand-writing and essays to pressed wild flowers and mounted cabbage white butterflies, from knitting, sewing and crochet to woodwork, art and miniature gardens, from cake making to model making, and the judges had an unenviable task so high was the standard.

There were refreshment tents for the patrons and members, and also for the general public, a licensed bar, and a wealth of trade and country craft stands. It was a day when the whole village dressed up and stepped out to enjoy a memorable day in a carnival atmosphere being entertained by Morris dancers, a band, and many novelty attractions. Though the show has survived and in recent years been injected with new enthusiasm it is a mere shadow of its forerunners, and maybe indicative of our changing world.

The three Church of England schools of Holy Trinity, St. Peter's and St. Luke's had until 1938 educated the children of the village right up to school leaving age. In that year the High School was built as a secondary school to accommodate the older children. Originally called the Formby Senior Council School, then the Formby Modern School, and later the Formby County Secondary School, it was always known as the New School, and even today many of the older local residents refer to it as such. I attended the school for only a short time meeting children from the other schools of St. Peter's and St. Luke's, many of whom remain my friends today.

Travelling up and down Long Lane to school we passed Rimmer's farm set in the fields and where and old carriage and a hearse were for many years parked

The School Choir, 1947

School Play, 1947

alongside and in which the hens used to nest. We once saw a pig being slaughtered as we came home and the screams from that pig are as real today as all those years ago.

The atmosphere at the school was a happy one and the plays which the school produced were especially memorable. On one occasion Russell Brown, the music and art teacher, went with some of the senior boys after the evening's performance to my mother's shop with a large tin bath. She piled it high with chips which they took back to the school to feed the hungry performers. As the school attendance grew a prefabricated extension known as Shinto was added. The school had an excellent choir and competed successfully in several music festivals, including our own Formby Music Festival, travelling as far as Freckleton, with my contribution being as a member of the "Shrimp's Choir" and offering such renditions as "The Trout", "Oh, lovely peace" and "Nymphs and shepherds".

My main recollections of the school are of the cookery and needlework classes. These are indelibly printed upon my mind never to be erased. Both subjects were taught by Mrs. Armitstead, known to us all as Aggie Fo – Aggie I suppose as it was not too fashionable or complimentary, and Fo because when she counted out the numbers she always pronounced four as foe. To say we were terrified of her was an understatement. Miss Reily at Holy Trinity had been an authoritarian, respected and later revered. A more awesome presence could not have been imagined, and so, at the tender age of eleven, we went as lambs to the slaughter. Our first needlework lessons were to make a cap to be worn in the cookery class. I left the school after two years having unpicked the cap fourteen times, it still uncompleted and looking more like a floor cloth. It was quite commonplace for Aggie to shut one of us in a cupboard for some minor and probably unwitting misdemeanour. We scrubbed the tables, always scrubbing "the way of the grain" and waiting for the crash of the rolling pin on those same tables in recognition of some mistake or other on the part of one of us. Her temper was legend. In fairness, however, it has to be said that many of her pupils gained skills which stood them in good stead for life and have just cause to be grateful to her. I cannot in all honesty claim to be one of them.

It is only with hindsight that it is realised just what a difficult job our teachers must have had with such large classes of such mixed abilities, but whatever the standard of education success rarely comes to those who fail to seek it by their own determined efforts, and many past pupils have indeed attained success in all walks of life. The school ceased to be the County Secondary School when it became comprehensive and took the new name of Formby High School. It was officially opened on 10th October 1972 by the then Secretary of State for Education, Mrs. Margaret Thatcher. That the school was such a happy place has been borne out in recent years through the popularity of the reunions, with past pupils flocking back to meet not only their fellow pupils but their teachers too.

From the age of thirteen I attended the Southport Technical College travelling there each day by train and always cycling to the station and leaving my bicycle at Alfie Formby's cycle shop close to Formby Railway Station. My brother and I both left our bikes at Alfie's shop as it cost 8d per week – a penny cheaper than at the Station cycle park. Both cycle parks were crammed full and it never ceased to amaze me how Alfie could always extricate the right bike from the tangle of machinery no matter what time we arrived back to collect it.

The back of Dick Goulbourne's cottage at the end of Duke Street
(The Blundell Arms is to the right)

The railway station was for many years a joy to use. The porters, including Dave Bullen, Harry Bannister and Les Pooley, took great pride in caring for the platform gardens, and Formby regularly won the prize for the best kept gardens with a colourful display most of the year. The waiting rooms, too, were pleasant and inviting places with blazing fires in the winter and vases of flowers in the

Cross Green: The Blundell Arms (now The Cross House)

summer, and everything polished and clean with not a sign of graffiti or vandalism.

The porters often filled in their time between shifts playing bowls on the immaculate green of the Railway Hotel, and in fact bowling greens were an essential feature of every public house in Formby. There was great rivalry in the bowling league with many teams competing. The local hostelries of the Grapes, Blundell Arms, Railway, Freshfield, Royal, plus the Tin Tab in Timms Lane, Holy Trinity, Gild Hall, Duke Street Park, and the Conservative Club were all members of the league.

My father was a keen bowler playing at varying times with Holy Trinity, the Blundell Arms, and the Conservative Club, and reaching the final in the cup the year before he died to be narrowly beaten by Councillor Jimmy Rimmer. My uncle, Joe Ashcroft, actually died on the bowling green of the British Legion in the final of a match which apparently overtaxed his heart with the tension of the game – surely an almost perfect way to end one's life!

The greens were beautifully tended and created quite a pastoral scene when spectators were able to lazily watch the skills of the bowlers in the tranquil calm of a summer's evening. The age of the motor car has resulted in all these bowling greens bowing to modern day progress and becoming car parks, with just six remaining – the Park, Conservative Club, Holy Trinity, Tin Tab, Gild Hall and the British Legion.

The Park was really nothing more than an expanse of greenery, purchased by Dr. Sykes, our very respected G.P., and given to the local council to be used as a park in perpetuity – something, on his own admission, not entirely the magnanimous gesture it might at first seem as his house overlooked the area, and by this benevolence he was ensuring his home would continue to have a pleasant

Formby F.C. Cup Winning Team 1947:
Back row: Ginger Leatherbarrow, Arthur Briscoe, Bill Moran, Ned Moran, Billy Wright, Taffy Jones, Walter Paterson, Dick Sergeant.
Front row: Dennis Jones, Kirby, Jimmy Ball, Harry Gannon, Tommy Cain, Taffy Edwards

open aspect. A gesture nevertheless for which we all have cause to be grateful. The only amenities in our park were a bowling green and a putting green with the picturesque thatched pavilion adding a rustic touch to the surroundings.

Dr. Sykes was also a patron of our local football team which, following the second world war, was highly successful with a thriving supporters' club of which we as a family were members. We all regularly attended the Brows Lane ground, savouring the hot Oxo at half time, and followed the team on away matches to such faraway places as Burscough, Skelmersdale, Marine (at Crosby) and Prescot, travelling by coach and regarding the outings as very lengthy journeys.

Billy and Chummy Blanchard were stalwarts of the club and the cup winning team of the Moran brothers, Tommy Cain, Harry Gannon, Ginger Leatherbarrow and the like were our heroes. The football hooligan had not yet been born and the idea of invading the pitch would have been anathema to the supporters then. The football ground was also used for baseball matches with Hector Bonallo and his distinctive American accent a popular player.

Very few local people travelled to the larger clubs of Everton or Liverpool though many held allegiance to one or other of the clubs. We were not yet into the age of the motor car and the accessibility of the Formby team assured them of the local support. My father's visit to Wembley in 1950 to watch Liverpool lose to

Arsenal was the highlight of his short life and the furthest distance he ever travelled.

* * * *

The church played an important part in my formative years, and from a very early age my father took my brother and me to Holy Trinity church with him every Sunday morning at 11 a.m. During our childhood Canon Dawson was our vicar, a bachelor who lived in the vicarage in Freshfield Road.

In our early years the congregation was summoned to the services by the ringing of the bell which was tolled by Ted Aindow who lived in one of the small thatched cottages in Gores Lane. When the bell became unsafe it was replaced by a gramophone record which was amplified from the belfry, but eventually it became very worn and the sound distorted and the bells were abandoned altogether.

The church had an attractive childrens' corner with a variety of books and appealing pictures and was where the flags and standards of various guides, scouts and other groups were displayed.

Canon Dawson introduced the unique Christmas wreathing service in which we all took part. This involved carrying long garlands, made of evergreens by the women of the parish, which we paraded round the church. About eight children carried each wreath and the ends of each one were attached to a rope suspended from the high pillars near the roof of the church. We all walked up to the altar to collect our wreaths then positioned ourselves round the sides of the church waiting for the appropriate moment when Canon Dawson's voice would boom forth "Let the church be wreathed". The child at the head of each wreath would then pull the rope and the sheer delight as the wreaths all rose heavenwards shone in the eyes of us all. Sometimes the rope would stick or the wreath get caught on an ornate part of the pillar and that would bring Miss Dean rushing down with her pole to release it. The beauty of the church at Christmas was breathtaking, and I doubt that any of our

Canon Colin Towers Dawson

parents had a dry eye as the church was being wreathed. It is most pleasing that the custom has survived to the present day.

My brother and I were members of the Sunday School which met in the parish hall every Sunday afternoon whilst the Children's Service met in the church. I never quite knew the criterion for this segregation but I loved the Sunday School and the teachings of Miss Heaton, Miss Liverseed and Miss Walsh who practised such patience with us all. We were given enchanting little books with small squared sections on each page clearly marked with each Sunday's date and every week we received a picture stamp which we would stick over the appropriate

Holy Trinity Church

square. I'm sure everyone else was as anxious as I was never to miss a week in order to get the stamp. Our Sunday School outings each summer were to the exotic reaches of Ainsdale Boating Lake or Churchtown's Botanic Gardens where we eagerly explored these foreign parts and enjoyed every second. The church also had a thriving youth club where we played table tennis, snooker and billiards, and where we suffered, or in most cases enjoyed, our first grown-up dances. Across the front of the stage in the parish hall was a row of electric light sockets which never seemed to have any light bulbs fitted. We found that by sticking our fingers in the sockets an electric shock ran up our arms which caused us all great amusement but could have had dire consequences.

Holy Trinity church has always been used for the Remembrance Day services when all the local organizations in any way concerned with the patriotism of our land, such as the British Legion, W.V.S., scouts, guides, police and of course all the services from Harrington Barracks and Woodvale joined together on the nearest Sunday to 11th November for the parade to the War Memorial. For a good many years after the war these parades were most moving and heartrending occasions, with the poignant last post of Jack Whiteside's cornet dying into total silence as "we all remembered them". The crowds thronging the Village were packed solid as the seemingly unending parade terminated at the War Memorial where countless wreaths or simple poppy crosses were laid, many by the wives and children made widowed and fatherless through the bitter conflict. The weather was always very dismal and often very wet and cold but the elements had no effect on the multitude who turned out to pay their respects.

When the war ended there was great jubilation throughout the land, and as in all areas of Britain we here in Formby held street parties to celebrate our victory. We joined with the Flaxfield Road residents to hold our party in their road. The long trestle tables ran down the centre of the dusty road, union jacks and bunting fluttering aloft, and despite the rationing everyone managed to provide a table fit for a victorious triumph over our enemies. We also had the privilege of the chairman of our council, Jimmy Rimmer, being in attendance, not in his official capacity, but as a resident of Priesthouse Lane.

Games were organized for the children, and a huge bonfire with an effigy of To-Jo, perpetrator of the Japanese atrocities, perched high on top was built on the field at the beginning of Flaxfield Road and Bull Cop where the sports were also

The Queen's Coronation celebrations 1953: Flaxfield Road street party

held during the day followed later at night by the dancing. My uncle Miles was taking part in the men's race when he suddenly went into a tremendous sliding skid. His racing feet had hit a cow pat sending him sprawling along the field.

When darkness descended the bonfire was lit amid yells and whoops of delight and the dancing began to the accompaniment of an old wind-up gramophone and a piano which had been pushed into the field. For once we were allowed to stay up late that night and were able to remain at the celebrations in an atmosphere of great excitement for the children and sheer utter relief for the adults in the knowledge that the horrors of war were over and the hope of a peaceful new world was in prospect.

This community spirit was repeated a few years later when our King died, heralding a new Elizabethan age with the coronation in 1953 of his daughter, the very young Queen Elizabeth II. We were still in the grip of the austere aftermath of the war years with rationing still in force, but with the Coronation celebrations came a wave of optimism for the future made even more joyful with the conquest of Everest by Hillary and Tenzing coinciding with this very momentous occasion.

During and immediately after the second world war Formby still remained the quiet rural place it had always been. Much building work had been carried out between the wars in the 1920's and 1930's when the Little Altcar area became built up with Altcar Lane, Marina Road and Kent Road providing what was then a very substantial area of housing with most of the properties being bought by the wealthier business families for rental to their employees and others. Small developments had also taken place in many other areas of Formby, but nevertheless the housing situation after the war was far from satisfactory and had meant that many families were living in less than ideal conditions in 'The Huts' in Broad Lane beyond the by-pass. The unhealthy environment and the acute need for better housing heralded the start of the council's building programme with the building of Alderson Crescent, Royal Crescent, Kings Close, Sealand Close, and parts of Lonsdale Road, Andrews Lane and Queens Road. Up to this time there was very limited council property in Formby.

I well remember one lunch time in 1946 or 1947 cutting through Long Lane via Alderson Crescent building site. I was with two friends on my way from school to my grandmother's house in Graburn Road. I always called at my mother's shop to collect my dinner and then went on to my grandmother's to eat it. The three of us were running through the newly planned-out site when I leapt across what I thought to be a solid patch of sand. It turned out to be a sand covered lime pit! I sank down to my waist, floundering about in the white sticky mess and getting further and deeper into trouble. I had raced ahead of my friends, Joan and Eileen, who stood looking on in horror as I thrashed about in the gooey lime. Joan threw me the belt from her school mac, and the two of them stretched across to yank me out. I eventually emerged caked in white slime splashing the revolting stuff all over them. We all traipsed along Church Road past Wilson's Garage to the astonished stares of the garage men and the fury of my mother when she saw my ruined clothes. The embarrassment of leaving a trail of white splodge with every step I took paled into insignificance alongside the reception which greeted me at the chip shop. I was sent to my grandmother's still caked in lime where I was cleaned up, whilst my mother had to pedal off home on her bicycle to Priesthouse Lane to try and find me something to wear. Children then did not have the extensive wardrobe of today's children and she had a very difficult job finding me alternative clothing. The indignity that day after all I had suffered in the lime pit was complete when I was forced to go back to school in the only other coat I possessed which was far too small for me and a hideous shade of brown.

Despite this council development the extent of the building had little impact on the way of life and character of Formby. The real changes were to come a decade or two later and were to change the face of Formby forever.

The thatched cottages were an accepted part of the scene in Formby whether they were wattle and daub or the more sturdy and conventional brick, and up until the late 1950's over fifty were still in existence and dotted all over the area. The row of brick cottages in Halsall Lane where Bob Wright grew his famous roses

The cottage of Wright's Rose Growers in Halsall Lane: now The Cloisters shopping complex

were not thatched but were most picturesque with a colourful display of flowers in their well cared for gardens, and the beauty of laburnum trees cascading their yellow flowers made a spring time show of splendour. The abundance of so many trees added to the general attractiveness and the tiny backwater of Furness

The first pair of cottages in Halsall Lane
(now replaced by an optician's and other shops)

Bob Howard's cottage, School Lane

Avenue was probably unknown to those not in the immediate vicinity. When the developers moved in to this lovely and rural corner and the cottages and trees disappeared to make way for a shopping complex it must have come as a tremendous blow to the Furness Avenue residents to have been so suddenly exposed to the outside world from their previous obscurity.

Many of the white cottages, charming as they were, could not realistically have been expected to survive into the present age. Many must have been very damp and insanitary, and like everything else in this world had only a certain life expectancy. Unhappily some of the better maintained met the same fate as the rest when the power of big business stormed in and the few remaining cottages now stand as a reminder of our past and an enhancement to their surroundings lending some character to an otherwise mundane landscape of bricks and mortar.

Our village was governed by the Formby Urban District Council with certain aspects of local government, such as Education and Libraries falling under the jurisdiction of the Lancashire County Council. All our local government officers were based at the Council Offices under the leadership of John Breese, the Clerk to the Council, and all of these officers lived locally, were known to us, and were easily approachable should the need arise.

The upkeep of our roads was largely the concern of the local council, but the main road through the district was the responsibility of the County and this was where Bob Sutton made his mark. Bob lived in Watchyard Lane and could be seen

Formby Council 1955:
Councillors Ted Pearce, Jack Dean, Peggy Beeston, Bill Alderson, George Kershaw,
Jimmy Rimmer, Christopher O'Neill, Mrs. Neep, Jack Hawkins.
Behind: Harold Turner, John Breese, Ron Thorpe

every working day trundling his dust-cart and brushes along Church Road and sweeping the street clean with the deftness of an artisan. Dick Dickinson who lived in Altcar was the other Lancashire County Council road sweeper who looked after the Altcar stretches of roads keeping the grass verges neatly trimmed with the long sweeps of his scythe and often calling in on the residents for a cup of tea. Our own local council employees undertook the cleanliness of all other roads in Formby and many different men were engaged in this work including Tommy Tierney from New Road who tragically lost his foot in a road accident.

Our councillors were naturally all local men living in our midst, some of them the sons of previous councillors, and all of them deeply entrenched in local knowledge and history. In a village community life was comparatively uncomplicated, and expectations not unduly high. Our affairs seemed to be in capable hands and most people showed little concern for the matters of local government and were reasonably content. All this was to change with the enormous development of the 1960's when village life began to crumble.

As the influx of new residents progressed there was a desirability for these people to become a real part of the community and for some of them, quite rightly and properly, to become involved in local affairs. The inevitable result was that the newly elected councillors eventually outnumbered the older local ones. It appeared puzzling to many local people that having come to a rural area through its attraction as such, these same newcomers now found the need to change the image to that more closely resembling the places they had left. The simple life was disappearing, making way for the sophistication of suburbia with the accessibility of the big city. The administration of a small population of country folk by like-minded fellows with such local names as Rimmer, Dean, Norris, Alderson, etc. is now in the annals of history and though we still have local councillors resident in

Formby their roots are newly laid, and we now rest under the umbrella of a much wider conurbation with local decisions being made by representatives not always wholly familiar with all the areas under their control.

In the fifty years since the war there have probably been more changes in Formby than at any time in its history. Today we have a population approaching 30,000 and the status of a town. It is still a pleasant place to live and I shall never leave it. I count myself more than fortunate to have known Formby as a village – to have been born when I was, and where I was. My generation had very little in the way of material assets though compared with our parents were affluent. We experienced a war in comparative safety when we were too young to fully understand its significance and danger, yet old enough to remember it and even enjoy it. We lived in a less materialistic age, and though we had little we had wealth beyond measure in the freedom we had to go where we chose, when we chose. Living close to nature gave us an inner sense of compassion and love for animals and our environment. To hurt or vandalize living things be they creatures or plants would have been abhorrent. We grew up in a world of innocence and with a healthy respect for our fellow men. We were very, very lucky.

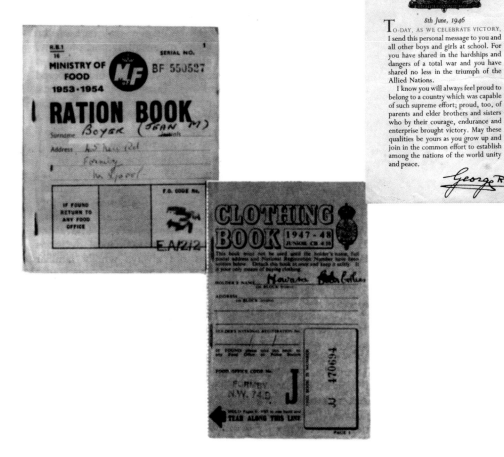

THE POEMS

Through bitter darkness and despair,
I sadly bore the pain,
Until the sadness sparked a light,
Which made me live again.

From all the wretched hopelessness,
Which seemed my fate in time,
The joy of precious days gone by
Poured out in words of rhyme.

Those simple melancholic poems,
Some happy and some sad,
Touched chords of pure nostalgia for
The times we'd all once had.

The copies flew around the world,
More tears than mine were shed
By kindred souls in foreign lands,
For youthful dreams now dead.

Not dead but just forgotten
In the mists of yesterday,
Brought back to life in times of loss,
To think about today.

The memories of a gentler age
Are treasures to be shared,
When we lived the simple village life,
And everybody cared.

THE VILLAGE

The name on the street map is shown 'Chapel Lane'
But that name's hardly known and not used,
'The Village' is how it has always been known,
And no one is very amused.

A traffic-free zone is what some people want,
Let the cars travel through others say,
Does it really much matter the locals retort,
It's been ruined and spoilt anyway.

The character's gone is the general lament
Of those old enough to recall
When the Village was just what its name would imply,
Full of shops for the needs of us all.

Old Bill Swift, Mr. Bills, Tilly Woodfin & Co.,
Just two banks and a shoe mender man,
Soapy Smith, Mrs. Clark, Charlie Stevens were there,
And they all fitted into the plan.

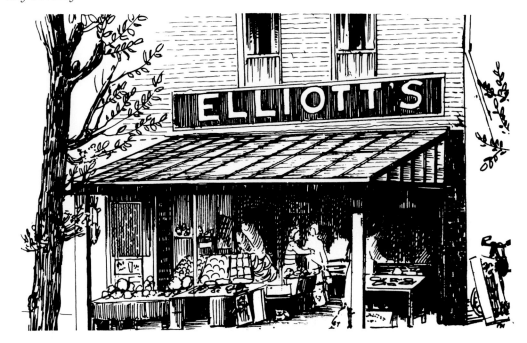

Then the banks and building societies came,
The estate agents, offices, too,
Accountants, solicitors all filled the space
Which big business had needed them to.

The family firms which had been here for years
Have all gradually faded away,
No Rimmers, no Aldersons, Elliotts or Wrights,
What a shame they weren't able to stay.

But the big chestnut trees are still spreading their leaves,
And the 'conkers' still blossom and fall,
And the children still come to collect them each year,
Though the damage they do would appal.

It isn't the same, and it isn't as nice,
But it's still not a bad sort of place,
Time couldn't stand still and we had to move on,
But we've used up so much of the space.

So 'The Village' is still what it always has been,
The hub of community life,
Let us leave it alone, let it rest for a while,
Just at peace from upheaval and strife.

THE QUEENS

A clapped out piano sets the scene,
With a woman sitting near the screen,
Pounding the keys for our delight,
Down at the Queens on Saturday night.

The noisy film reels clatter round,
Producing the pictures and the sound,
Not always synchronized quite right,
Down at the Queens on Saturday night.

No sleazy sex or violence,
Just films to cheer not cause offence,
Old Mother Riley or Pearl White,
Down at the Queens on Saturday night.

George Formby strumming on his uke,
Will Hay with cane and reading book,
Dorothy, Bob and Bing take flight,
Down at the Queens on Saturday night.

Sixpence, ninepence, one and three
Was what you paid for entrance fee,
Squeaky seats and flickering lights,
Down at the Queens on Saturday nights.

Sally Houghton and old May,
Flashing their torches down the way,
Ushering films in black and white,
Down at the Queens on Saturday night.

No one cared if the film broke down,
It didn't even bring a frown,
It was quite expected that it might,
Down at the Queens on Saturday night.

The slow decline in movie shows
Meant sad farewell, the Queens must close,
The lights were dimmed, we said goodnight
To the dear old Queens on Saturday night.

OUR LADY'S SCHOOL.

I watched so sadly as a crowd
Of bricks and mortar tumbled down,
Oak beams and rafters sturdy still
Were smashed beneath the wrecker's drill.

This seat of learning once revered
By boys and girls of yesterdays
Had stood so proudly through the years
Of wars, depression, changing ways.

But now it lies a flattened mass,
Born of Victoria's craftsmen true,
Fine architecture built to last,
But gone forever from our view.

Praise God not mammon we were taught,
But somehow we forgot that prayer,
The riches gained from what we've lost
Have laid our souls and conscience bare.

Lost generations softly sigh
Beneath the tomb-stones standing by
What have they done that men may say
Our Lady's School has passed away.

VIKING VILLAGE

This Viking village now has gone
From dreamy lanes and spreading fields,
Where yeoman farmers tilled the soil,
And fishermen brought in their yield.

A far cry now from village life
Of blacksmith, squire and rural scene,
When cottages adorned the land
Their thatch from crops the reaper gleaned.

A simple, carefree, close-knit clan
When man would help, not hinder, man.
Where did it go? What have we lost?
Much richer now, but at what cost?

The fields, the ditches, lanes are gone
As progress madly marches on,
Where are the trees that stood so tall
And beautified each spring and fall?

The Rimmers, Mawdsleys, Aindows, Wrights,
Diminished sadly from the fold,
Are shadowed now by names quite strange
From places spread around the globe.

A sprawling, noisy, busy town
Which now transcends that lazy life,
Where residents don't settle down
But travel on to higher sights.

From both ends of the social scale,
Coarse diction through to cultured tone,
Few local accents still remain
As indication of their home.

To those whose ancestry goes back
Through countless generations here,
A certain sadness shows a lack
Of comprehension, thoughts unclear.

How did this transformation come?
Why was it here they chose to stay?
This village where life was hum-drum
Has gone forever, far away.

How glad are those whose roots lie deep
In humble, honest Viking earth,
For they still see with eyes that weep
The memory of their place of birth.

JOAN HOLDEN'S SHOP

Joan Holden's shop was a paradise mess,
Whatever you asked for she always said yes.
Buttons and tea-towels, slippers and socks,
Hankies, pyjamas, or shoes in a box.

Underwear, cotton reels, needles and thread,
Knitting wool, collar studs, sheets for the bed,
Trousers and dresses, ribbons and pins,
Tea-cosies, hair-nets, gloves for the twins.

Elastic, shoe laces, braces and bibs,
Dressing-gowns, jewellery, even pen nibs,
Material for deck chairs or curtains or shirts,
Buckles and hair combs, aprons and skirts.

Coat-hangers, belts, and hair clips and slides,
Cardigans, jumpers, and lots more besides.
In fact when you visited Joan Holden's shop
You knew you would never catch her on the hop.

Her passing has left a remarkable gap,
Where will Dad go for that natty flat cap?
Her shop wasn't classy, or tidy, or neat,
Quite the reverse, but it couldn't be beat.

Eccentric, hard-working, and totally good,
She'll long be remembered, if not understood.
With Maisie, and Nora, and Josie as well,
There was nothing you wanted that they didn't sell.

THE VILLAGE SCHOOL

At the end of the village was Trinity School,
Three class-rooms that's all, and three teachers to rule.
Miss Reily, Miss Culshaw, Miss Heaton were they,
Who taught us and helped us at work and at play.

Miss Culshaw was clever 'cause she drove a car,
Miss Heaton was pretty and younger by far,
Miss Reily, the headmistress, famed and renowned,
So tall and so frightening, she bellowed so loud.

She'd a voice like a man, and she had a strange hat
Which she wore all her life, we were certain of that.
At adding and take-aways and spelling too,
We daren't get it wrong, we were terrified to.

The fear inculcated by Lilian R,
Would be frowned on today as too ruthless by far,
But beneath all the bluster and outward veneer
She was kindly and caring and not too severe.

Now when we look back to the days of our youth,
We surely can say with absolute truth
We were happy though disciplined, safe yet prepared
For whatever life offered by teachers who cared.

BROWS LANE

The Village stops and then Brows Lane
Continues on with shops again,
Like one continuous thoroughfare,
But once those rows of shops weren't there.

The Post Office was all that stood
Beside the bank as right it should,
Then Trinity School was next in line,
Attractive building, stout and fine.

Right opposite a lovely house,
The Elms at first its name pronounced,
A change of ownership had meant
The Priory came and The Elms then went.

Great elm trees growing in the grounds,
Plants in profusion all around,
A pretty corner quite serene,
So normal to the Formby scene.

A parrot in his cage swung high
Outside the door, and passers-by
Would whistle loudly to the bird
Whose strong reply was clearly heard.

Just memories now recall that scene,
Where such tranquillity had been,
The planners took it all away,
And nothing's left of yesterday.

ASHCROFT'S CHIPPY

The queue was a product that war time had bred,
It was something expected of all,
No shoving or pushing, no moaning or rushing,
We patiently waited our call.

Our rations were meagre, our money was scarce,
But we blithely accepted our lot,
With a war on we knew that things could get worse
And were thankful for what we had got.

Wherever we went to was always a chore,
But nobody seemed much to care,
The butchers, the bakers and candlestick makers
Had little to serve us with there.

But the busiest place and the much longest queue
Was the Chippy so cheap and so good,
It was friendly and warm and steam ran down the wall,
And good value was well understood.

Church Road, Formby
The Old Council Office

M E Sibley

The chips were just coppers and so were the fish,
And the batter bits tasted a treat,
They fell off the fish, cost a ha'penny a dish,
So who cared that we couldn't get meat.

What a haven it was, what a saviour of life,
It was packed to the doors every day,
Good hot nourishing food to feed many a brood,
And the mothers quite able to pay.

The soldiers and airmen poured in every night,
Met their girl friends and all of their mates,
They'd no money to spare but they loved to be there
In the best place to meet all their dates.

That Chippy was Ashcroft's – the one we loved best,
It was second to none without doubt,
They worked harder than most and sold cod that could boast
Would taste better than scampi or trout.

Those days are long gone and the war has been won,
And the Chippy well answered the call,
It fed us and reared us, it warmed us and cheered us
When we all had our backs to the wall.

Whoever would think that a Chippy could be
So important in war and in peace,
But whoever remembers that Chippy today
Knows the happiness served with the grease.

WALLIS'S FAIR

Flashing lights and blaring sound,
Bobby horses whirling round,
Great excitement for us all,
"A penny ride" the man would call.

Round and round the horses flew,
Children screaming as they do
When wild excitement reaches heights,
Amid the maze of fairy lights.

The whole of Formby came each night
To sample all the fair's delights,
The Bay Horse field was quite transformed,
And everybody's hearts were warmed.

They'd all the things to bring real joy
To man and woman, girl and boy,
Rolling pennies, throwing mops,
Swingboats, waltzers – they were tops.

You'd even win a threepenny bit
If all the tins your mop could hit,
And then you'd have another go
To try again with one more throw.

Too soon the week would fly away,
The caravans packed and on their way,
The lights extinguished, music gone,
Wallis's Fair was travelling on.

THE SHORE

Long summer days,
School holidays,
Always it seemed to be warm,
Sandwiches packed,
Off we all tracked
To the shore like bees in a swarm.

Off on our bikes,
Even on trikes,
Our parents knew we were fine,
Sun, sand and sea,
Nothing could be
Better for kids at that time.

Sandhills were steep,
Starr grass grew deep,
We ran and chased through it all,
Laughter and joy
For each girl and boy,
Tossing an old tennis ball.

Nothing to pay,
Free every day,
We splashed and swam in the waves,
Jellyfish found,
Digging around,
Sand tunnels made into caves.

Exotic shells,
Lovely harebells,
Pebbles so smooth and so round,
Morning till night,
Loving the sight
Of the sea washing in on the ground.

Tired and spent,
Dirty we went
Back home exhausted to bed,
Happy to be
Here in Formby,
With our playground the shore just ahead.

RIMMER'S

On the corner of the Village was a shop,
With the name emblazoned right across the top,
That name was part of Formby's heritage,
Quite symbolic of our former Viking age.

Rimmer's was that proud and famous name,
And their shop was full of fruit and fish and game,
Their windows were a lovely sight to see,
Piled with fruit and veg. in perfect symmetry.

Great huge pyramids of apples firm and round,
Next to oranges shaped in a perfect mound,
All the veg's you could ever hope to need,
Neatly stacked and on display for us to feed.

M.E.Sibley 76 ©

Mr. Jim was on the side with all the fruit,
And Mr. Bob the fish and poultry followed suit,
Mr. Bill the market transport organized,
And Miss Nellie ran the van delivery side.

Miss Shan and Elsie Bridge kept the accounts,
While Dixie Ashton weighed the fish in right amounts,
Mrs. Rimmer, Mrs. Ward and Marcia, too,
Along with Betha made a really first-class crew.

For a hundred years the family served us well,
And they always would as far as we could tell,
But there sadly dawned the day the blinds came down,
When our village woke and found it was a town.

THE PRIEST HOUSE

The Roman Catholic faith was strong,
And tolerated in that day,
A church was needed for the throng
Of worshippers to kneel and pray.

The church was built along School Lane,
And mass was celebrated there,
Until the Orange monarchs came
And put an end to sacred prayer.

The Priest house standing quite close by,
So stoutly built by Formby's squire,
Stood empty now and wondered why
God's love for man by man should tire.

Religious differences prevailed,
And Catholics once more were outcast,
Their hearts were rent, they wept and wailed,
But still their faith held strong and fast.

Their church for worship was closed down,
But that would not deter the flock,
The Lord with mercies would them crown,
Their faith would stand firm as a rock.

In secret they assembled then,
Along the lane at the Priest house,
"Watch yard" the cry would warn the men
To hide and keep quiet as a mouse.

Two hundred years have rolled away,
The fortunes of the house have changed,
Irreverence followed till the day
Its use was fully rearranged.

Chapelhouse Farm

A farm house later it became,
With pigs and cows around the land,
Old Teddy Mawdsley was the name
Of the new occupant on hand.

The Priest house days were numbered now,
Another war had sealed its fate,
Evacuees replaced the cows,
Soon history would evaporate.

The 1950's came around,
And Formby's building boom began,
That great historic house came down,
A victim of expansion's plan.

Those unconcerned with history
See just a pleasant road today,
Religious strife and mystery
Lost in the past of yesterday.

THE MAY BLITZ

A direct hit from Jerry's bomb
Made Liverpool look like the Somme.
Where can we go? What shall we do?
Our homes are gone, our families too.

A dreadful week with no respite
From Hitler's wrath and Nazi might,
The terrace houses all aflame,
What price to pay in freedom's name.

Why is this happening to our port?
The people's war is being fought.
Why pick on us? What have we done
To tantalize and rile the Hun?

A full week passed and still they came,
The Messerschmitts to kill and maim,
The awful carnage, blazing fires,
The sky alight like funeral pyres.

We've had enough we'll have to go,
Our friends in Formby, they will know
Where we can rest and get away
From all this horror night and day.

So weary – just for peace they pined,
By any means that they could find
They left their ruined city for
Some refuge from that evil war.

What utter bliss, what calm and peace,
True friends to help, the noise to cease,
Refreshed, restored in clean fresh air,
A world away from fear and care.

The Blitz was done, the city scarred,
What bits were left were black and charred,
But Churchhill said we'd win the war,
We knew we could – we'd win, and more.

The city would be built again,
Lots of the people would remain,
But Formby's rural country face
Would see a change affect the place.

And so it was – it grew and grew,
And lost the charm the locals knew.
The war must take most of the blame
Why Formby now is not the same.

FORMBY

We knew it once when we were small,
But did we really see at all
The beauty we just took as ours,
Whilst playing in the fields for hours.

The trees we climbed and hid inside,
Their trunks and branches spreading wide,
The brambles scratching racing legs,
The bird's nests full of speckled eggs.

The farmyard barns with bales of hay,
Beside the shippon where each day
The milkman's hands coaxed forth the milk
With rhythmic movement smooth as silk.

The countryside which met the sea,
Wide open spaces, wild and free,
The seagulls wheeling overhead,
How will it look when we are dead?

No fields, no farms, no trees to climb,
Our children now don't have the time,
Life rushed away at frantic pace,
We hurtled on through time and space.

We were to blame, we did not try,
Whilst living we let Formby die,
It grew, it flourished, then it burst,
We watching as progress did its worst.

Our ghostly spectres now look down
On an affluent suburban town,
And shake each sad bewildered head,
At how it looks now we are dead.

CHURCH ROAD

From the top of Church Road right down to Cross Green,
What a mixture of rural delight,
Some nice houses, three farms, several shops and a school,
With the police station there on the right.

Bubbles Dickinson's hardware and chandlery shop,
Right opposite Greenhalgh's place,
Mrs. Cairns on the corner past Bobby Neale's pies,
And the café for feeding your face.

Bradley's, Yeoman's, then Cranshaw's, and Tommy McGee
Cutting hair for a tanner a go,
Mr. Golding and 'Brookie' with mouths full of tacks,
Mending shoes with a new heel or toe.

Ashcroft's chip shop came next, and then over the road
Frankie Wright with a marvellous stock
Of cigarettes, sweets and a host of good things
From a tea pot to carbolic block.

Next door Boardman & Tetlow's for grocery goods,
And the Co-op just opposite there,
Wilson's garage for petrol for automobiles,
And a pump to fill tyres full of air.

The Gild Hall so popular Saturday nights,
Where the girls met their future husband
At the dances with Bernard and Norman and Jack,
Playing well in their fine three piece band.

Police Station and Whitehouse Farm

Bill Hunter's farm first, Jossie Rimmer's the next,
And their cows used the road like a track,
Herding along from the farms to the fields,
Then for milking they all herded back.

The rosy red apples on Jossie's big trees
Were temptation to all of the boys,
But six policemen right opposite worked like a charm
And the orchard was safe from their ploys.

Next to the police station old Mr. Parr,
With his garage constructed of tin,
He mended our punctures and fixed up our bikes,
And sold cans full of blue paraffin.

Rothwell's stores were across with Bob Hogg at the till,
Serving bacon and bread and the like,
Very handy for mothers who met out their tots
From Our Lady's at four every night.

Stevens & Hooks with their haulage firm next,
Past the school where Ma Pep ruled the roost,
Then the Bay Horse with Alcocks, both Lily and May,
So run down they'd no business to boost.

Some more great big houses, then right at the end
Walker's Farm with the pony to stroke,
What a wonderful stroll down a major main road,
Where each step of the way someone spoke.

For those who recall those far halcyon days,
When our lives were much simpler than now,
We were lucky to know just what Formby was like
When the village lived under the plough.

TO THE BROOK

Straight down Bull Cop and out over the field,
Hop over the stile, our happiness sealed,
With jam jars and fishing nets and old tin cans
Clutched tighly for what we could catch with our hands.

Our fishing nets made with a nail and a cane,
Old stockings the net as we ran down the lane
To the ditch by the brook where the tiddlers and frogs
And jack sharps swam round in the reeds and the logs.

All day we would play catching all that we could,
Fill the jam jars with tiddlers and handfuls of mud,
Then back home we went past the barn and Lowe's Farm,
Scruffy children wet through but free from all harm.

What a great way of life with no worries or cares,
A tin bath in the living room, then up the stairs
To our dreams of tomorrow when we'd all start again
With our jam jars and fishing nets off down the lane.

THE GALA

Bank Holiday Monday, the sun always shone,
The village turned out, every single last one,
To join in the races and happy side shows,
And meet all the neighbours that everyone knows.

PROGRAMME.

Children's Fancy Dress Parade.

Parade at War Memorial at 1-30 p.m. prompt.
Interval 5 to 5-45 p.m.
Refreshments at Moderato Prices in the Hall.

The Committee has power to alter any handicap.

EVENT 1—*100 Yards Flat Race, Men.*

	HEAT 1	yds		HEAT 2	
1	H. Lamar	4	9	Jas. Lloyd	1
2	W. Rimmer, C.L.	7	10	H. Cockcroft	4
3	Hy Jackson	7	11	John Fenner	7
4	Ed. Mawdsley	8	12	Ted Edwards	8
5	R. G. Norris	10	13	W. H. Hall	10
6	R. Leddy	13	14	John Barton	13
7	E. Moon	13	15	R. Wareing	4
8	Jas. Rimmer, C.L.	8			
	1st 2nd			1st 2nd	

HEAT 3

		yds
16	D. Postlethwaite	5
17	S. Scarisbrick	7
18	Jos. Mawdsley, M.H.	7
19	Jos. Rimmer, L.A.	9
20	Jos. Steneth	9
21	Hy. Mawdsley	13
22	D. Salmon	1
23	J. Moore	4
	1st 2nd	

The rose queen so pretty with full retinue,
The band playing well as they came into view,
Along to the field just behind the Gild Hall,
Where the longed for performance was waiting for all.

Descend from the wagons then on to the stage,
Where the rose queen sat down helped along by her page,
The crowning was done and we all clapped and cheered,
The photographer snapped them and then disappeared.

The kid's fancy dress was a popular class,
With Snow White, Formby's triplets, a big beer glass,
Such ingenious ideas made from old odds and ends,
By the Mums and the Dads and the aunties and friends.

The sports and the races of all different kinds,
The children excited and out of their minds
At the prospect of winning a prize or a cup
If they got to the finish without tripping up.

The sack race, obstacles, plain running track,
The ladies race with 'Little Nell' at the back,
She was such a good sport, overweight and rotund,
But she ran like a good 'un to swell the church fund.

The highlight was always the great Formby Mile,
As the men and the boys set off with a smile,
Peter Bradshaw, the champion, was there at the last,
To pick up the cup as the winning post past.

Tommy Ledger was shouting and taking the cash,
As the big 'Wheel of Fortune' whizzed round in a flash,
When the finger stopped moving and came home to rest,
You knew if you'd lost of had feathered your nest.

That August Bank Holiday came every year,
Accepted and cherished as something held dear,
But as our sleepy village grew up and got lost,
A whole way of life disappeared to our cost.

Wicks Lane, near
Green Loons Farm.

BYGONE DAYS

Country folk with country accents,
Everyone knew everyone,
Leafy lanes and grassy meadows,
No one thought of rushing on.

Buttercups and four leaf clover,
Celandine and hollyhocks,
Flowers growing in the hedgerows,
Children blowing dandelion clocks.

Lots of dusty lanes to wander,
Daisy chains and marigolds,
Many ditches filled with frogspawn,
Cattle in the old pinfolds.

Making hay from dawn till sunset,
Stooks of corn set in the fields,
Farmers bringing in the harvest,
Toiling as the church bell peals.

Butterflies fluttering gently round us,
Autumn conkers on a string,
Oak and elm and ash and poplar,
Sycamore pods fly like a wing.

Blackberry picking in the evenings,
Dewberries growing by the shore,
Gorse and vetch and foxgloves blooming,
Who could ever ask for more?

Is this memory just a daydream,
Passed and gone just like a kiss?
How can we convince our children
Formby once was just like this?

TASKER

A tumble-down shack and a man from the wars,
Whose life seemed so simple without any cause,
Some old mongrel dogs and a battered tin pan,
The sandhills were home to this solitary man.

We knew him as Tasker and thought him quite odd,
A remote and strange character, off he would plod
With down-at-heel shoes and tattered old togs,
As he trailed from the shore with his sack and his dogs.

His knowledge and culture belied by his looks,
His life just revolved round his pets and his books,
He'd rejected a world he could not understand
For the plants and the wild life the sea and the sand.

He lived very frugally, liked his pint pot,
The cold and the wet seemed to bother him not,
Throughout all the seasons his life was the same,
He survived snow and rain and when the winds came.

Looked down on by many for what he commends,
His dogs were his family, the seagulls his friends,
His life style for him was contentment sublime,
And to live close to nature was never a crime.

No home, no possessions, no job, and no wife,
He did nothing, went nowhere, wasted his life,
Why should we remember and talk of him still?
He's part of our folk-lore, and that's why we will.

THE EMBASSY

The Embassy cinema so plush and so grand,
Where the lads and the lasses would go hand in hand,
Jack Mawdsley in uniform smartly attired,
Greeting the patrons, both young and retired.

A clip round the ear if the boys misbehaved,
Then across to the Grapes for his thirst to be saved,
Back for the interval shining his light,
As though he'd been there for the whole of the night.

Stephanie Hilton was there at the box office flap,
Our tickets shot out from a brass ticket trap,
We'd then go inside as the queue moved along,
Take our seats for the show which would never go wrong.

Red velvet seats, well upholstered and clean,
Lovely carpets, posh lights and a big flashy screen,
This was no flea pit for any old scruffs,
The elite were the patrons in fur coats and muffs.

Two-and-threes up the stairs to the balcony seats,
Where the upper crust classes would go for their treats,
Technicolour films with no hitches or gaffes,
And cartoons designed to produce lots of laughs.

Downstairs in the one-and-nines on the back row
Were the sweethearts who always missed half of the show,
Paying far more attention to what went on there,
Than to watching the dancing of graceful Astaire.

At the front in the ninepennies just past the rail,
The noise from the youngsters would rise up the scale,
Cricks in their necks looking up at the screen,
Which was too high above to be properly seen.

The interval lights would illumine the place,
And the girls would go out then to powder their face,
While the boyfriends would buy them an ice-cream or chocs,
Or a packet of fags and a Swan Vestas box.

If the film had been sad we would then mop our eyes,
Blow our noses and smile as we got up to rise,
And file down the aisles to get to the doors,
Where Jack Mawdsley was standing on duty of course.

We all loved the Embo and queued every night,
To see Hedy Lamarr or a good cowboy fight,
What a long time ago do those memories seem,
But it's only last week when you just sit and dream.

THE VILLAGE BOBBIES

They had no need for walkie-talkies,
No need at all for Panda cars,
Our bobbies here used Shanks's pony,
And never went to seminars.

No brass-hats breathing down their necks here,
No forms in triplicate to write,
Just leisured strolls around the village,
Keeping watch by day and night.

We knew them all and they knew us then,
Respected, held in high esteem,
These seven men were our protectors,
Reliable, trusted, first-rate team.

Then Formby was a quiet back-wash,
Open doors, no bolts and bars,
Crime was almost non-existent,
And hardly any motor cars.

Fred Beswick was the tall and lean one,
Small moustache and big flat feet,
We all felt safe with Fred amongst us,
Pounding round his Formby beat.

Norman Brooks, the quiet shy one,
Played piano in the band,
But don't forget he's still a copper,
Toe the line, or feel his hand!

Bob Greenhalgh was the big rotund chap,
Crime detection was his game,
Sergeant Coulthard at the station,
Watch your step – they knew your name!

George Davidson and big Bill Hoptroff
Were the men we all admired,
Plus P.C. Rooke, the mounted policeman,
All hoped they'd stay till they retired.

In such a law-abiding village,
Seven policemen seemed a lot,
But pay was low and no inflation
Meant the best was what we got.

Men of honour, poorly paid then,
Unsocial hours, but quite content,
Our Formby bobbies were our mentors,
And we missed them when they went.

F.U.D.C

Once we had a district council,
Once we knew our place,
Once our chairman, Jimmy Rimmer,
Was a well known face.

Once we had our own officials,
Once we knew them all,
Once we used our Council Office
Like our own Town Hall.

Once when Harold Turner ordered,
Once they heard the shout,
Once our workmen knew their workload
They would all turn out.

Once Bob Sutton swept our roads clean,
Once our park was neat,
Once we had a thatched pavilion
Where we all could meet.

Once when John Breese was the king pin,
Once we knew the score,
Once when Formby was just Formby
We seemed to matter more.

Now we have no Formby council,
Now we've lost our way,
Now we're just a part of Sefton,
Completely gone astray.

THE LIBRARY SHOP
(LANCASHIRE COUNTY LIBRARY)

It was a wondrous place to be
When you were only just turned three,
And then when you were over four
The great delights were even more.
From five and six were better still,
So many things to cause a thrill.
Seven, eight, nine, ten, as minds awoke,
Came endless treasures for young folk,
For you could go there on your own,
Without your Mum or Dad – ALONE!

Where could this pleasure palace be?
The fairground, park, or by the sea?
Those venues all give real delight,
But only if the weather's right.
This paradise of endless joy
Was free to every girl and boy,
By READING you could live each word,
Be brave or clever, strong or scared.
Those days had no expansive hall,
Or endless stock for one and all,
A tiny shop supplied the need
Of those whose hobby was to read.
Despite its very modest size,
That library shop enthralled our eyes,
No lettered person with degree
Behind the desk in old Formby,
Just Mrs. Derbyshire in charge,
And literary wants were none too large,
She frightened us a little but,
But then most grown-ups always did,
Her long black dress and glasses small
Perched on her nose to see us all.
How greatly things have changed today,
Technology now leads the way,
That tiny library shop has gone,
Replaced by a much grander one,
But it's so nice to think back when
How simple things were when you're ten.

THE MILK ROUND

Saturday morning,
Daylight was dawning,
Out of our beds we shot,
Down to the farm,
Peaceful and calm,
Where the horse waited ready to trot.

Each of us took turns,
Loading the milk churns,
On to the old milk float,
Ladles were ready,
Dolly stood steady,
The reins loosely tied at her throat.

Bert Lawton was waiting,
And anticipating
How many children would be,
Bright-eyed but yawning,
At seven that morning,
Aboard for the ride that was free.

Riding the milk round,
Over the rough ground,
Bumping along with the horse,
This was like paradise,
Nothing could be so nice,
Heaven was like this of course.

Stop at each house gate,
Stagger with milk crate,
Down the front path to the door,
Fill up the milk jug,
Or the old pint mug,
Sometimes a tip was in store.

Back to the stable,
Ready and able
To unload the churns on the floor,
Into the dairy,
White-washed and airy,
The milk round was over once more.

This was the way then
We used to play when
The T.V. set hadn't been born,
Countrified pleasures,
Were our simple treasures,
Each Saturday morning at dawn.

THE BOAT HOUSE

In childhood days we never knew
The history of the lifeboat crew,
We didn't know we'd led the way
And launched a boat in Liverpool Bay.

To us the boat house was the shop
And café where we bought our pop,
Its sloping roof down to the shore,
And gaping massive wide front door.

Cold cobbles covered with blown sand
We walked upon, bare feet to stand
And change the bottles we had found
For copper pennies large and round.

A huge enclosure quite close by,
Beside the sea, beneath the sky,
Where all our bikes were in a stack,
Unlocked and safe till we came back.

The sea was clear, the shore was clean,
Hard ridges where the tide had been,
Wrecked boats and driftwood were our toys,
Sandhills resounding with our noise.

As setting sun joined sea and sky,
Back to the boat house we would fly,
Collect our bikes and ride away,
What perfect end to perfect day.

THE SWAMP

In winter months when snow lay deep,
And all of nature seemed asleep,
Down to the swamp we'd make our way,
And spend each frosty day at play.

The ice formed solid as a rock,
Dozens of children all would flock,
To slide and skid between the reeds,
Tentative steps to dizzy speeds.

No expert skaters; raw recruits,
No proper skates; just wellie boots,
We slipped and fell and staggered back,
Not caring if the ice should crack.

As winter's grip released its hold,
We bid goodbye to ice and cold,
The swamp returned to soggy slush,
With spiky reed and straight bulrush.

Now Gardner Road lies on the top
Of our dear swamp beyond Bull Cop,
Where gentle pussy willows grew,
When all the world to us was new.

ASPARAGUS

Down by the pines the asparagus grew,
A food much beloved by the affluent few,
In pure Formby sand by the edge of the sea
It was planted and grown, this delicacy.

Jimmy Lowe was acclaimed as Asparagus King,
His crops were world famous and bundles he'd bring
To sell in the village from humble small shops,
And transport on his lorries, these wonderful crops.

The gentry, the royals, all partook of his wares,
His daughters worked hard as the labours they shared,
Such lovely young girls slaving into the night,
In a season so short and a schedule so tight.

Just casual help and all hands to the pump,
A frantic work load before they could slump,
And know that their efforts were their own rewards,
In supplying this food to both princes and lords.

Formby asparagus was famed and renowned
Throughout all the country and it could be found
On fine royal plates and in great hallowed halls,
At society weddings and county hunt balls.

Lowe's asparagus fields can no longer be found,
No more feathery ferns in that poor barren ground,
As agricultural industry withered and died,
Pine Tree Farm disappeared with the incoming tide.

HARRINGTON BARRACKS

Hundreds of houses cloak the land
Where once the regiments did stand,
Young soldiers shattered from Dunkirk,
Back from a nightmare they'd not shirk.

In rags and tatters they were clad,
The lucky ones who were just glad
To have survived the beaches where
So many friends they'd left back there.

The peace of Formby's quiet lanes,
Stark contrast to the battle pains,
From bloody beach to silent shore,
These weary men were home once more.

Green beret and the khaki cap,
Where was this Formby on the map?
A place they'd never even heard,
Now here their billets they all shared.

Formby was teeming with the troops,
Marching feet and stamping boots,
Battalions lined up on parade,
And children watching unafraid.

Exciting times for children's eyes,
Sweet innocence, a priceless prize,
Oblivious of the cruel war
That brought us sights unseen before.

Those soldiers left, a few returned
To make their homes and livings earned,
In this small village once unknown
They laid their roots and called it home.

The years passed by, the barracks died,
Fields, trees and flowers all expired
As houses sprang up smart and new
To change that lovely, rural view.

When we look back across the years,
When times were hard with many fears,
How could we ever visualize
That vast estate before our eyes?

Such natural beauty all around,
So many wild flowers to be found,
Now they're all gone and in their place
A homestead for the human race.

It had to be, it had to grow,
But we were lucky we could know
The way it was in times gone by,
When what we loved grew up to die.

V.J. NIGHT

Long trestle-tables down the middle of the road,
Sandwiches, jellies and cakes by the load,
Despite the food rations and those dreadful B.U.'s,
War was over at last - we knew we wouldn't lose.

Victory was celebrated all round the land,
And here in little Formby the parties were grand,
Great bonfires with To-Jo propped up on the tops,
And in the fields we were dancing amid the cow flops.

Union Jacks, lots of bunting – a wonderful scene,
Kids united with Dads they didn't know and hadn't seen,
Life was good once again, deprivation would be gone,
We could pick up the pieces and simply carry on.

The men and the boys who were lost in the war
Paid the ultimate price for our freedom once more,
Sadness and joy intertwined with relief
That a bright new tomorrow could be our belief.

When we sang and we danced back in 1945
The future looked good and hope very much alive,
Life went on, people prospered, the welfare state came,
Bringing apathy, greed, and nothing was the same.

Life today is much easier in very many ways,
But those dark days of Hitler seemed happier days,
When we all pulled together and did what we could
To help one another in a place that was good.

What's happened here in Formby is mirrored round the land,
Places grow, people change as progress is planned,
But did it need to change quite so dramatically,
That now we're just another place with no identity?

THE MARMALADE CART

Here we had no main drain sewerage,
Here the cess pool flowed,
And every Friday, early morning,
The chariot hit the road.

Here we had no sanitation,
Here the cockerel crowed,
And every Friday, early morning,
The chariot hit the road.

Here we had endangered species,
Here the natterjack toad,
And every Friday, early morning,
The chariot hit the road.

Here the bucket down the garden,
Here the candles glowed,
And every Friday, early morning,
The chariot hit the road.

Here was Hagan on the back seat,
Here to fetch the load,
And every Friday, early morning,
The chariot hit the road.

When we think of bygone Formby,
A picturesque abode,
Do we forget that every Friday,
The muck cart hit the road?

THE WAR MEMORIAL

Armistice day,
Cloudy and grey,
The forces, the police on parade,
Processions so long,
The people would throng
In respect of the sacrifice made.

Fresh in the minds,
Memory finds
The time when those lost lives had been
The husbands and sons,
Destroyed by the guns,
In two wars that were wholly obscene.

Khaki and blue,
Everyone knew,
As they marched from the church to the cross,
With all civic heads,
To honour the dead
Of the wars that created such loss.

The cross stood erect,
A mark of respect,
In a corner of our village plot,
The names which it bore
Were with us no more,
For eternity now was their lot.

The memorial stands
On Weld Blundell land,
A gift to the villagers here,
That never shall we
Forget what we see,
And be grateful for all we hold dear.

A symbol of pride,
The shops alongside,
All their names, like the men, long since gone,
As we hurry on by,
Do we stop and think why
These young men were denied to live on?

They fought and they died
That we could abide
In an island of freedom and choice,
Though their Formby has gone,
Their names will live on,
Through their sacrifice we can rejoice.

Such growth and such change
Would today seem so strange
If those heroes returned from their rest,
For the Formby they knew,
With the fields wet with dew,
Has exploded like bombs in the west.

Estates now abound,
Where once was the ground,
A carpet of flowers and grass,
Let us never forget
That we all stand in debt
To those names etched in stone as we pass.

HOLY TRINITY

Our Church in Formby came to birth
In eighteen-eighty-nine,
She rose so proudly from the earth,
A symbol of love divine.

A monument from man to God,
A home for all to share,
The comfort of his staff and rod,
In-built with love and care.

A building to his glorious name,
A sanctuary of peace,
A haven where the faithful came,
And here their fears released.

Life's differing fortunes down the years,
The good times and the bad,
The jubilations and the fears,
Here shared, both warm and sad.

The evils of the first world war,
The dreadful bitter loss,
We shall remember evermore
Reminds the reredos.

The joy of marriage solemnized,
The miracle of birth,
The parting grief of sad demise
At journey's end on earth.

The wreathing and the gift of toys,
Mothering Sunday flowers,
The Easter eggs for girls and boys,
The harvest and God's powers.

The guides, the brownies, scouts and cubs,
The youth club and young wives,
The school, the bowling, tennis clubs,
All milestones in our lives.

An old yet ever youthful church,
All changing yet the same,
A loving, caring, hopeful church,
To the glory of God's name.

The choir stalls ringing with the sound
Of voices raised in praise,
Oh, Lord, we pray let grace abound
In all the coming days.

And may our Church live day by day
Into eternity,
That unborn congregations may
Bless Holy Trinity.

MRS. MITTON

A hundred years she lived and more,
In fact a hundred and four,
And in that time she left our shore –
The year nineteen-o-four.

She thought Australia would be fair,
And sailed away to sea,
But six months later she got there
And missed her old Formby.

Australia was a barren land,
So dusty and so hot,
She and her husband hand in hand,
Back on the ship they got.

Straight back to Formby they both came,
And opened up her shop
In Mitten's Lane – which took her name,
And there was glad to stop.

The smallest shop you'd ever find,
The best stock in the land,
So dark the kids could rob her blind,
But no – they'd all be banned.

This pokey little white-washed place
Was full of everything,
Tinned food and soap to wash your face,
Bread, cakes, and balls of string.

Potatoes, firewood, veg. and fruit,
Sweets, biscuits, matches, too,
Cinnamon sticks and liquorice root,
And paper for the loo.

Set in the fields in clean fresh air,
Right opposite the farm,
She'd never be a millionaire,
But could live in peace and calm.

No trace today of that small shop,
No sign of where she'd been,
No indication of the spot,
Which now is Smithy Green.

FORMBY HIGH

Amid the fields and ploughshares
This edifice appeared,
A blot upon the landscape,
But needed said our peers.

It housed the pre-war school kids
Who had nowhere else to go,
In a lovely brand new building
Looking like the Earls Court Show.

They came from Holy Trinity,
St Peter's and St Luke's,
To start a new and different life,
With implements and books.

They'd never heard of science,
Bunsen burners full of gas,
Iron filings, blobs of mercury,
And Miss Parry head of class.

The boys were taught their woodwork,
And the girls to cook and sew,
Mr. Nelson was our idol,
And old Aggie scared us so.

The Browns brought out our culture
In both music and in art,
And sports and games were uppermost
And closest to the heart.

Blundell, Formby, Scarisbrick,
Were the houses of the school,
And sports day was the highlight,
Competition was the rule.

Now fifty years have passed away,
And new generations swot
A different type of learning
Than their forbears ever got.

More academic skills are taught,
Technology's the rule,
The education now required
Is light years from our school.

The school laid down the guide lines
Which set us on the track,
The rest was really down to us,
And now we can look back.

Just look around our Formby now,
With houses by the mile,
All built, maintained and serviced
By those kids from Formby High.

Good joiners, brickies, handy men,
Gardeners, plumbers, sparks,
They came in on the building boom,
And in business made their marks.

And so the school goes on today,
With kids who work and try
To emulate their parents
Who once went to Formby High.

MURIEL SIBLEY (1)

We were so blind, we could not see
The things we loved and lost,
The cottages, then tree by tree
Into the past were tossed.

Our fields and lanes and ditches deep,
So slowly went away,
We shed no tears, we did not weep,
We lived just for the day.

Then into Formby came the one
Who saw what we could not,
Her bicycle she perched upon,
And with her camera shot
Each building as it bit the dust,
Each leafy lane that fell,
Her records captured for our trust,
The place we'd known so well.

With paint brush, film and artist's pen,
Such beauty she'd record,
Quite unappreciated then,
We locals would have scorned.

How could we know so long ago
How fortunate we were,
When Muriel came and said hello,
And stayed her life to share.

We owe so much to her today,
A precious record now,
Of how our lives were yesterday,
Mrs. Sibley take a bow.

DOCTOR TREE'S SURGERY

We know that coughs and sneezes
Will quickly spread diseases.
We know the things we're all supposed to eat.

We know that high cholesterol
Is like low octane petrol,
And makes our engines tick not quite so sweet.

We know that booze and nicotine
Are poison like the wicked queen
Laced in the apple for Snow White to eat.

We know that lack of exercise,
And sausage, bacon, eggs and pies
Are full of things that really aren't a treat.

White flour and sugar too refined
Are foods we know that are defined
As just as bad as eating bright red meat.

And fruit and veg with pesticides,
Plus chicken and the rest besides
All narrow down the menu we can eat.

Salmonella and listeria
Cause some of us hysteria,
And fill the doctor's surgery each week.

So when we know all this today
Why do we still persist to say
We're here again to see our poor G.P?

The doctor's at our beck and call,
Why don't we just forget it all?
Then she'd be bored and not run off her feet.

Finally –

In this soccer mad mecca of Merseyside, and with the changing climate of easy travel and the growth of Formby, our own little football team has become completely overshadowed by the outstandingly successful first division teams of Liverpool and Everton, with the familiar red and blue now predominating over the orange and black of the past. The tragedy of Hillsborough touched us all claiming the lives of three of our young people and focusing the world's attention upon us. Hillsborough is already part of our history.

HILLSBOROUGH

It's gear, it's fab, it's here again,
We're on the Wembley trail,
We'll slaughter Forest, Norwich, too,
We know we just can't fail.

Scouseland's going to win that Cup,
It's good as ours, we know,
The reds or blues, it's in the bag,
For Merseyside to show.

The whistle blew at Hillsborough's ground,
The crowds still pouring in,
All herded up and penned like sheep,
To see their heroes win.

The roars of scouse encouragement,
Rose loudly to the skies,
Come on you Reds, died on their lips,
As horror filled their eyes.

The surging crowds, the screams of pain,
The panic, and the fear,
The carnage as the buckled rails,
Left no escape from here.

Trapped in the snare like cornered rats,
The anguished cries rose up,
Of frantic souls in terror now,
Robbed of that Wembley Cup.

The devastation all around,
Such madness named as sport,
Young lives snuffed out when just begun,
Their tragic days cut short.

The game was stopped, the war was lost,
The troops condemned to die,
That peaceful Anfield army wrecked
Beneath the April sky.

The glory that was Liverpool,
The pride of Merseyside,
Lay lifeless on a battle field,
Whilst round them others cried.

No hooligans, no one to blame,
No lessons learned it seems,
First Ibrox, Bradford, and now this,
Are football's shattered dreams.

Is this the end? We've had so much,
Why us? The plea goes up,
Please God be with us in our need,
For Satan's claimed our Cup.

Surrounding design by David Mills

HILLSBOROUGH

FORMBY REMEMBERED

A Century of Change

FOREWORD

In 1989 when I decided to write my last book, *My Formby*, I embarked upon an exercise which gave me great pleasure. It was a labour of love in which I endeavoured to put together some sort of record of the only place that had been my home and the place I could never imagine leaving. No other person had attempted it in quite the same way and it seemed to me a worthwhile task which I have never regretted. My earnest hope was that the book should create interest and enjoyment in jogging many more memories into recalling yet more incidents, people, and places which I had not mentioned, and this would appear to have been achieved.

The book's immediate success surprised me with copies travelling the world and bringing unexpected praise. I have never claimed, nor could I, to be an authority on Formby. My knowledge consists of that acquired through having always lived in Formby, and I know with utter certainty that there are many others with far greater knowledge than I.

My writing is from the heart and is aimed at a reading public, of any age, who enjoy to wallow in nostalgia whilst at the same time perhaps gleaning odd snippets of information which may add to the interest and build up the picture of the Formby of a bygone age.

I suppose it was almost inevitable that the omission of so much of our past should call for a sequel. I have been reminded of countless stories which had lain hidden in my memory, and also learned of endless more which were previously unknown to me. An older generation than mine has seen a Formby of even greater changes and I have now enlisted their help. They have dredged from the past the most fascinating tales, and I have also included other memories from my contemporaries as well as including more recent events which should be quite fresh in the memory.

In this new book my material has come not from any documented sources but from the authentic accounts of real people, and through these memories and observations I have attempted to extend the picture of Formby as it used to be, and I hope the result will please and delight all those who read it and maybe nurture the desire for more deeper research into our most interesting history.

Talking and listening to our older generation has been one of the most enlightening experiences and also one of the most rewarding. They have lived through such vast changes that their Formby is quite different from my Formby. The oldest of my informants was 99 years old John Tyrer and many more in their 70's and 80's have been so willing to talk and recall the way Formby was in their younger days, and I have been more than privileged to listen.

It seems an indisputable fact that Formby has a certain fascination and warmth of feeling for all who have had connections with it, no matter how deep or fleeting, and by meandering over a century of change some of those bygone memories will be rekindled as we witness Formby's growth from a sleepy village to a suburban town.

Today we all take so much for granted the services and amenities which our forebears never knew or indeed could have imagined. We drive along the roads of Formby with no thought of how things were before they were there, and probably our only thoughts might be of the disgraceful state in which they have been left as they are dug up and thrown back with monotonous regularity in order to avail us of those very services our ancestors were denied.

We perhaps complain when the odd streetlight is out of order, and as we enter our centrally heated homes and luxuriate in a hot bath after relieving ourselves in our syphonic flush toilets what possible reason could we have for thinking it was ever thus? And yet within the living memory of a large, though diminishing, number of people it was all so very, very different.

* * * *

At the beginning of the 20th century Formby was mainly fields, and what roads existed were earth or dirt track, and with the fashion of the day being long sweeping ankle length skirts the ladies of the village must have grown accustomed to their soiled and muddied clothes particularly during the winter months.

Around the time of the first world war some of the more well used roads such as Chapel Lane, Freshfield Road, Rosemary Lane, Halsall Lane, Church Road and Three Tuns Lane became cobbled, and apart from the obvious advantage to mankind these surfaces also greatly helped the horses in gripping the roads more easily.

At about the same time it was decided that a main sewer should be laid through the village, and this began at the Grapes Hotel end of Church Road and ran the full length of the main road to the Royal Hotel in Liverpool Road with extensions branching off along School Lane as far as the Village and also into Raven Meols Lane. Enormous and hitherto unknown problems were encountered when the sewering began, and so complicated were these problems that several firms actually suffered bankruptcy. The 'running sand', so peculiar to Formby because of its low lying position, caused ruination to the first contractors who carried out the work in their usual manner laying pipes to what they considered an adequate depth only to find the next morning no sign of those pipes – they had completely disappeared with the water, and the sides of the trenches had fallen in.

Formby village at night looking west.
Barclays Bank now stands on the site of the thatched cottage (near right)

Formby was originally a bog land and it was probably the monks from the Altcar priory near Hightown who set about the task of draining the land by making cuts to take the water away. It is likely that the area known as The Waterings in Liverpool Road was the silt bed as this particular patch was always very fertile producing three or four crops a year for each nurseryman who worked it, and making the succeeding businesses of John Tyrer, Jimmy Dickinson, and Sam Lytle very successful enterprises, and it was here in the rich soil of The Waterings that young Douggie Knight learned his craft which took him in later years to consistently claim the country's highest awards for his rock gardens at the top national flower shows, including the Chelsea Show where he attained the honour of being presented to the Queen in recognition of his achievements.

In very much earlier days it was also here that boats used to be moored before the course of the River Alt was re-routed, and John Tyrer recalls the land being so wet that it was quite commonplace for him to find cockle and razor shells on the ground before the sewering began. With the ground often under water one of his workmen fell face down in a shallow ditch after imbibing rather more than was good for him one pay day, and but for John's quick action would certainly have met a watery grave. About seventy years later this same area, now developed as Lytles Close, was the scene of a quite amazing sight as the members of one family sailed out of their front door in a canoe following the serious and calamitous flooding which occurred as the water rose to an unprecedented level ruining property and possessions, and necessitating the use of sandbags for the protection of all the houses in the vicinity.

It was, therefore, a monumental task at the beginning of the 1900's when the sewering commenced, and after very costly experiments it was discovered necessary to sink boards down the sides of the trenches to prevent them from collapsing. Eventually it was a firm called Monk & Newall who mastered the art and Formby's first sewers were laid. However, it was only the centre of the village which was connected to the system and a great number of households still relied on the traditional dunny, or bucket in the garden.

During the 1920's and 1930's many other properties progressed to septic tanks or cess pools, quite disgusting facilities which remained until the 1950's and were often situated close to the houses making them a definite hazard to playing children who frequently fell in emerging caked in the most revolting mess imaginable. The infamous 'marmalade cart' which was used to remove the effluent from all the households reliant on the outside privy, which again even as late as the 1950's was a considerable number, became immortalised in the song chanted by the children who kept as far away as possible from the filthy stench as the chariot trundled on its weekly rounds:

> *The corporation muck cart*
> *Was full up to the brim,*
> *The driver over-balanced*
> *And found he couldn't swim,*
> *He sank right to the bottom*
> *Just like a heavy stone,*
> *And everyone could hear him sing*
> *'There's no place like home'.*

Although those days are now long gone, quite incredibly today there still remain a very limited number of households (in Kew Road for example) reliant on the septic tank, and still encountering problems reminiscent of fifty years ago, and possibly still producing the finest home grown rhubarb as their forbears did before them!

Being a country village there was not considered to be a need for street lighting and it was not until around the time of the first world war that the odd gas lights appeared. They were very few and far between and were lit by a lamplighter who went round each night at dusk and then returned about midnight to extinguish them. Two of the lamplighters were Henry Lovelady and a little man called Teddy Mercer who reached the gas mantles with the aid of a small ladder. The lamplighters were later made redundant when around 1920 an automatic pilot light was fitted which controlled the lighting times.

* * * *

The emergency services, such as the fire and ambulance, which today are available at the raising of a telephone receiver were in the last century either non-existent or run on voluntary lines.

Formby's first fire station was for a brief period in Cable Street before moving at the beginning of the 1900's to the corner of Old Mill Lane and Church Road on the site which much later became the home and surgery of the dentist, Mr. Bracewell.

The fire engine (or probably more accurately the fire cart) was housed in a type of large shed, and in the nearby garden was the stump of a massive tree on which

Old Mill Lane with Willow Grove to the centre left and Church Road ahead where Formby's old Fire Station was situated prior to the site becoming the dental surgery of Mr. Bracewell. Behind the trees on the right was the farm of Miles Formby (later Aughton's) and now a dental surgery.

was erected a huge bell which was rung as a fire warning by Mrs. Bond, who along with her husband, was the resident caretaker of the old adjoining Council Offices. The fire engine was dragged to the fires by horses which were hired from various owners for the purpose, one owner being Rimmer Cabby from Gores Lane, so nick-named (as were most people) because of his hire cab business, and it was a great thrill for the neighbourhood children to watch Rimmer's horses galloping like the cavalry the length of Old Mill Lane on their way to the fire station.

The total work-force was probably no more than six, and in cases of dire emergency when no horses were readily available the men themselves would pull the fire engine to the fire.

Eventually building contractor Ernie Meadow became the fire chief and from his home on Brows Lane (on the site of the present Luncheon Club) the brigade was summoned to the fires by the firing of a maroon. This was a most unpopular method for the local neighbours who suffered near heart attacks at the sudden explosions almost on their doorsteps, and it must have come as something of a relief when in 1927 the Formby Council Offices were built in Freshfield Road and provision was made in the new building for a fire station.

During the second world war there became a need for extra men and machines and more space was required so the station moved again, this time to the Embassy Buildings in Piercefield Road where the necessary room and sleeping accommodation for the men was available.

Formby's early fire brigade at the Council Offices yard

The regular fire brigade consisted of little more than half a dozen part-time members and as the war progressed the acute need for more assistance saw the formation of the Auxiliary Fire Service (the A.F.S.) when those men not enlisted for active service in the forces were recruited into either the A.R.P (the Air Raid Precaution), the Home Guard, or the Fire Service. The regular brigade bore the awesome responsibility of protecting Formby from the war time fires, but with such limited resources relied heavily on the A.F.S. particularly for fire watching duties.

Volunteers came from all walks of life in the local community including Council workmen Bill Guy and Jack Brennan who lived in ideal locations directly beside the Council Offices and in the early years of the war were thus on the spot for call-outs to the council yard station.

There were probably about fifty volunteers, some of whom were waterboard man Jack Ackers, Jack Wright, Harry Boyer, John Walton, Eddy Thomas, Tommy Threlfall, George Lowe, and my father, Dick Rimmer. In addition to the fire engine the service also had several trailer pumps which were towed to the fires by lorries commandeered from local coal merchants and haulage contractors such as Mr. Boardman and Joe Fryer.

Formby escaped lightly from the bombing with only a very few properties suffering direct hits, but it was the May blitz on Liverpool in 1941 which created such havoc and has been recorded in history as one of Britain's darkest hours. Jack Wright recalls the horror of being one of Formby's A.F.S. crews drafted in to the city to do what they could to help. News had come of the impending raids and the Formby brigade had arrived on the first day, with driver Eddy Thomas at the helm, to find the department stores of Lewis's and Blackler's engulfed in flames and the whole city, it seemed, alight. Windows were all blown from the buildings, all communications were down and for a full week the Formby brigade remained in Liverpool battling against Hitler's onslaught, their families at home not knowing whether they were alive or dead. They had gone in emergency just as they stood up with no money, clothing, shaving equipment – nothing. They were dispatched to the blazing Mount Pleasant billiard hall and then to the School for the Blind at Brownlow Hill which had been requisitioned as their billets, but on arrival found it totally destroyed by a bomb. They then transferred to the University campus at Pembroke Place and each day fought the raging infernos as the German bombs relentlessly rained down on the city night after endless night. Silcock's cattle feed warehouse was ablaze with a huge five hundred gallon petrol tank alongside the building in danger of explosion, and the Formby brigade were sent to save the tank from the flames. With no water supplies available they found the only water in the canal in Love Lane close to Tate & Lyle's sugar refinery and from there they pumped what water they could, training their hoses on the tank and miraculously keeping it from igniting. Inside Silcock's laboratories were cages of rats used in their experiments and as the men fought the blaze they could see these poor creatures trapped in the inferno squealing in terror with no hope of rescue. Another nearby warehouse housing hundreds of tins of baked beans was hit and as the Formby men battled to bring the fire under control the tins exploded and they found themselves knee-deep in beans as they squelched around the ruins.

With the railway line out of action and a total breakdown in communications it was impossible to contact their families who, as far away as Formby, could all clearly see the night sky over Liverpool ablaze from the raging fires, many of them convinced that they would never see their menfolk again. But like a messenger from the Gods one of their fellow A.F.S. colleagues quite incredibly managed to get through to Liverpool. Johnny Mawdsley, the painter and decorator from Three Tuns Lane, somehow rode through the carnage of Bootle and Liverpool on his motor-bike, located the men and rode back again with the joyful news that they were all safe.

After a week of ceaseless attack, with fires raging continuously, countless lives lost, and the city in ruins, these exhausted, unshaven heroes of the A.F.S. abandoned their vehicle, caught the train from Bankhall Station with the electric line restored, and returned home to the peace of their village and the arms of their loved ones, thankful to be living those few short miles away from such mayhem.

The war continued but nothing again equalled the horror of the May blitz, and probably the worst the A.F.S. were called upon to deal with were the blazing pine woods near to the Formby Golf Club, set alight by incendiary bombs, and the bombing of Woodvale Aerodrome site when it was in the course of construction.

In 1945 when the war ended many of these A.F.S. men remained in the fire service as part-time volunteers easing the burden of such regulars as Ernie Meadow, Harry Dobson, and Billy Wareing. After the traumas of the war years the peacetime force experienced many lighter moments and although volunteers the men took their commitment seriously assembling for fire-fighting practice once a week. On one occasion one of the men, Harry Boyer, had brought along his small daughter, Winnie, to watch operations. Either by some freakish accident or through sheer incompetence another of the men turned his hose full on with the little girl in direct line of the full force of water which knocked her completely off her feet. My father was one of the brigade, and it was probably the only time in his life that anyone ever saw him lose his temper at the crass stupidity of his colleague as he scooped up the dripping child and tried to comfort her as she screamed hysterically with the shock of the experience.

As during the war in the event of a fire the men were called out by an alarm which was fitted in each member's house and also by the sounding of the fire siren from the fire station. The siren had originally been the air raid siren and its loud wail could be clearly heard all over Formby. It was all very reminiscent of Dad's Army with men to be seen frantically pedalling their bicycles or running at breakneck speed in the direction of the fire station at the sound of the siren, where they would leap on to the fire engine and head for the fire.

Obviously the delay inevitably incurred in this procedure meant that any serious fire could often be well ablaze by the time the brigade arrived to put it out. The whole operation was decidedly amateurish despite the dedication of the men and in today's highly sophisticated and technological firefighting age the antics of the fire brigade might appear farcical.

On one occasion the siren had sounded informing of a fire and all those men within earshot had abandoned their work and fled in the direction of the fire station. One man on his bike had arrived at the station only to find he had just missed the fire engine – not an uncommon occurrence, but being the public spirited citizen he was he leapt back on his bike and pedalled furiously round to the fire which happened to be in Cable Street and not too far from the fire station. By some herculean effort he arrived at the fire ahead of the fire engine, saw smoke billowing from the house, flung down his bike, and flew down the garden path brandishing his axe ready to batter down the door. Quite why, or what he would have done next is pure speculation because at that precise moment the fire engine, bell clanging, arrived just in time to save the door becoming matchwood and to extinguish the fire.

On another occasion one of the thatched cottages on the corner of Southport Road and Ryeground Lane suffered a chimney fire which attracted all the children in the neighbourhood. The excitement mounted as dozens of pairs of small eyes stared in anticipation of the fire setting alight the thatch. The loud wailing of the siren filled the air, and then round the corner came the fire engine. Two men quickly found the fire hydrant whilst a third man fixed the ladders against the cottage wall and across the roof. He then came down, collected the hose and carried it back up the ladder to the top of the chimney where smoke was belching forth. Carefully he pointed the hose down the chimney and let fly with an enormous burst of water flooding the house with the filthy black sooty deluge whilst down at the bottom the other two men worked like Trojans with brushes sweeping the dreadful mess out of the front door of the cottage to the accompaniment of wild cheers from the audience of wide-eyed children on the pavement.

Probably one of the most serious fires our Formby brigade attended after the war was that near Hightown when the 'rubber dump' ignited. This was a gigantic pile of old tyres which was mysteriously set on fire and which blazed for weeks like some ritual funeral pyre despite the attempts of several brigades to bring it under control. The acrid stench of the burning rubber could be smelled for miles around and eventually, much to everyone's relief, the fire burnt itself out.

In 1964 a new fire station was built in Church Road under the control of Lancashire County Council and staffed by full-time personnel all highly trained in fire-fighting techniques, and all a very long way in operational terms from those part-time voluntary efforts of a loyal band of amateurs, but in geographical terms very close to Formby's very first fire station.

* * * *

Mention of Jack Ackers as an auxiliary fireman cannot fail to evoke vivid memories of a character known to everyone in his time, and I make no apology for including him yet again. As a young man Jack served his time as a plumber with a builder called Bill Tracey (one time water-board official and also part-time fireman), who although not a particularly successful businessman, was responsible for some good class properties in Formby. Jack never actually worked at his trade but joined the Water Board where he was known to the whole village as 'The Water Man'. He was also a born comedian.

Never a man to hurry, Jack cycled around the district with his water board rods strapped to the cross-bar of his bike and was a positive mine of information. Whenever he was asked to help out in cases of emergency out would come his notebook and as he carefully flipped though the pages impressing upon the poor unfortunate householder how very busy he was he always ended every conversation with "But seeing as 'ow it's you I'll fit it in some 'ow". The fact that the last date in his book was 1926 seemed totally irrelevant to him in 1950.

He was the man everyone called upon to refit washers to their dripping taps. His charge in the 1950's for this service was 2d per washer, but Jack's generosity knew no bounds and it was almost the norm for him to say "but seeing as 'ow it's you I'll not charge you this time, but I'll accept a glass of beer instead" – the beer of course, costing several times more than the price of the washer.

Jack knew every house in the district where he could expect some liquid refreshment and regularly did the rounds. Early on in his career he had one particular watering hole in Wrigley's Lane where a friend of his nicknamed Rimmer Screbe lived. Screbe lived in a small cottage on the site of Wrigley's Close

Jack Ackers, sporting his customary watch and chain, outside his retirement home in
Willow Grove after moving from his Kenyons Lane Water Board house in 1961.
He was suceeded by Southport man Peter Prescott whose appearance and
sunny disposition so closely resembled his predecessor

where his wife kept some pure white Aylesbury ducks which were a picture as
they waddled about against the background of the lush green grass which
stretched back along Green Lane as far as St. Peter's Church. Very often the ducks
would lay away and anyone finding the eggs and returning them to Mrs. Rimmer
would always be rewarded with the equivalent number of hen eggs in exchange.

One day Jack decided to quench his thirst by going to visit his friend Screbe.
Screbe had a huge Alsatian dog almost the size of a donkey which never left his
side and was the essence of obedience to his master, but to everyone else was a
roaring monster. Not knowing whether the dog was at large Jack took the
precaution of going through the back yard, carefully bolting the door behind him
with the intention of creeping across the yard to the house door. He'd barely taken
two steps when the dog burst from nowhere towards Jack who that very morning
had just been issued with his brand new Water Board uniform coat. Trapped in the
small yard with this wild beast after his blood he whipped off his coat to fend off
the animal which was barking and growling like a thing possessed. Screaming and
yelling for help at the top of his voice he was heard by Screbe who came to his
rescue by calling the dog to heel only to find the shaking figure of Jack standing
holding just the collar of his new coat. According to Jack the remainder of his coat
lay in shreds strewn around the yard from the ferocious attack by the dog.

Not content with having his own private refreshment stops Jack was always in
with the crowd at drinking times in one or other of our local hostelries, and more
often than not would find himself squashed in the corner seat making it
impossible for him to get out without causing a major upheaval and creating
havoc amongst the other drinkers and total disturbance to the entire room. This

was never any problem to Jack. Rather than put everyone to such trouble he would sit it out accepting every drink that came his way, and on reaching his round would contentedly lean back in his chair and pronounce "Well, I'm stuck 'ere, but what does it matter who pays so long as we're 'appy".

Yet another of his tales was of the time he was leaving a house after his usual Water Board duties when a neighbour called to him in a very distressed state telling him about a plague of cockroaches in her house, and asking if he knew a remedy. "You've come to the very person" said Jack, "I've got exactly what you need at home and I'll bring you some next time I'm passing". True to his word Jack delivered his magic powder reassuring the woman that once she'd used it as instructed she would have no further worries. A fortnight later Jack was once again in the area when the next door neighbour of the 'cockroach woman' came out to him in a terrible state. "Mr. Ackers", she wailed, "I don't know whether you can help me, but my house is over-run with cockroaches and I can't get rid of them". "Don't you worry" said Jack, "I've got the very thing at home and I'll bring you some". Jack's quick brain immediately diagnosed the situation and realised that the first woman's plague had been driven out by his powder into her neighbour's house. But Jack was never a man to be beaten and he returned to the second woman's house with his powder and his instructions. His triumphant answer when relating this tale was that neither neighbour was ever again plagued with cockroaches because with his powder scattered alternately first in one house and then in the next, although it didn't kill the pests, their constant journeying back and forth from one house to the next eventually resulted in "the buggers all dying of exhaustion".

M.E. Sibley

Bull Cop. Pinfold.

The Pinfold where five lanes met – Priesthouse Lane, Flaxfield Road, Bull Cop, Watchyard Lane and Kenyons Lane in which the Water Broad house was situated.

Jack's wicked sense of humour was not always appreciated as for instance when one rather aristocratic lady called him out for advice because she was very worried at the discolouration of her water. "Perhaps you'd better consult Dr. Tobin" chuckled Jack.

Jack always professed to be an accomplished pianist, and was indeed very fond of music, but it would appear that the only piece he could actually play, and that was only about half a dozen notes, was 'Dolly Day Dreams'. He enjoyed trips with his pals into Southport to the Palladium Cinema on Lord Street, where this naturally very garrulous man would silence his companions with "Shurrup – it's 'th'organ" and would sit completely entranced at the melodious tones from the instrument. The film was quite incidental to the sublime pleasure he always derived from 'th'organ'.

In conclusion this neat and tidy little man, who was certainly not over fond of work, brought a wealth of humour to our village life and his happy disposition and relaxed manner seemed adequate compensation for his lack of motivation in his job. In today's frantic world Jack's philosophy on life is perhaps to be envied, and in his own words "What does it matter so long as we're 'appy".

* * * *

Prior to the second world war Formby had no ambulance service, and should the need arise for hospital treatment, emergency or otherwise, whatever means of transport available was used. As there were very few private cars this usually meant hiring one of the local taxi firms of either Rimmer's, Wright's, Martin's or later Schofield's.

During the second world war Formby's first ambulance service was set up by the Red Cross and was run on voluntary lines from the yard behind the Council Offices by a man from Marina Road, Mr. Jones. He was joined by a neighbour of his, Bert Brook, who although having no knowledge whatever of first aid was able to drive and also had the added and unusual advantage of being on the telephone.

These were the only two volunteers and they each permanently left their bicycles propped up outside their respective front gates ready for a quick departure in case of any emergency which came to them via the police and Mr. Brook's telephone. The two men would then pedal as quickly as possibly to the council yard where they would get out the ambulance, which was an old hearse, fill up the radiator with water and make their way to the waiting patient or accident victim. The arrival of a hearse whilst lying sick or injured could hardly have been a comforting sight to the poor patient, always assuming they were still alive after all this delay.

In 1948 with the formation of the National Health Service, engineered by Nye Bevan, the ambulance station moved to the Embassy Buildings in Piercefield Road alongside the Fire Station and a purpose built Commer ambulance was purchased which turned out to be a converted bread van. The vehicle almost shook the patients to death despite it being incapable of reaching 20 m.p.h. but nevertheless was a decided improvement after the hearse.

The workforce was increased to nine members under the authority of Lancashire County Council and the men worked four round the clock shifts with two men on each. They were supervised by a chief officer, first Mr. Edwards and later Mr. Davies.

Night duty was usually very uneventful and the men often retired to bed for a few hours sleep. One night Mr. Jones awoke about 3 a.m. to answer the call of nature and got out of bed in the pitch dark fumbling for the light switch as he did so. The next second there was an almighty blast from the siren as he hit the wrong switch and almost frightened the wits out of both himself and Mr. Brook, and no doubt woke up the whole of Formby at the same time. This same sort of disturbance was often experienced by the patrons of the Embassy cinema if a fire occurred during the showing of a film, when a slice of the picture was lost through the deafening crescendo from the siren in the adjoining building, and whether the nearby egg-packing station behind the building suffered any disasters through the sudden shock of the siren is only speculation, but the unexpected racket from such close quarters could quite conceivably have had dire consequences when dealing with produce as fragile as eggs in transit.

The ambulance station remained at its Piercefield Road home for almost twenty years, and then with the continuing growth of Formby was resited at a purpose built station in Kenyons Lane in 1968.

* * * *

As Formby emerged as a village small shops began to open up, many in the front rooms of private houses, to provide the various needs of the people. One such shop was in Old Town Lane where Mrs. Wright, the mother of taxi drivers Bella

An early view of Formby Village looking east before the construction of the roundabout

and Steve Wright, opened up her front room to sell mainly the produce of her garden. Ninety-five years old Margaret Rimmer recalls as a small child being sent to Mrs. Wright to buy a penny pot of herbs to make soup which always consisted of a carrot, a piece of turnip, a parsnip, and a bunch of herbs. On very special occasions, and probably only once or twice a year, Margaret was given a pomegranate which should have cost a halfpenny and was a luxury she could never have afforded so this made the gift a special treat indeed.

The Post Office, Old Town Lane

Potter's was another small cottage in Gores Lane which sold cooked meats, and eventually many independent businesses were founded so that by the end of the 19th century, a recognised shopping centre was established in Chapel Lane in addition to other small outlets scattered around the village.

Formby was predominantly a Catholic community and early on in the 20th century Father Carr, of Our Lady's Church, had been instrumental in helping

Formby Laundry in Coronation Avenue.
Their advertisements stated: Shirts and Collars a speciality;
Fancy Work and Flannels carefully treated; Good family trade

many of his parishioners to set up in business, and one of these enterprises was the Formby Laundry run by the Tickle family with their large number of daughters. They were originally established behind Hurst's chandlers shop in the

Village before later moving to Coronation Avenue which was formerly named Cockle Lane.

The laundry van was a familiar sight around Formby, and with its advertised 'large lawns for open air drying' proved a very successful business and seemed almost an institution. However, with the advent of the washing machine and the launderette in the 1950's the need for a laundry began to wane and with the changing times the Formby Laundry finally ceased trading in the early 1960's.

Unfortunately for some of these small businesses the owners did not have the advantage of even a basic education and they foundered, but of those who did flourish they must be applauded for their tenacity in thriving with little or no knowledge of commerce, and prospering through sheer hard work and determination.

Probably the most well-known and longest established business was that of Rimmer's on the corner of the Village. Founded in 1844 by Richard Rimmer it

Rimmer's shop at Christmas with founder Richard Rimmer (centre) surrounded by some of his family: Janie (2nd left), Nellie (3rd left), Bobby (5th left), and Billy (7th left). The T.S.B. now occupies the corner site of the Village

passed down through the family selling fruit, vegetables, poultry, and fish for over a hundred years. Richard became a local councillor using his business as an electioneering slogan – 'Vote for Rimmer, ducks for dinner' and setting the precedent for his son James who in later years established the record of being Formby's longest serving council chairman.

Traditionally Rimmer's windows were a display of splendour and at Christmas time a quite incredible sight. Such was the demand for poultry at Christmas that the family and their staff worked literally day and night plucking and dressing the birds which were then festooned around the outside of the shop suspended from the overhead boards and laid out on tables across the front of the pavement. Apart from those villagers who kept their own poultry Rimmer's were the main suppliers of Christmas fare to the rest of the village, and the necessity for the intensive work schedule to supply on time left everyone concerned utterly exhausted by Christmas but nevertheless with a feeling of great satisfaction.

Rimmer's was synonymous with Formby and it was with disbelief that we saw the shop's closure in the mid 1960's and was the first indication of the major changes which lay ahead for our Village.

The first butcher's shop to be opened in Formby was before the first world war in Long Lane at Eccles Farm (later to become Rimmer's). Since those early days many more butchers began trading and Charters of Chapel Lane must rank as the longest established reminding us even today of the self-sufficiency of our village with the large cow's head displayed in the shop and which was slaughtered at Ag Shaw's farm in Kenyons Lane during the early years of their trading.

The second world war years undoubtedly created the worst problems ever experienced in the meat industry when each butcher was only allocated the most niggardly of rations for each of his registered customers. Rationing apart some families were in no position to afford even their meagre allowance of meat, but, as in all small communities, the circumstances of most people were well known to the tradespeople, many of whom were kindly individuals, and despite the austerity of the war years the shop keepers all did their best for their customers.

One such butcher was Harold James. Harold was a popular and generous man whose shop was situated opposite the Railway Hotel on the corner of Formby Street, and he knew better than most those villagers who were in less than comfortable circumstances.

Although we were a farming community the strictest regulations were in force which prevented the slaughter of any animals without a licence, but on more than one occasion Harold James decided, sometimes with the aid of his young son, Harold junior, to bend the law somewhat as a means of helping those less fortunate than himself. In collusion with any equally public spirited farmer he would drive his old car across to Altcar where an illegally slaughtered pig would be surreptitiously bundled into the back seat of his car. One never to be forgotten night two pigs had been killed and young Harold was instructed to sit on the pigs and keep them hidden from prying eyes as they drove back to Formby. As they travelled along with the youngster astride the pigs the car suddenly juddered to a halt as Harold senior slammed on the brakes, and leaning across to the passenger side, he opened the door and said "Get in, Bob, we'll give you a lift", and into the seat fell the ample frame of Bob Greenhalgh, our village detective. Young Harold almost died of fright at the sight of the policeman sitting only inches away from the dead pigs beneath his legs. Perspiration poured from the boy as he sent up fervent prayers that their illicit cargo would not be detected, convinced that both he and his father would be clapped in jail for their heinous offence if the policeman discovered their crime.

The journey took only minutes but to young Harold seemed an eternity as he sat terrified and bathed in sweat on top of the pigs. They reached the police station and bid goodbye to Bob who eased himself out of the car with barely a glance at the boy and an amiable farewell to his father as he slammed the car door behind him. Some time later Harold junior, looking an unlikely Santa Claus, ran the length of Raven Meols Lane and Formby Street depositing small parcels of pork and bacon on the doorsteps of needy customers all of whom were totally ignorant of the ordeal undergone by the boy now delivering their welcome and anonymous gifts.

An even closer brush with the law came one night when Harold James had gone to Bond's farm in Altcar, once again to collect an illegally slaughtered pig for his customers. The Formby police made regular patrols around all the farms in the district, including Altcar, making sure that no illegal killings were taking place, and it was just as Harold was about to leave the farm with the dead pig that the policeman arrived. Dick Bond, the farmer, and Harold had a prearranged plan for such an eventuality and they immediately picked up the pig, which was hurriedly wrapped in sacks, and rushed into the farmhouse heading straight for the bedroom where they dumped it into the bed. Harold laid it on its side and pulled up the bedclothes to cover it and then lit a candle which he placed beside the bed before swiftly disappearing. In the meantime Dick had gone to confront the policeman, ranting and raving at him for doubting his integrity and telling him that he'd never been so insulted in his life. "You can search every inch of this farm, inside and out" he roared, "And I defy you to find any trace of a pig being killed. But if you go in the bedroom don't you dare wake my mother. She's very ill and fast asleep and if you so much as go near that bed I'll let you have both barrels of this gun right between the eyes". The policeman mumbled an apology and said he had received information which had to be acted upon, and then proceeded to search the outbuildings. He then came into the house going in and out of every room and on reaching the bedroom he silently opened the door, saw in the flickering candlelight the recumbent shape of Dick Bond's sick old mother, and gently closed the door.

Bills Lane farm cottage off Raven Meols Lane, for many years the home of the Mawdsley family, and close to Lea Farm where the Fletcher brothers sold duck eggs

The acute shortage of meat during the war combined with the paltry rations led to a variety of substitutes including the unpopular and very suspect whale meat. Customers were extremely wary about buying such foodstuff despite it not being rationed like the normal meat supply, and so Harold James devised a plan to tempt his customers.

He filled his window with the most luscious looking steaks which he advertised as Del Monico steaks – a very grand sounding title for his whale meat and a ploy which worked admirably as sales soared. One of the most critical of his customers was one of Harold's own employees, Tommy Howard, who carried on at great length at the outrageous suggestion of eating something so disgusting as whale meat. Tommy spent much of his time at the home of the James family at Valley House and enjoyed many meals with them, and when one evening he got up from his dinner praising Mrs. James to the skies for the delicious rump steak she had prepared for them all he was almost struck dumb when she informed him that he had just eaten one of his hated Del Monico steaks.

Harold James was such an amiable man it seemed strange that his dog should appear the complete opposite of his master. Occasionally, and without any apparent provocation the animal would fly at any other dog which might approach the shop. One day a Mrs. Sole was passing with her dog on a lead when the butcher's dog set upon it and a tremendous fight ensued. Harold stood convulsed with laughter as the two dogs, one still tangled up in its lead, fought like mad things. Mrs. Sole threatened to release her dog if Harold didn't call off his dog, but Harold seemed to be enjoying the performance too much to do anything until Mrs. Sole let go of her pet and the two animals raced inside the shop where the most terrible fight continued resulting in the shop being wrecked and the chopping block being overturned. And the jovial Mr. James very quickly became a very sober man.

It was a sad day indeed for Formby when this popular figure who was also well known in golfing circles died at the early age of 51. But fortunately for Formby and its people his son carried on with the business so that the name of Harold James remained in Formby for many years until in 1967 he eventually moved on for a spell in Canada and the business changed hands.

* * * *

In the early part of the century employment was in short supply throughout many parts of the country and consequently many of the working classes travelled far and near to seek work, and it was in this way that Formby found itself home to many young people who arrived to live in at the various big houses in the district as servants and maids, gardeners and coachmen to the Liverpool merchants and business men now living in the fresh air of the Formby countryside.

Josie Goulbourne was just one who in 1921 at the tender age of 13½ came from her home in Liverpool to take up residence and employment at Shaftesbury House in Raven Meols Lane. The House was a private asylum built in 1864 by Dr. Stanley Hays Gill as both a residential family home and an exclusive private asylum for the mentally ill. In its later years the House became known locally as the lunatic asylum, but it was in fact a very caring establishment run by old Dr. Gill, his son Dr. Eustace Gill, and Dr. Thompson who also lived in at the House. It was a magnificent building set in seventeen acres of grounds with lavish living accommodation for the family which included the founder and his wife, his son and his wife and their five young children. Tragically young Dr. Gill died at an early age leaving his widow with the children, the youngest of whom was only a

Raven Meols Lane in 1932 before the building of Park Road (on the right). The small curly-haired child is the late John Aindow, the Eccles Crossing signalman, outside the family cottage which was later demolished to make way for Walker Close. The motor van parked opposite Shaftesbury House was that of Mr. Peek who delivered paraffin door to door.

few months old. As well as the private accommodation the house comprised of four hospital wards – one for men and three for women – and a separate rear block for the staff which numbered approximately twenty and consisted of kitchen maids, pantry maids, nannies, nurse maids and the nursing staff of the asylum.

Life below stairs was arduous and the hours long with only half a day off each week. The maids would rise at 6.30 a.m. clean out the grates and make the fires, take up the hot water to the family in their bedrooms, prepare the tables and the food, and generally attend to the extensive work around the house. The work was unending until 10.30 p.m. when, after placing the hot water bottles in the beds and taking up the hot water for washing, these young girls would fall exhausted into their beds.

When their recreation day came round the girls were required to sign themselves in and out of the house, and their greatest delight was walking the length of Raven Meols Lane bordered on either side by ditches and with its abundance of thatched cottages on the journey down to the shore or the pinewoods. Probably the prettiest stretch of all was along Kings Road with its high hedges full of dog roses bordering the fields of Walker's farm where their cattle grazed long, long before the land became Duke Street Park.

Walker's Farm on the corner of Church Road and Altcar Road in 1930. The farm still stands but the out-buildings have been demolished together with the barn which was situated opposite the farm in Altcar Road beside the path to Formby Fields. Their original farm was in Duke Street

Despite the hard work and long hours the years Josie spent at Shaftesbury House were happy ones with one of the highlights being the concerts which took place on the stage at the asylum for the patients and often for the Raven Meols Lane neighbours who were invited along to the performances.

The asylum continued as such for many years and with the death of the resident Dr. Thompson a new doctor was engaged, Dr. Erskine, and a new house built for him on the site of the orchard. Eventually the asylum closed and the magnificent house was taken over by the Catholic Social Services and was re-named St. Vincent's and used as a reform school. Sadly in 1990 the school was closed and the building and land sold for development and yet another of Formby's stately old houses disappeared along with the ghosts of a bygone age and way of life.

* * * *

Whilst domestic service created much employment in Formby the village still remained essentially a farming community right up to the end of the second world war with most employment being connected with the land. With dozens of farms scattered around Formby the farming year was always eventful and the farms themselves hives of activity. The winter was perhaps the quietest of the seasons with January and February seeing the farmers attending farm sales and auctions buying up stock and machinery from neighbouring farms in preparation for the coming year. February also heralded the arrival of the threshing machine when the bitterly cold east winds often prevailed and the men stood perished to the bone as the great machine threshed the corn separating the wheat from the chaff and leaving the remaining straw to be baled for use as bedding in the stables and shippons with any surplus being sold to other stables in the area. Some of the bales of straw were also piled up to form a wall within the barn to store potatoes, and it was these bales which created the magical playgrounds for us all as children.

Feeding the cattle in a field opposite the Methodist Church, Elbow Lane at its junction with Duke Street. The cottage in the background was the home and shop of Mr. Barrett the shoe maker

As winter gave way to spring the preparations began for sowing the crops with the men hand-cutting sets for the potato planting. The older farm hands were often designated this job and in the warmth of the shippon or stable they would riddle the potatoes, then expertly cut each vegetable leaving the necessary sprits which formed the seed. The land was ploughed in the spring and fertilized with the farm's own manure from their cattle and the crops were sown. Chemical fertilizers were unheard of, and each year the crops were rotated with perhaps one year corn, the next potatoes, the next oats, the next swedes, etc. Hopefully ensuring a good annual yield.

The yard of Whitehouse Farm opposite the Police Station,
then the home of Jossy Rimmer, and now a row of shops.

The farmers were always dependent on nature and the weather often determined their work and the results of their labours. A wet winter would mean a poor crop of hay, but a mild and drier winter could mean two crops if the farmer was lucky. The haymaking began in June when the hay was cut, spread out for drying, tossed about with the pykle, baled, and finally stored in the barns to provide the winter feed for the cattle. One of the strangest sights at haymaking was that of the Robinson brothers from Lovelady's Farm in Little Altcar riding on top of their hay cart in full working gear but wearing bowler hats.

The busy harvest time followed in July and August with the cutting of the corn when it was gathered into sheaves, arranged in stooks and the farmers prayed for good sunny weather to reap the rewards of all their earlier hard work. Unlike today the stubble was never burnt off but was later ploughed back into the land.

The cornfields were always an attraction to us all as children when the stooks became miniature houses as we hid inside and often watched the rabbits as they scampered about and the birds as they pecked at the bits of corn that had fallen from the ears.

As the year progressed into October the potatoes were lifted and as well as the regular farm workers along came the Irish labourers and the children in their hoards to pick the potatoes in their annual 'spud picking' holidays. And very soon the round would start again – cattle, crops, and children all taking part in the continuing process of farming.

Jimmy Lowe was one of Formby's most versatile farmers who originally farmed at The Nurseries on Liverpool Road which was most conveniently placed close to the

Jimmy Lowe, the asparagus king

blacksmith's forge, and his eldest daughter, Emily, found it a fascination at the beginning of the century to watch the mail coach stop at the nearby Royal Hotel on its journey from Southport to Liverpool whilst the horses were changed, presumably to be re-shod before continuing on to Liverpool.

Jimmy was also renowned, not only locally, as the asparagus king and in the very short season transported basket loads of his luxury crops from his Pine Tree Farm at Freshfield to customers the length and breadth of the land. He also carried out arable, dairy, and pig farming from his Bull Cop farm, Devon Farm, as well as growing fields of blackcurrants which were a source of revenue to the local school children. But popular as Jimmy was he was not noted for his charitable benevolence and paid very poor rates for the picked crops. After hours of picking at 1½d per pound nobody exactly made a fortune and some of the more enterprising lads would plunge their baskets of blackcurrants into the nearby ditch thus increasing the weight when they were banged onto the scales and

Jimmy Lowe's daughter, Dolly Maitland, and Ronnie Harrison bringing in the asparagus harvest at Pine Tree Farm

Jim Sutton and Harry Bannister boxing the asparagus in the bunching shed at Pine Tree Farm

Jimmy Lowe's team of horses and men

Jimmy Lowe with his daughter, Vera, at the plough. The field later became the blackcurrant field
and the fields behind now form part of the Formby By-Pass

hoping and praying that the wet fruit would pass unnoticed, always explaining
with angelic innocence if questioned that they had accidentally squashed the fruit.

During the second world war one of the youngsters who earned his few
coppers in this way went on in later years to much loftier heights by becoming an
M.P. and holding ministerial office with the Conservative party as Education
Secretary, Chairman of the Party, and Home Secretary, but as an evacuee in
Southport he often travelled out to Formby where along with all the other war-
time children Kenneth Baker diligently picked his way along the blackcurrant
bushes filling his basket as he went.

In addition to his farming Jimmy Lowe also served as a local councillor
pronouncing from the hustings 'Vote for Lowe the man you know'.

Jimmy Lowe's son-in-law Bob Strong, successfully took over the farm after the second world war but experienced a disastrous loss on one particular day when he had planned to deliver one of his pigs to a fellow farmer in Lydiate. Very much in the mould of his father-in-law, Bob carefully watched the pennies and after much haggling had negotiated an acceptable price for his pig and arranged the delivery. Unfortunately the pig had other ideas and as Bob and the entire farmyard chased the animal towards the lorry it rushed and veered in all directions determined to avoid the wagon at all costs. For nearly an hour the pig and the men played cat and mouse around the yard until eventually the exhausted pig was cornered on the lorry back-drop and pushed on board. Bob was furious at the wasted time and effort and furiously sped off to Lydiate. On arrival he opened the back of the lorry and there lay the pig as dead as a door nail, obviously the victim of a heart attack after all the exertion in the farmyard. Bob took one disbelieving look at his expensive dead pig and almost had a heart attack himself.

* * * *

The rural nature of Formby made the blacksmith's forge a necessity in the village and was still in regular use until the 1950's.

One of the best known smiths was old Alma Wood whose unusual Christian name was given to him for arriving into the world in September 1854 to coincide with the victory of the battle of the Alma River in the Crimean War. He originally hailed from Bury but came to Formby as a carpenter and wheelwright to work at the smithy attached to the Waterings, a large house in Liverpool Road which was the home of the Lovelady family. Eventually he married Catherine, the daughter of the house, and later moved further along the road to the smithy near the Royal Hotel.

The Liverpool Road smithy with Alma Wood (arms folded) and John and Joe Robinson with a small relative in 1900

Two of his sons were killed in the first world war, but his third son, Bert, returned home from the fighting, and though suffering deafness through shell shock, worked with his father making the barns and the potato carts for the local farmers. The two men working from simple pieces of wood and using no measurements were able to create a complete cart in the tradition of the true craftsman, from the wheels, including the spokes, to the body, to the shafts, polishing the wood until it was as smooth as silk. Once the wooden wheels had been made they were hooped by placing the iron bands into the red hot fires of the forge, the bellows often being pumped until the fire glowed red by Alma's young granddaughter, Julie, and then hammered into place around the wheels, charring the wood as the sparks flew. The wheels were then plunged into a nearby pond to be cooled and boiling alive the inhabitant frogs much to the distress of Julie. The final stage was the painting and signwriting on the cart with all of these skills being undertaken by the same craftsmen.

Julie Daly, Alma's granddaughter recalls two huge cart horses arriving from Sutton's of Park Farm towing a farm cart to be repaired by her father and grandfather. When the work was completed this small twelve years old child was given the job of driving the horses and cart back to the Raven Meols Lane farm. Never having done anything like it before the only instructions she was given were to pull left on the reins to go left, right to go right, and back to stop. Delirious with joy at being trusted to ride along with such beautiful animals this tiny girl completed the journey sitting aloft of the horses and arriving at the farm as triumphant as the Queen of Sheba.

* * * *

My grandfather, Robert Rimmer, at Altcar with his horse and cart which he took each week to
Liverpool market laden with farm produce c.1900

In addition to farming, though to a lesser and declining degree, the sea provided a livelihood for the shrimpers, cocklers and other fishermen of the village. Amongst the many local fishermen was Jimmy Meadows, whose granddaughter, Margaret Kilshaw, remembers the hard and industrious life of her grandfather. He not only fished the waters but also made his own deep bottomed carts and his nets which he took down to the shore and staked across the sand waiting for the incoming tide to bring in the haul of whiting, fluke, and other flat fish. He caught cockles from Taylor's Bank and, of course shrimps by the shoal, and clad in his high rubber waders and his sou'wester he demonstrated his great strength by lifting unaided on to his cart the heavy massive nets full of fish which he transported back to his home in Cheapside where the load was tipped on to a scrupulously scrubbed white top table to be cleaned and sorted before he set off on his rounds of the village to sell it.

Many of Formby's fishermen were ruled by superstition and Jimmy was no exception. The porch of his house was made from the wood he had salvaged from the shore, and before every fishing trip he would always touch a certain solid oak beam to give him luck on his way.

In the 1920's one of his daughters, Madge, owned an old three-wheeler van which she used as a mobile fish shop, and about twenty years later towards the end of the second world war when his granddaughter, Margaret, was only ten years of age she was expected, along with all the rest of the family, to spend every Sunday afternoon at the kitchen table picking shrimps for the certain favoured and more wealthy customers who were able to afford to pay double for the privilege of having the shrimps ready prepared for the table.

Throughout his fishing days Jimmy was entrusted with the responsibility of collecting all the fishing rents from his fellow fishermen which were payable to Jonathan Formby, of Firwood, who held the fishing rights.

In addition to his fishing Jimmy was also one of the lifeboat crew alongside the famous Aindow family, and always carried the following prayer with him on his rescue trips:

> *Mother pray you for each big ship*
> *That on the ocean floats*
> *And I will lie and speak to God*
> *About the little boats*

By this time the lifeboat was kept in Birkey Lane from where it was towed by horses along Raven Meols Lane and down to the shore with the horses wading into the sea up to their bellies until the boat was afloat.

During the second world war Jimmy progressed to the coastguard service and witnessed one of the saddest sights of the war when he discovered the body of a young handsome blond German airman who had been shot down on the shore. It was an experience which made a lasting impression upon him and at the time moved him to tears.

It was quite commonplace for the cargoes of wrecks to be washed up on the shore, and many were the times that crates of whisky and oranges found their way to his family who relished such flotsam regardless of the salty taste to the fruit which during the war was in such scarcity.

The Formby Lifeboat recognised as the first in existence in Britain
which operated from 1776 to 1918

The Old Lifeboat House in Birkey Lane. The house next door was a public house licensed to sell
beer and tobacco only and was known as "Mary Neale's"

Eventually the cockles began to become tainted with mud, and the shrimping supply declined, and with advancing age Jimmy turned from the sea to the land carrying out gardening jobs and carting sawdust from the new Burrough's spade handle factory alongside the Royal Hotel. Like most of his kind he continued working almost to the end of his days in 1962 and just at the time when the Formby he knew so well was about to change out of all recognition.

The launch of the Formby lifeboat

* * * *

Apart from these rural occupations the Power House became one of Formby's major employers after the first world war when the electrification of the railway line ensured work for a sizeable number of local men who walked across the fields to Hogs Hill to work as greasers, labourers unloading the coal, and other allied jobs under the direction of manager, Mr. Creagh who was always a familiar sight around the village with his shiny leather leggings and mounted on his majestic horse.

Before even the advent of electricity and on until the 1950's coal was transported to the Formby Gas Works in Watchyard Lane from the Woodvale

The Gas Works in Watchyard Lane, opposite Cable Street, (now Smithy Green)

Station sidings of the Cheshire Lines Railway. It arrived by steam train from the Lancashire coal fields and was shovelled by hand on to carts which were then towed by horses to Formby. Two of the carters were Rupert Howard whose home was attached to the Gild Hall, and Billy Rimmer from Little Altcar, who, along with several others, often managed to transport two loads of this back-breaking cargo in a day.

Above: Eccles Crossing looking inland to Raven Meols Lane and Formby Street.
The signal box was then on the right when William Rice was the man in charge

Below: Eccles Crossing in 1912

The coal was piled at the Gas Works which at that time was owned by The Formby Gas Company where it was processed to provide the gas for the whole of Formby, as well as to make tar and coke. The gasometer was situated on the site and one of the early managers was Jack Buckley assisted by his brother Fred, and later Neville Murphy and Mr. Norris. Shortly after the second world war when coal was still in short supply and coke was a very grateful substitute Mr. Norris would often tease the children queuing up for the sacks of coke by asking who could do gazintas. "What's gazintas?" the children would ask, "You don't know gazintaas?" he'd reply, "What sort of school do you go to when you don't know two gazinta four, four gazinta eight."

The Gas Works became defunct in the 1950's and the site later formed part of the Smithy Green estate.

The various shops, coal merchants, building firms, golf club, and railway also provided employment for the village, but times were changing and as the internal combustion engine took hold small garages and haulage companies were established providing further employment for the local people.

One of Formby's earliest garages was the Formby Motor Co, founded just after the first world war by Isaac Buckley and situated next to the Royal Hotel. The garage held the agency for Morris cars and sold new cars to the public, many of whom were unable to drive. With no such thing as a driving test in those early days drivers usually taught themselves to drive by trial and error, but one of Mr. Buckley's employees, Jack Wright, was a very versatile young man who combined the skills of driver, mechanic and also instructor to any new customers who required his services. Jack later went on to gain the rare qualification for the time of driving instructor by passing the R.A.C. examination in Liverpool in 1938. Amazingly for a garage The Formby Motor Co. had no petrol pump on the site and petrol had to be brought from the Anglo American Oil Co. in Southport in two gallon tins which at the time cost 11d per gallon (just under 5p in today's currency).

The company ceased trading during the second world war and was taken over by Sculpher's and today The Telegraph Garage stands on the much extended site with their car wash just behind what was once a row of tiny white-washed cottages.

Wilson's was yet another prestigious garage business established on Church Road in the early days of the motor car, and still continuing today under the new ownership of Chapman & Mawdsley.

But it was through the vision and ambition of one young man called Noel Woodward that Formby began to undergo a radical change to its traditional rural image.

In 1917 when 18 years old Noel Woodward began mending bicycles and gramophones in an old army hut in Old Mill Lane little could anyone have imagined that from such humble beginnings would grow a business which would dominate the life of Formby and bring employment to hundreds.

Wilson's Garage and house, Frank Wright's sweet shop, Boardman & Tetlow's grocers, and cottages which were finally a garden centre before demolition. Chapman & Mawdsley's Garage now occupies the Church Road site

Noel's father, Harry Woodward, owned a smallholding in Old Mill Lane where he grew chrysanthemums, rhubarb, and other seasonal crops which on three days a week Noel would take for his father to Liverpool market in his old motor truck. Although very unreliable and prone to frequent break-downs Noel would load up his truck every morning at 5 a.m. and together with 14 years old Gerry Norris would set off for the market to sell his produce. On arrival Noel would leave Gerry in charge of the truck whilst he went into the market café for a pint of tea and a bacon sandwich. Eventually the pair became well known to the other traders and one day a builder approached Noel and suggested that as he came from Formby where there was plenty of sand it might be a good idea if Noel would bring him a load. So Noel decided that on the days when he wasn't delivering the fruit, vegetables, and flowers for his father he would take the sand. He did so well in the first year that he made enough money to buy a lorry. This enterprising young man continued this upward trend working hard and buying a new lorry every year for the next twelve years. With his expanding fleet of lorries he found it necessary to move from Old Mill Lane and went to Old Town Lane, and then, as the business continued to grow, on to Cable Street taking on more local boys as employees with each new lorry he bought.

Some of his earliest employees were the brothers Gerry (his original young partner) and Frank Norris, brothers Billy and Arthur Lovelady, Joe Rimmer, Stan Scarisbrick, and Arthur McLoughlin, who all learned to drive simply by using the lorries.

In 1932 they moved to the new site building their garage on what seemed the back of beyond. But Noel Woodward, ever the shrewd businessman, must have got wind of the impending new by-pass to be cut through the fields. The rest of Formby must have wondered at the madness of building in such a God-forsaken spot with the showrooms facing out onto open fields instead of the then main road. Five years later they were facing the new by-pass and on full view to all the passing traffic.

From the start of their business and right on until the 1950's Woodward's carted tons of sand from Formby and the loads had to be shovelled by hand. The work was arduous and back-breaking especially when, as was often the case, the sand was wet. The men used what was known as a number eleven shovel which could hold almost half-a-hundredweight of sand, and the implement was polished and

One of Woodward's early lorries with drivers Harry Jackson and Miles Rimmer (my uncle)

cleaned to perfection which made the process of cutting into the sand more efficient. Then in the early 1950's following a very severe storm the Admiralty brought in a law preventing the removal of anything from within half a mile of the high tide mark. Formby Council enforced this law which meant that Woodward's had to then go further afield for their sand, carting from along the coast at Ainsdale and even going inland for it. This side of the business became increasingly difficult until in 1973 they ceased the sand haulage and diversified into the motor trade, and being the main Leyland agents for the area began to buy up other agencies including the Salford firm of William Senior.

Woodward's held a lifelong reputation of treating their workforce with fairness, and back in the 1930's when there were no paid holidays for any working man they showed real generosity to their employees by treating them all to a free day out by charabanc to Blackpool. Each man was given a free meal and a ten shilling note – almost a fortune when wages were approximately £2 per week – and group photographs were always taken, some of the men on the dodgem cars, and right up to the end of Woodward's days these photographs were still displayed in their office.

Woodie's, as they were affectionately known, were the main employers for Formby and probably most families had some connection with the firm either through family or friends. Most of Formby's early tradesmen were apprenticed at Woodward's and to the firm's credit produced some of the finest skilled men in a

Aerial view of Woodward's Garage on Formby By-Pass.
The 5½ acre site is now Tesco's superstore

wide variety of trades such as engineering, mechanics, joinery, painting, sign-writing, and metal-work.

Sadly in 1987, sixteen years after the death of Noel Woodward, the business closed, and the once immaculate building which had stood for over half a century as a fine landmark in Formby fell into dereliction, and its demolition in 1990 to make way for a superstore marked the end of an era.

Woodward's was so much a part of Formby that it will probably never be forgotten, and the young lad whose mania for motor bikes led to the foundation of the firm which bore his father's name, H.W. Woodward, was by any standards a quite remarkable and honourable man. A very human aspect of his life illustrates the truth of those words in the following story.

When Noel Woodward was about 19 years of age and the proud owner of a motor bike he was already well established in business repairing bikes. He became friendly with a girl from Downholland, Ellen Prescott. By all accounts she was a lovely girl and quite tragically contracted T.B. at the age of only 18 years. Noel visited her regularly and a deep affection developed between them. Sadly with a terminal illness such as T.B. marriage was out of the question, and eventually at the age of 32 Ellen died. Noel in the meantime had married but his feelings for Ellen must have been very strong for he never forgot her. Ellen's mother lived to be 85 and every Christmas throughout her long life Noel sent her a hamper of food and luxuries, a practice which he continued throughout the austerity of the war

One of Woodward's body building shops

years, still finding foodstuffs when it was almost impossible to do so. Ellen was his first love and despite a happy marriage she obviously held a very special place in his heart, and that place was perhaps filled in some small way by him never losing touch with her mother, and maybe only accepting the loss when an old lady of 85 joined the daughter she had lost such a long time before.

WOODWARD'S

From a small and humble acorn
A mighty oak tree grew,
A bike shed down in Old Mill Lane
With the workers just a few.

The vision of those local lads
Whilst mending wheels and spokes
Became a dream to realise
For those young Formby blokes.

They saw the great potential
As the motor car came in,
Noel Woodward and the Norris boys
They all set out to win.

They built a place of high prestige
Beside the new by-pass,

Some of Woodward's staff beside the demolished Garage in 1990:
Gill Norris, Cyril Hall, Arthur Sutton, Brian Tickle, Mick Bradshaw

With garage, workshops, offices,
And showrooms with plate-glass.

They used a mighty workforce
Made up of local men,
And ran a haulage business
Carting sand and chippings then.

The business grew and flourished well,
The jewel in Formby's crown,
Employment here for everyone
With no travelling into town.

Mechanics, drivers, fitters, clerks,
Just no one could go wrong,
Directors working with the rest
To guide the firm along.

Woodward's was a landmark here,
And always would remain,
With branches spreading round about,
An established famous name.

It seemed as solid as a rock,
Unthinkable to say
That Woodward's would begin to crack
And disappear one day.

But sadly with the changing times
That sign of Formby's pride
Began to feel the winds of change
And its fortunes took a slide.

Now racing wheels flash past the site
Where once their lives began
As shining monsters on display
To tempt life's fickle man.

And just as man returns to dust
Poor Woodie's does the same,
Ignoble end to splendid past
Will soon bear Tesco's name.

* * * *

Despite the growth of the motor industry it was not until more recent years that car ownership became so prevalent and during the second world war very few people owned cars and those who did belonged to the upper classes. There was also a shortage of petrol and to travel in such an elitist form of transport was something most people only dreamed of. It was, therefore, the most wondrous treat for us as a family to ride, just once a year, in a taxi to visit our grandparents in Altcar. At all other times we either walked or rode on our bicycles.

The taxi driver was always either Steve or Bella Wright, the brother and sister team mentioned earlier, and two of Formby's real characters. Bella was no beauty and always wore a type of peaked pork pie hat and sported a black coat which boasted the most radiating shine from the constant sliding in and out of her taxi. Bella's mastery of the art of driving had to be seen to be believed. Her appearance

Formby village with the new bank on the corner of Halsall Lane
but before the construction of the roundabout

gave the air of complete professionalism, but to experience her expertise was quite something else. It has to be remembered that she was almost alone on the roads of Formby and took full advantage of that fact by always driving in the centre of the road and rarely using more than second gear. Her clientele were the gentry from the big houses, and almost exclusively ladies, whom she ferried around treating them with near reverence. She would alight from her taxi, open the passenger door, flinging wide her arms as she swept aside the lower classes in order to usher her passengers unimpeded into Derbyshire's shop to exchange their library books or into Hetherington's hairdressers for their Marcel waves, all the while bawling on top note to 'make way for Mrs. So-and-so' in her best authoritative tone.

Her brother, Steve, was a large, hefty, red-faced man who alternated his working day between the Freshfield Hotel and his taxi, but who was to us a knight in shining armour as we climbed inside his beautiful car, savouring the rich smell of leather from the luxurious upholstery, and for the brief journey to Altcar we were not only transported in distance but also in imagination becoming almost royalty as we relished the joy of four wheels.

Another of Formby's early taxi drivers and well known car mechanic was Johnny Houghton whose garage business still survives in Phillips Lane through his grandson. Johnny was yet one more of our real characters whose bark was far worse than his bite, and who owned one of Formby's first M.O.T. appointed garages.

Phillips Lane

Originally a gardener Johnny received no formal training as a mechanic and picked up his skills as he went becoming adept at his trade and very much in demand by the local motorists. One eminent Southport surgeon whose home was in Formby relied heavily on Johnny and had an agreement with him for his car to be regularly serviced, cleaned and repaired on Sundays – a day normally sacred to Johnny and indeed the one day in the week when the whole of commerce and industry closed down. Johnny obliged the surgeon because of his special circumstances until one day the doctor criticised Johnny's work. Obviously accustomed to great subservience from his hospital underlings, the surgeon was taken aback at Johnny's reaction, the mechanic being no respecter of persons, and rather grudgingly the surgeon apologised. But the harm was done and Johnny would have none of it. Unused to such treatment and quite alarmed at the unexpected turn of events the surgeon began to offer profuse apologies which had not the slightest effect on Johnny who told his customer in no uncertain terms what he could do with his car. Many months later, cap in hand and almost on his knees, the surgeon returned to the garage and pleaded with Johnny to accept his apologies and continue with their business arrangement, and Johnny, having proved his point and had his fun, relented.

Johnny many times came to my rescue when in 1964 I paid the grand total of £15.10s for my first old banger, a 1947 Austin 8 with a gear stick like an umbrella, a windscreen which opened out from the bonnet, very rickety running boards, and little orange side flap indicators which only worked with a hearty slap from inside the body of the car. It was, in short, a heap of rubbish, but to someone officially qualified to drive but totally lacking in experience it seemed the ideal way of really learning to drive. Unfortunately the M.O.T. was introduced whilst I owned my ancient relic, and so I trundled it round to Johnny who, after insulting my vehicle with every known expletive, then issued me with the necessary document of road worthiness which to this day I still regard as something of a minor miracle.

After the making up of Formby's roads just after the first world war they remained almost traffic free up to the 1940's and even by the 1950's were reasonably quiet. As the motor car became master potential drivers found it a far less nerve-wracking experience learning to drive than do today's learners, and many were taught by family or friends without any formal instruction although the driving test was just as much an ordeal then as now.

Probably all of my generation who had no access to a car learnt to drive with Formby's first and only driving school, the Wrightway School of Motoring, under the watchful eye of one of our ex-postmen, Dave Wright. My own lessons were in his Hillman Minx saloon which seemed to me, when my only transport was an old B.S.A bike, like a Rolls-Royce.

Dave was a very patient teacher and instructed many learner drivers who sorely tried that patience to the limit. Two middle-aged sisters who lived in Altcar Road became proud owners of an Isetta bubble-car and decided they would like to learn to drive properly despite it being quite legal for them to drive unaccompanied with their vehicle being a three-wheeler, and so they enlisted the services of Dave. The access to the car was through the front of the vehicle which opened out like a door and when closed meant there was precious little protection inside. The first and only time Dave accompanied one of the sisters he sat rigid with terror as she zoomed into top gear and went like the clappers keeping only inches away from the vehicle in front. Brakes were slammed on with gay abandon, and the journey along the bypass into Southport and back left our intrepid instructor an almost broken man. As Dave emerged from the car just thankful to be alive he asked "Don't you ever consider that you might be too close to the car ahead, going at such a speed? After all there's nothing but a thin piece of metal between you and the boot of the car in front". "Oh no" she replied, "We never think of that, and the brakes are awfully good". "Well" said Dave, more sure than he'd ever been of anything in his life that nothing on earth would get him back inside that death trap, "I honestly don't think there's anything more I can teach you". And with self-congratulatory looks of real triumph these two gentle ladies beamed all over their faces.

Another very much younger driver, and a great personal friend of mine, learnt to drive on her father's farm tractor. She took to it like a duck to water so that when the time came to take to the road in a car she was very proficient in the art. She sailed through the driving test and was then, and is still today, an excellent driver, but one incident at the very start of her motoring days belied that natural talent and was a less than auspicious start to her later successful taxi driving career.

It happened on a summer Sunday afternoon with not another car in sight and will forever remain a mystery, but the result was that her car crashed into the 'No Waiting' sign outside the Post Office knocking the top clean off the signpost. The impact also knocked the headlight off the car which just happened to be an ex-lord mayor's Humber which she had borrowed. With utter horror at what had occurred, and in a terrible state of shock, she picked up the 'No Waiting' sign and the massive battered headlight and drove immediately to the police station to report the accident. "Was anyone leaning on the sign at the time?" asked the policeman. "Of course there was no one leaning on the sign" she snapped. "Then there's nowt to worry about" was his droll reply. That did little to console her so

Formby Police Station. The section on the right was for many years the home
of a serving policeman

she went round to the home of Harold Turner, our Council surveyor and clerk of works, who showed just as little concern as the policeman. The next morning as we all met on the station on our way to work this dear friend appeared carrying a huge shopping bag bulging with the headlight inside it on her way to try and get a replacement in Southport. We all howled with laughter and treated the matter as some hilarious joke – a joke that turned decidedly sourer when six months later, and on Christmas Eve, Marjorie Strong received her first and only police summons to date for careless driving and damaging public property.

* * * *

Formby's social scene may have appeared tame by city or town standards, but there was a real community atmosphere and we did have two cinemas and several church halls where a variety of social events were regularly held making it quite unnecessary to travel outside our village for entertainment.

The Queens was our first cinema situated in Three Tuns Lane, and originally named the Picturedrome. It was opened in 1912 and probably the most important person, after the projectionist, was the pianist who accompanied the silent films. There were several talented performers including Liverpool man Noel Crickett, Tom Coward, and local girls Alice Houghton, Gladys Lovelady, and Mrs. Murphy.

The first owners of the Queens were Mr. & Mrs. Simcock who lived behind the premises. It was later taken over by a Mr. Palin and then in 1925 by Southport man, Mr. Alexander Knight, who renamed it the Queens. Mr. Knight also owned cinemas in Ormskirk, Clitheroe, Tarleton, and in Devonshire Road, Southport all of which bore the same name as ours, and it was on one of his many journeys between Tarleton and Formby as he was transporting the highly inflammable film reels in his car that the car caught fire and he was burnt to death. His son, Douglas, then took over the cinema for a time. The last owner of the Queens was George Dacre who tried without success to continue running it as a cinema before it finally ended its days as a roller skating rink in 1957.

It seems a strange coincidence that conversely our second cinema, The Embassy in Green Lane should have started its life in 1928 as a roller skating rink and eventually ended its days as an ice rink. The intervening years as a cinema were magical years for the film going public of Formby who enjoyed an entertainment unequalled in later years.

Before the advent of television we were richly catered for with our two cinemas each of which were markedly different in status. The opulence of the Embo, as it was fondly known, with its velvet seats, plush carpets and highly decorative wall panels, stood in marked contrast to our local fleapit, the Queens, but our surroundings were only of secondary concern compared with the actual filmshows. At the Queens we were all assisted or controlled by female usherettes, whilst at the Embassy along with the girls we also had the resplendent uniformed figure of Jack Mawdsley and later the less imposingly clad Dick Ashcroft and Roy Cruikshank, whose heads became silhouetted against the screen as they were caught in the shaft of light from the projector on their patrols along the aisles and across the front of the house.

From the 1930's to the 1950's the pictures was a great social occasion for all with no barrier to age or class and provided the entertainment for the whole village. The stalls catered for the youngsters and the less affluent whilst the balcony was definitely an indication of one's elevated status.

In stark contrast to today's young people who go out for the night at nine or ten p.m. our film performances usually finished by 9.45 p.m. which was considered quite a late hour, but it was not only the thrill of watching a film in comfortable surroundings which created such pleasure but also the congeniality of socialising with friends and acquaintances followed by a trip to the local 'chippy' on the walk home.

The supervision of the youngsters was quite strict, and in general the behaviour acceptable if sometimes on the noisy side but trouble brewed at one evening performance when a young lad had taken into the cinema with him a box of white mice which escaped half way through the evening. The pandemonium which followed resulted in the culprit being yanked out by the scruff of the neck by commissionaire Jack Mawdsley and together with the whole row of his friends being banned from the cinema for a month – a terrible penalty which ensured that Reg Clegg never again repeated the offence.

Dancing was always a popular pastime and from the time of the first world war dances continued for over fifty years at each of the church halls with the most popular being the St. Peter's dances at the Victoria Hall with its magnificent sprung floor.

In the early days Formby was full of young people living in at the various big houses in the district as servants and maids and the dances were the main attraction for them all. In most cases all these young people in service were expected to be back at their residences by 10 p.m. but many used their ingenuity in inveigling the coachmen or butlers into lending them keys so that they could comply with the regulations by clocking in on time and then sneaking out again when the master and mistress of the house had retired to bed.

During the 1940's and 1950's dancing at the Gild Hill to the Melody Maker's Band or the Clarkson Woods Band was the big night out, and Friday nights at Harrington Barracks were known as the three G's nights – The Grapes, The Gild, and The Girls, and it was at the Gild Hall that many romances began and blossomed into marriage.

One of the highlights of the wartime church hall dances were the spot and raffle prizes and when young Ray Mawdsley won half a dozen eggs his mother greeted him with more joy than had he been the prodigal son returning home with such coveted produce.

Again during the second world war concert parties flourished offering entertainment which though decidedly amateurish was very popular and enjoyable. Just after the war 'The Follies' was an annual show staged at the Congregational Church Hall featuring all local people, like the Butlers, the Humphreys, and the Suttons, and their simple acts of comedy sketches and singing were a delight. The company went on to be renamed the Harry Whitehouse Players after their founder and continues to entertain to the present day.

The Gild Hall Band: Jack Cooper, John Whittle, Norman Brooks and Bernard Norris

The Holy Trinity Parish Hall also staged concerts organised by the very youthful son of a local builder, and a budding entrepreneur with an eye to the main chance. When still only fifteen years of age he arranged charity shows consisting of dancing acts, very often featuring the Peggy Whitton Dancers, ventriloquists, singers and comedy sketches. This enterprising youngster entered into an agreement with Mr. Gilbert from the Bon Bon sweet shop in the Village for the provision of soft drinks for one of his concerts which Mr. Gilbert happily supplied on credit secure in the knowledge that the boy's father was a successful business man. Anyone knowing Mr. Gilbert might find such an act of trust incredible so completely out of character was it, and when it later transpired that the benefiting charity, The Daisyfield Orphanage, was an ingenious piece of fiction and that the boy was unable to pay his debts, it came as a profound shock not only

The corner of Whitehouse Lane and Church Road with Whitehouse Farm,
now a row of shops opposite the Police Station

to Mr. Gilbert but also to the people of Formby that anyone could conceivably have succeeded in diddling the wily Mr. Gilbert. His protestations and pleadings to the lad's father fell on deaf ears, and for probably the one and only time in his life Mr. Gilbert came financially unstuck when the builder berated him for his foolishness in transacting any sort of business deal with a minor – and a particularly unreliable minor as his son.

A much more ambitious and professional offering at the Holy Trinity Parish Hall were the plays performed by The Fellowship Players which were founded in 1947 and whose first production was Terence Rattigan's Flare Path. The standard of acting was always of the highest quality and the company is still enjoying acclaim and success in their new venue just around the corner at their own Little Theatre in Rosemary Lane and performing under their new name of The Formby Theatre Club.

In addition to the pictures, the dances, and the concerts, the whist drives formed an integral part of village life and were enormously popular events with several being held each week organised by a variety of organisations including the local churches.

Blind Tom Balshaw was one of Formby's keenest players as well as being one of the most well-known characters. Known to everyone as an expert piano tuner he had at one time owned a shop in the village where he sold musical instruments, and next door to his shop his wife ran a haberdashery shop which later was taken over by Parker's. Tom lived in a bungalow in Davenham Road and was a familiar figure as he tapped his way round Formby with the aid of his white stick. In his younger days he quite amazingly went ice skating and rode a tandem with all the confidence of a sighted person, refusing to allow his disability to interfere in any way with the life he lead. He attended as many whist drives as was humanly possible always playing with his own special pack of Braille cards, and it was a rare occasion indeed when he was not amongst the prize winners.

The whist highlight of the year was undoubtedly the Altcar Christmas Whist Drive which was held at first in the Old Vicarage and then in the new and tiny Parish Hall. Tickets were always at a premium with the Formby people clamouring for them alongside the locals.

The Hall on the night was packed solid with barely room for any of the players to change tables throughout the game, but despite Tom's blindness his handicap passed almost without notice as he moved easily from table to table. In fact many people tended to completely forget that he was blind.

The draw of the Christmas raffle was, if anything, more eagerly awaited than even the whist drive itself with produce and livestock in abundance as prizes, and all donated by the local farmers. The first prize was traditionally a six weeks old piglet, followed by turkeys, chickens, pheasants, ducks, geese, potatoes, carrots, and the usual festive fare of chocolates, wines, spirits, and cigarettes. So generous and numerous were the prizes it was a very unfortunate player who came away completely empty-handed. The only drawback to success in my own experience was the time my mother won a pair of ducks to be collected just before Christmas from the donating farmer; in this case Jimmy Aspinall. My cousin, Anne, and I went to the farm to collect the birds only to be confronted by the said ducks still running around the farmyard. Jimmy quite expertly caught them, necked them, and handed them over to us complete with feathers and still twitching. My quite irrational fear of feathers rapidly turned the euphoria of winning the ducks to near terror, and the journey back to Formby probably broke all records as the pair of us raced straight to Rimmer's poultry shop in the Village where Dixie Ashton promptly plucked and dressed the birds ready for the oven.

* * * *

The Conservative Club in Three Tuns Lane was another popular venue for whist drives particularly after the second world war, and such was the obsessive interest in the game that as recently as the miners' strike in 1973 when there were total electricity blackouts the whist drives continued with the players using candles. There was even one occasion when there was a bomb scare in the middle of a whist drive and everyone was urged by the M.C., Joe Forshaw, to leave the building as quickly as possible and to go in an orderly manner down the stairs. Incredibly many refused to move as the hands they were playing were potential winners and it seemed more preferable to be blown sky high than forfeit a winning hand.

The original Conservative Club was not in Three Tuns Lane but was situated in a house in Chapel Lane next door to the present McDougall's chemist's shop where meetings and whist drives were held when the club was in its infancy just after the first world war.

Its new premises were originally built in 1894 by Formby Brothers as a church men's club for Our Lady's Church under the direction of Monseignor Carr and later Father Gardner. It remained as such for about thirty years and was then sold to a man named Campbell who continued to run it as a club. Unfortunately Mr. Campbell omitted to acquire the necessary licence permitting the sale of alcohol and the club was raided by the police, Mr Campbell was prosecuted and banned from ever holding a licence, and the club was closed down for a period of twelve months. Then in 1926 a group of club members, amongst them Arthur Holden, Bob Wright, Jack Wilcox, Dick Rimmer, Bill Alderson, and S.J. Lister, formed the Conservative Club which was officially opened by Lord Derby. It was not then, and is not today run by the Conservative Association but by the club members themselves who do, however, support the Association and allow them the use of the club rooms.

Its social functions have continued uninterrupted throughout its history despite the upstairs rooms being requisitioned by the King's Regiment during the second world war before the building of Harrington Barracks when the premises became billets for about a hundred soldiers.

In those early days at Three Tuns Lane, with the Picturedrome next door, the club had a building situated behind the property which housed a donkey engine driven by gas which generated the electricity for the club itself as well as for the lights and the projection of the black and white silent films at the cinema. This generator also provided the electricity for the nearby shops of Needham's,

The Conservative Club president, Councillor Jimmy Rimmer, receiving a picture of the House of Commons from M.P. Sir Douglas Glover

Ackers', Rimmer's, and Alderson's, and these premises were the first in Formby to receive electricity. The Rimmer family, of fruit, vegetable, poultry and fish fame, lived on the premises of their business and numbered six children in all. Their natural mother had died and they were in the care of an extremely kind and doting step-mother who, against the instructions of their father, allowed them to stay up late at night while their father was out along the road at the Conservative Club. She knew instantly when he would be coming home as the minute the lights went out at the Club so they did too at the house and this was the warning for the children to all scamper off to bed before he arrived home.

The only other electricity available at this time was at the Formby Golf Club which had its own generator.

As the advantages of electricity became apparent the company engaged in the industry was anxious to introduce the commodity to more customers, and as there was a certain apprehension on the part of the public towards such a revolutionary new product a promotional offer was made to the people of Formby in the early 1920's for them to have their houses wired free of charge. One of those to take up the offer was the Wright family in their small Halsall Lane cottage (now the Cloisters) little realising how very fortunate they were in receiving an amenity which at a later date was to prove a very costly acquisition.

Unfortunately for the company they greatly underestimated the future demand for electricity and installed a cable which was not strong enough, and to their cost had to replace it with a double cable to cope with the extra load.

During and after the second world war the Conservative Club was a popular rendezvous for our off-duty policemen whose quiet Formby postings must have been the envy of their colleagues in other areas of the Lancashire County force.

Halsall Lane with Norburn's bakery (later Price & Jones) on the right. The entrance to Furness Avenue is now The Cloisters car park, and The Gallery shopping complex now replaces the bakery

Crime was almost non-existent until an unprecedented spate of burglaries in 1947 left the whole village in a state of nervousness. People had never been in the habit of locking their doors until these break-ins were now making it necessary. It was

Formby's plain-clothes detective, Bob Greenhalgh

a puzzlement to everyone and something quite alien to this hitherto law abiding and close knit community. The police stepped up their regular patrols and one night P.C. Fred Beswick accidentally stumbled upon a barrel of apples hidden behind the War Memorial, and obviously the stolen property of Rimmer's greengrocers just across the road. Fred reported his find to both the owner of the shop, Jimmy Rimmer, and also to his detective, Bob Greenhalgh. Bob instructed Fred to stand guard over the apples and to stay well hidden in the bushes in the certain knowledge that the thief would soon return for his booty. Bob then clocked off duty and into the Conservative Club where he met a fellow officer and relayed the saga of the apples to him. The two policemen stayed at the club until closing time and then together went across to the freezing Fred who was still patiently guarding the apples in the shadowy undergrowth. "No sign of anyone yet" said Fred, "Just stick it out" replied Bob, "He's sure to show up soon" and with that Fred's two colleagues departed leaving him on duty. The next morning poor Fred, frozen to the marrow, left his lonely vigil and clocked off duty having seen no sign of the burglar. It was many weeks later when Formby and the police force itself were shaken to the core that Fred realised the reason for his fruitless night's work when the burglar was caught red-handed robbing a newsagent's shop in Freshfield and was identified as the very policeman who had been Detective Constable Greenhalgh's drinking companion in the Conservative Club.

Today the Conservative Club continues at its Three Tuns Lane premises and whilst the Club had always been leased from various breweries, in 1990 the present landlord, Boddington's, made an offer to sell their interest to the Club, an offer which was accepted and which hopefully assures the Club of an optimistic future.

* * * *

Another leisure pursuit which has been a long time favourite in Formby is football, and Formby's first team was formed just after the first world war and was named Formby United. The matches were played on a field off Raven Meols Lane backing on to Phillips Lane. Shortly after this the team became known simply as Formby Football Club and moved to the Brows Lane ground. As there was no proper fencing around the ground a makeshift fence was erected which was made from the canvas used for aircraft wings during the first world war, and this ensured that spectators could not see the matches without first having to pay to come inside the ground. This temporary fence which encircled the whole of the ground eventually fell into disrepair and was replaced by a more attractive wooden fence. Also around this time a stand was erected through public

The corner of Brow's Lane and Rosemary Lane with the Football Ground on the left and the Luncheon Club now on the right

subscription. Even so far back in its history Formby was intent on fielding the best team possible, and unfortunately for the local boys their talent was not always of the standard required and, as today, the teams were recruited from outside Formby.

Another football team of a high standard playing at the same time as the official Formby team was the Formby Holy Trinity team which played behind the Brows Lane ground opposite the Methodist Church on a rented field belonging to Walker's farm and slaughterhouse in Duke Street. Walker's was the only farm in Formby to have suffered an outbreak of foot and mouth disease – a tragedy which had threatened ruination to them with the slaughter of all their livestock in a giant bonfire. However, the Formby people rallied round and through their generosity made it possible to re-stock the farm and for them to continue farming.

The early Formby football team flourished with such worthy players as our G.P. Dr. Sykes playing alongside goalkeeper Bob Wright, the founder of the famous rose grower's firm, and bandsman Bob Eccles. The team continued its success throughout the 1930's becoming champions on several occasions with a very loyal following. The club had a thriving supporter's club and the team played to a high standard winning many more trophies. Some very notable players graced the pitch including Bert Trautmann the German goalkeeper who played for St Helens following his time as a prisoner-of-war, and who later went on to play first division football for Manchester City and will probably be best remembered for his part in their F.A. Cup victory in which Trautmann completed the game suffering a broken neck.

Formby Football team 1932/1933
Jonathan Formby is seated 5th left. Standing immediately behind him is Dr. A. B. Sykes

The present club is experiencing many difficulties, and a fire in 1990 only added to those problems. The ground itself is privately owned and under the terms of the lease will always remain as Formby's football ground providing matches continue to be played on a regular basis. With dwindling support recent years have seen the club becoming more and more dependant upon the popular car boot sales to boost their finance, but certain opposition to these sales has restricted their frequency and deprived the club of much needed revenue. Should they find themselves unable to fulfil the leasehold conditions the ground would certainly be in jeopardy, and in the event of the club becoming defunct there would seem little doubt that being situated as it is in a prime central part of Formby the site would constitute rich pickings for the developer and a once fine club which has been so much a part of our village life will be relegated to the annals of history.

* * * *

Formby's Flower Show was founded in 1893, the year in which John Tyrer was born, and as it heads for its centenary so too does John who understandably is its oldest member.

The first show was held in a small tent on the cricket ground, and then it moved to Holy Trinity Parish Hall when during the first world war all proceeds were in aid of the Red Cross. It later moved to the corner of Wicks Lane and Freshfield Road on a big field belonging to Collinson's who were in the shoe trade in Liverpool and who lived in Barkfield Avenue alongside the railway line. At this

Formby Flower Show 1950
Some of those left to right: Ted Mawdsley (Mayor's officer), Miss Harley,
Chairman of the Council Capt. Hutchinson, Formby's M.P. Sir Ronald Cross,
Mr. J. F. L. Formby and Mrs. Formby, Mrs. and Mr. John Breese

time the show was purely and simply a flower show with classes for the gentry and their gardeners to compete against one another, and there were also classes included for the cottagers to compete.

It was a happy social occasion for everyone to meet and mingle, and part of the marquee was screened off for afternoon tea. The Formby Band was always in attendance playing with their usual aplomb and creating a very jovial atmosphere on the day. It was the one day in the year which was eagerly anticipated by the whole village, and the one day when just everybody turned out.

Just before the second world war the show was briefly staged in a field in Deansgate Lane but its outlandish location was unpopular and this site was quickly abandoned.

A farm lorry acting as a grandstand at Formby Flower Show, 1949
The boys left to right are Ronnie Harrison, Freddy Gordon, Howard Corless and Derek Rimmer
(my brother). The girl standing wearing the hair ribbon is Ursula Rimmer

The show probably reached its peak following the second world war when its proud boast of being the finest one day show in the country went unquestioned. By now being held on Duke Street Park the farming classes drew enormous interest, and with Formby being mainly a farming community there was a wealth of local talent with all the farmers exhibiting. The entire length of the Duke Street side of the park was taken up with the cattle and horses which all arrived very early in the morning to be washed, groomed, and decorated for the show.

One of the most popular classes was the best decorated horse and cart in which no expense or hard work was spared. The animals were magnificent and groomed to perfection with gleaming brasses and harnesses, and coats shining like silk. The floats and carts were, too, a display of artistry and ingenuity.

One year following the parade of entries the announcement was made over the loudspeakers that Bill Hunter had been adjudged the winner. Proudly he led his horse and milk float round the arena and towards the judges to collect his prize only to be told that a mistake had been made and he wasn't the winner after all but only the runner-up. His disappointment can only be imagined, and the heartlessness of the judges in making such a mistake almost unforgivable.

The popularity of the Flower Show, more recently known as the Formby Show, has waned considerable over the years with the show today being a very inferior version of its forerunner.

The nostalgic memories of massive marquees filled with vegetables and flowers, wide varieties of entries from the children of the village, and the vast exhibits in the farming classes can only lead to despondency at the poor quality of the present day show.

In its heyday the show was Formby's highlight. The villagers then would have regarded foreign travel as likely as space travel, when even any sort of holiday was unheard of to most. The show met a social need which gave happiness to a small community steeped in rural tradition. The growth of Formby, the pressures in education for academic achievement, and the changing social climate have meant the sacrifice of simple pleasures, and whilst we are so very close to the show's centenary there can be no sadder situation than that of attempting to preserve something which has been so special but which now shows such signs of regression. It would indeed be heartening to recapture those halcyon days and preparations are already in hand towards that end with the hope of renewed enthusiasm from the many local organisations, but so much sheer hard work is involved in the presentation of the Show and so much disappointment must result in watching its decline that its future must be questioned.

Our annual Gala was a treasured and valued occasion which we reluctantly yet inevitably lost. On its recent record it might appear just as inevitable than once again the price we have to pay for our growth and affluence is the loss of yet another of our finest traditions.

Formby's Band has probably been playing at the Show since its inception and has always had a fine reputation. The Band has been in existence since before 1900 and some of its earliest bandsmen were all named Aindow – Halsall Aindow, Big Jack Aindow, Billy Aindow, Gil Aindow, and Ted Aindow, and whilst some of these early members were unable to read and write they could incredibly read music and played with consummate skill.

The Band was originally brass and in addition to the Aindows consisted of men like Bob Eccles, a man of varied talents who worked as a gardener for Jonathan Formby and also played in the local football team, Jim Goulbourne, another gardener at Job's in Lifeboat Road who played the drum, and together with a total of about twenty members they made up a very accomplished group of musicians. Jack Whiteside came along a little later as a virtuoso of the cornet and eventually leader of the Band, and they practised at his Kings Road home just opposite Phillips Lane.

In the very early days of the Band they were very much in demand in Liverpool for the parades and always played at the front being followed by the pipe and drum bands.

Wilf Wright recalls just after the first world war the band had been playing at a Gild Hall function and at the end of the performance were all merrily full of the right sort of spirit and shakily marched away from the Hall on their way back to Kings Road. When they reached the Village they struck up with a rousing tune and on reaching Elbow Lane all turned left – all that is except Jim Goulbourne whose big drum obscured his view, and he continued on along Brows Lane until a young lad ran after him shouting "Eh, mister, they've all gone down Elbow Lane". "It's all reet, lad" said Jim, "I know t'music", and carried on his lonesome way still belting all hell out of his drum.

Pine Tree Cafe, Freshfield Shore, owned by Capt. Hutchinson and which
eventually collapsed into the encroaching sea

Following the first world war the Band traditionally led the Armistice Day parade to the War Memorial, and almost as traditionally a character known as 'Snotty Bill' appeared heading the parade immediately behind the Band. His real name was Bill Rimmer (Butterbasson) from Watchyard Lane, and dressed in his tatty old overcoat and accompanied by his equally tatty old dog and with his ever dripping nose in evidence he marched along leading the procession of the forces and civic party creating quite a comic sight on such a reverent occasion, but his presence was never questioned and perhaps illustrates the simplicity and tolerance of village life.

Also around this time during the summer months the Band would go down to the Formby shore on Sunday afternoons and give performances for all the locals and visitors from Liverpool who were enjoying the seaside sunshine. One of the local vicars often joined them for a short service and hymns would be played making it all a very pleasant afternoon's entertainment.

The Band progressed to silver and from the 1920's until long after the second world war it was customary for them to play around the district every Christmas and New Year. They visited all the big houses accepting their festive hospitality at each call and also visiting every public house en route. By the time they reached the Bay Horse the carols were barely recognisable and the men legless with one of two of them having ended up in various ditches as they tottered round. One of the bandsmen eventually staggered home very much the worse for wear, and, fumbling to get through his side gate and into the house with his euphonium, lost his balance and crashed to the ground knocking over the dustbin and causing one almighty commotion. Hearing the hullabaloo his wife appeared, absolutely furious at his inebriated state, to find him lying amongst the debris muttering "Me instrument, me instrument, I hope I haven't dented me instrument". "I'll more than dent your instrument if I get my hands on you" she roared, and left him to sober up in the cold night air.

For many years the Band's Christmas tour was an anticipated part of the festive season, but once again as our village grew into a town the tradition along with the characters passed into memory.

* * * *

Up to almost the end of the nineteenth century Formby's administration came under the control of the West Lancashire District Council until 1905 when the Formby Urban District Council was formed. Their first council offices were situated in Moorhouse Buildings on the corner of Church Road and Old Mill Lane

Stoneyhurst Cottage, Priesthouse Lane, in the process of demolition
before its reconstruction in 1982

above what has for many years remained a fish and chip shop. The British Legion took over the premises when our new Council Offices were built in 1927.

In 1981 when the original thatched cottage in Priesthouse Lane was demolished to make way for the new one, an old shed in the garden was found to be housing a mound of papers. Both the cottage and the house next door, number 3, had been owned by Mr. John Dean, a local councillor and architect, and these papers must have been those in his official keeping for they were detailed specifications and estimates of the cost of building the proposed new Council Offices. These particular estimates, seen by the joiner employed on the site, showed the overall estimated cost to be £4,000, a princely sum in 1927 when the average semi would probably have been in the region of £350, but in the light of today's prices a positive gift. There was no indication as to whose estimates they were, but the contract went, perhaps appropriately, to Formby Brothers, today Formby's oldest building firm, who produced an impressive civic building which was the pride of the people.

All local authority work was fairly shared out between all the local builders and when a public clock was chosen for our Council Offices the contract went to the firm of Ward's builders. There being no such refinement as scaffolding in those

The Council Chamber

days the clock was erected on the building in a fashion reminiscent of a Marx Brothers film when Jimmy Goulbourne, a man of very slight stature, ascended a ladder supported only by a fellow workman, which barely reached the necessary height, and swaying about precariously in mid air Jimmy courageously battled against the forces of nature to fix the clock in place. That it failed to crash to the ground was testimony to the acrobatic skills and determination of the man, and the timepiece gave the finishing touch to our proud Council Offices. For many years the clock always kept perfect time and was the means by which we judged whether or not we would be late for school (and later work) in our race for the train.

In 1937, ten years after the opening of our Council Offices and following the abdication of Edward VIII, came the accession to the throne of King George VI and Queen Elizabeth. To commemorate the occasion it was decided to plant two horse chestnut trees either side of the front lawns each representing the new monarchs. The tree on the left of the building was dedicated to the King and the one on the right to the Queen, and it was a happy ceremony with many of the local school children in attendance. Nature sometimes has strange prophetic powers, and it seems uncanny that the tree planted for our King should wither and die, whilst the one for our Queen grew and flourished to become the sturdy specimen we see today and perhaps stands as a reminder of the long and healthy life of the lady who became one of the nation's best loved royals, the Queen Mother, and who was destined to spend most of her life isolated from the King she loved when his life came so abruptly to an end in 1952 whilst he was still a comparatively young man.

Hogs Hill Farm

The Council Offices also incorporated our official morgue, or mortuary, but before 1927 the morgue was an old black, tumbledown shed opposite Hogs Hill Farm on the site of the present Altcar Sewerage Works. Jimmy Goulbourne remembers as a small boy in about 1920 being terrified of going anywhere near the place so lurid were the stories conjured up by him and all his friends at what they might find inside. It was obviously a very basic place, to say the least, and dead bodies were deposited with little finesse or even human dignity.

Throughout history and right up to the middle of the 20th century Liverpool reigned supreme as a shipping port. The River Mersey was alive with vessels of all shapes and sizes from small boats to massive ocean going liners. The turbulent waters around our coastline, and particularly off Formby Point, caused many shipwrecks and claimed the lives of numerous seafarers, and it was a sad fact of life that bodies were often washed up on our shore.

At the beginning of the 1900's farmer Jimmy Lowe was given the contract to collect and remove any dead bodies to the morgue, and his daughter, Vera, never forgot the gruesome and haunting sight of being with her father as a very small child when he lifted a drowned seaman on to his big flat cart. The body had been in the water so long that the head fell off.

The water pump at the rear of
Hogs Hill Farm

As the Lowe family lived on Liverpool Road at the Nurseries (later Stott's cottage) opposite Marina Road and in close proximity to the morgue it may possibly account for Jimmy having the somewhat dubious honour of being appointed official body recoverer. Going back even further in time John Tyrer recalls the Railway Hotel acting as an unofficial mortuary. Being so close to the railway station it was presumably the most convenient resting place for any corpses until identification could be made by relatives arriving by train.

John recalls in the late 1890's accompanying his uncle to the Hotel and seeing the bodies of six drowned seamen, one of them black, all laid out on the floor awaiting identification.

The railway line, too, has also claimed a number of lives, and around the turn of the century one such victim was found by a group of local fishermen returning via Cabin Hill from a shrimping expedition. The body was badly mutilated and almost naked and the men picked it up and carried it to the home of one of the fishermen whose mother promptly found a clean shirt which, as a mark of respect, she placed on the body before it was taken to the morgue. Unfortunately the shirt happened to be the only decent one that the man possessed and the one he always wore when courting his future wife. When he later discovered the shirt to be

Altcar Lane cottages near to the old morgue and now replaced by modern houses

missing and his mother confessed what she had done he nearly went berserk and immediately roared out of the house and round to the morgue where he found the corpse, by this time as stiff as a board, clad in his best shirt. Determined to get the garment off the corpse at all costs he battled for almost half an hour pulling first one rigid arm and then the other in order to retrieve his precious shirt in one piece, and relieved beyond measure when eventually he succeeded and could meet the love of his life in true sartorial splendour.

This unpleasant aspect of life was perhaps made slightly less horrific when the new Council Offices were built in Freshfield Road and it became a legal requirement for the provision of a mortuary and the necessary inclusion was made. Jimmy Goulbourne recalls in his early days as a plumber with Dean's builders and funeral directors being instructed to deliver a coffin to the mortuary for a suicide case. No details were given, but foreman Jimmy Edgar gave his orders for Jimmy Goulbourne and two others to accompany him to the Council Offices to place the corpse in the coffin. It was customary for a policeman to stand on duty at the mortuary door until the body was officially removed for burial, but as the four men approached the mortuary they noticed that the policeman was standing quite some distance away. As they drew nearer they understood exactly why. The dead woman was a suicide by gassing case who had lain undiscovered for ten days. The smell was atrocious. The four men entered the mortuary and Jimmy Goulbourne pulled the sheet from the body and all four nearly passed out at the sight. The body was so discoloured it was every colour imaginable and was blown up to an horrendous size. Each man had to take an arm or leg and dump it in the coffin before rushing outside to be heartily sick.

Since the reorganisation of local government in 1974 our Council Offices have suffered a certain redundancy with many of the municipal departments being housed elsewhere in the borough of Sefton, and council meetings being held at the larger Town Halls of either Bootle or Southport. These once imposing offices now sadly show the signs of neglect with crumbling masonry and dilapidated paintwork, and the erection of a new clock to replace the one which for years had stood permanently at 2.50 p.m. only seems to emphasise the surrounding decadence. Regrettably the building would appear to face an uncertain future and only time alone will tell what fate awaits it.

Up to the formation of Sefton our Council had naturally been made up of local men, many of whom followed in the footsteps of their fathers, and all of them entrenched in local knowledge and with a deep concern for their village. Formby's

Formby Council Offices at 11 am on 8th February 1952 –
the Proclamation of H.M. Queen Elizabeth II

Close up of Council Chairman Peggy Beeston proclaiming our new Queen
following the sudden death of her father King George VI
Left to right: Mr. Gollan, Councillor James Rimmer, Harold Turner, Jack Hodge,
John Breese, Councillor Edwin Melrose, Mrs. Hodge

placid stagnation as a country backwater had survived many centuries with little change. The coming of the railway in 1848 had swelled the population slightly, but it was the end of the second world war which was to bring about the transformation of our village.

The destruction of Liverpool had left the city like one gigantic bomb site and with an urgent need for a re-housing programme. The city dwellers would have to move outwards and to the Formby Council alarm bells were ringing. Under no circumstances did they want their village to be used as an overspill area with sprawling council estates, and so, anxious to preserve Formby's village status, they embarked upon a private building programme as a means of attracting a more select and affluent influx of home-owning residents, leaving the parallel farming villages of Kirkby and Skelmersdale to take the overspill population. It was a plan of which many councillors were proud and appeared to them successful at the time. Undoubtedly they were faced with a dilemma and genuinely acted in Formby's best interests but with hindsight it was probably the start of many of Formby's present day problems as the emphasis continued to be almost exclusively on building houses, houses and yet more houses.

Formby's few established building firms now began to see the emergence of new companies and it was with the enterprise of Arthur Briscoe, a member of our football team and a man of great personal ambition, that the building boom began. Beginning in the early 1950's in a modest way his expansion and completion of the Park Road Estate at the end of the decade brought employment to a large number of local men and boys who all received a good grounding in their trades, many of them later going on to found their own businesses.

Two of these young apprentices seemed unlikely candidates for success when one day they were sent to collect a massive ladder from a property in Freshfield to bring to the site at the other end of Formby. The lads set off on their bikes for the

A newly built pair of bungalows in Southport Road in 1933.
Jimmy Goulbourne (fourth left) is the only Formby tradesman in a team of Birkdale workers

ladder which was of an enormous length. They each took hold of an end and then mounted their bikes and with the ladder stretched out between them pedalled with great dexterity the long length of Gores Lane and Halsall Lane. On reaching the Village roundabout the lad at the front cycled round the island whilst his pal behind was forced to ride out in such a giant sweep to negotiate the roundabout that he ended up flat on his face in the war Memorial garden with the ladder and his bike on top of him. They eventually resumed their journey along the Village and as they cycled down Brows Lane were confronted by a very distraught lady who rushed out of her gate shouting to them for help as her chimney was blocked causing clouds of smoke in her dining room. The pair leapt from their bikes and like true Sir Galahads positioned their ladder up to the roof after first instructing the lady to go inside and kneel beside the fireplace and watch for any falling object whilst they ascended the ladder to inspect the chimney pot. Minutes later there was the most piercing scream and the boys almost fell down the ladder and into the house where the lady stood completely covered in soot with a perfect shape of her anatomy silhouetted round the sooty hearth where she'd previously been kneeling. The two lads fled from the house after grabbing their unwieldy load and set off once again on their bikes to their building site hoping and praying that their boss would never learn of the chaos their intended act of chivalry had caused.

* * * *

In 1991 as the Gulf War raged in the Middle East and men from our community were involved in battle, we were reminded yet again of the evils and horrors of war. One of Formby's sons has lived through a number of wars and has vivid memories of them. His earliest recollection goes back to the year 1899 when John

Tyrer was just six years of age. John was playing near his home in Raven Meols Lane when he saw a group of men dressed in red tunics marching through the path from Hogs Hill to Raven Meols Lane where they continued on to the railway station. Young John excitedly marched alongside them and recognized some of the men as Dick Goulbourne, his brothers Bill and Harry, plumber Percy Evans from Halsall Lane, and a man who was a joiner with Dean's builders. On arrival at the station the Formby Band was waiting, and as the men changed from their red tunics into khaki battledress to board the Liverpool train the band struck up to bid farewell to the soldiers on the first leg of their journey to South Africa and the Boer War. Miraculously in 1902 when the war ended every one of those men returned home, and in 1900 when Mafeking was relieved John and all his schoolmates at St. Lukes School were given a day's holiday in celebration.

The Old Post Office in Brows Lane.
The first Holy Trinity School and modern Post Office replaced the building

The school in those days was situated on the corner of Kings Road and Raven Meols Lane, now the site of a block of flats, and had a total of 92 mixed pupils all squashed together in one small room under the care of just one teacher, Miss Amelia Smith, who had come to Formby from her home in Tamworth. A year or so later the infants were moved to a building further along Kings Road where they were taught by Miss Mayers, and very shortly after this in 1901 the overcrowding was greatly eased with the building of Holy Trinity School in Brows Lane.

The Tyrer family lived quite near to the school at Whitehouse Farm in Raven Meols Lane and were tenants of the Weld Blundells. At the nearby Park Farm opposite Kings Road, which many may remember as the home of the late Tommy Sutton, lived the Chatterton family who ran a charabanc hire business in Bath Street, Waterloo. Mr. Chatterton rented the farm for the hay and straw he needed for his horses which drew the charabancs, and employed as his groom local man, Joe Spencer. In 1897 Dicky Blundell celebrated his 21st birthday and all the Blundell tenants were invited to Ince Blundell Hall for the celebrations. They were transported by horse and charabanc and were followed by a second charabanc containing the Formby Band who were engaged to play at the party. Dicky and his

St. Luke's School, now replaced by Raven Meols Lodge flats on the corner of Kings Road

brother, though both were soldiers, never went to war and sadly died at an early age leaving just two sisters. One sister married Commander Montagu (who gave his name to Montagu Road) and the other married a Mr. Weld (whose name became immortalised in Weld Road, Birkdale). With no male heirs the Blundell line died out and the only male relative, though not closely related, was the well known writer and poet Alfred Noyes who is probably best remembered for his poem 'The Highwayman'.

Many of Formby's young men gave their lives for their country in both world wars and their names are commemorated on our War Memorial, a gift to the people of Formby for all time by Mr. Weld Blundell.

Our saddler, Ernie Bills, often spoke of the horrors of the trenches during the first world war in which many of his fellow soldiers were lost. Ernest was one of the lucky ones who returned home to pick up the threads of his life in the sleepy country village far, far removed from the obscenities of the French battlefields.

Here in Formby a regiment of Scottish soldiers arrived and were billeted in a wooden hut attached to Lowe's Farm in Bull Cop, and the colourful sight of an army of swirling kilts marching along the lane to what became known as the Boys' Hut caused many a flutter in the hearts of the village girls. The soldiers experienced a very bitter winter whilst in Formby and would massage their exposed knees with Vaseline to protect them from the severe cold. Presumably their stay in Formby was a stopping off point on their journey from the north to join the other British soldiers in France.

Although Formby escaped the real horrors of the first world war some preparations were made in case of attack and dug-outs appeared on the Poverty Field at Montagu Road, and the Bay Horse field, which at that time stretched as far as the old Our Lady's School and churchyard, was used for civil defence manoeuvres.

Mawdsley's cottage in the centre of the Village next door to the Midland Bank
and now a row of shops and offices

When peace came in 1918 there was jubilation in Formby and a peace parade was organised by all the local schools (St. Peter's, St Luke's, Holy Trinity, and Our Lady's) in which the local coal merchants and farmers decked out their lorries and wagons with flags and bunting and led the parade on a tour of the village. They all set off from Our Lady's School on Church Road and when they reached the Victoria Hall the children from St. Peter's left the parade to go inside to enjoy refreshments whilst the rest continued on to their respective schools. Alice Houghton recalls as an eight-year-old feeling very tired after the long march and relishing the meat pies which awaited them all back at Our Lady's School courtesy of Norburn's bakers.

World War One had been dubbed the war to end all wars but sadly only twenty years later we were once again plunged into a war which was to prove to be the beginning of the end of the village that was Formby.

At the onset of war in 1939 the nearest barracks to Formby were those at Seaforth, but as the war progressed and Liverpool suffered such devastation, including the bombing of the Seaforth barracks, soldiers were moved out to Formby and billeted in private houses. Harrington Barracks was then built during the war and the men transferred from the houses making way for the evacuees to take their places.

Inventories were taken of all properties and many properties were requisitioned to house evacuees, amongst them the present Maryland Home for the Elderly in School Lane which was at that time two semi detached houses and which then became home to two Bootle families, the Chapmans and the Morrises.

Situated so close to the Village, which was then a residential as well as a commercial centre, the Chapman boys would meet with the Village boys on a Sunday afternoon to play either football or cricket down the middle of the road.

They knew there would be no sign of traffic until 4 p.m. when Schofield's taxi came through on its way back to base in Halsall Lane leaving the road once more their playground for the remainder of the day.

Today we look back with astonishment on the antics of the Home Guard and the A.R.P. The simplicity and unsophistication of a bygone age conjures up pure wonder that we survived and won a war with such primitive methods and equipment, and though the Dad's Army image creates great hilarity we would be misguided in thinking it was all an episode to be ridiculed, for people lived in real fear and rose to the occasion of defending their country with courage and fortitude. History has shown us to be a nation of resilience and strength and that we are a people to be reckoned with. The civilian forces in Formby answered the call of duty admirably and must be counted as a contributory factor in our country's victory. The A.R.P. played an important part in the war effort by their vigilant patrols of the village. It was crucial to our safety that no lights were to be seen through any windows and it was the duty of the A.R.P. wardens to ensure that blackout regulations were enforced. 'Put that light out' became a familiar catchphrase and any culprit could be assured of a hefty fine for breaking the law. The Fire Guard was a branch of the A.R.P. and Formby must surely rank as the only place in Great Britain to boast its very youngest member in nine years old Richard Gardner, the son of member Dick Gardner, and the organisation's official messenger boy. Young Richard was issued with three asbestos sheets measuring approximately six inches square on which messages had to be written – paper would have been useless in the event of a fire – and Richard would pedal around Formby on his bike delivering his messages with the expertise of a veteran. Once a week the boy would join his fellow Fire Guards at either the Queens or Embassy cinemas where informational slide or film shows were given to educate the members in all aspects of fire fighting including the procedure should a plane or a parachutist come down, and practical manoeuvres were also carried out as a means of ensuring proficiency in case of enemy attack. One of the practice sessions involved a phosphorus bomb being tossed into the middle of the road at the junction of Moss Side and Deansgate Lane. The men were then expected to demonstrate their prowess in fire fighting technique by dealing with the bomb, but unfortunately Richard's father gave them little opportunity as he invariably shovelled it up and flung it in the nearby ditch.

Incendiary bombs dropped all over Formby and it fell to the A.R.P. to extinguish them with their stirrup pumps. Mr Aughton was one very cunning farmer near to the corner of Old Mill

Home Guard Peter Boyer

Lane and Church Road who saved himself untold work in watering his crops by reporting that bombs had fallen in his field, and then sat back in comfort whilst young A.R.P. warden Alice Houghton crawled all over his land with her stirrup pump putting out the non-existent bombs and watering his cabbages in the process.

The Home Guard also played an essential role in our country's defence by their regular patrols of the shore area as well as other parts of the village keeping watch for the threatened invasion. With a shortage of weapons the men were issued with broom handles as rifle substitutes for practice sessions and two of those Home Guard officers were Peter Boyer and Mr Bracewell, our dentist. These two men were one night on duty in a caravan in a field near to the Freshfield roundabout keeping watch for any German invaders. They had both fallen asleep and were awakened by the movement of the caravan which was being rocked back and forth. Peter Boyer, who by nature was a very nervous man, peered out of the caravan window fully expecting to see the enemy ready and waiting. His startled face registered utter relief as he saw the reason for the movement of the caravan as a horse gently scratched its backside against it. The two men banged on the sides of the caravan and yelled at the horse to go away doing their best to stop the rocking motion, but the horse continued his exercise unconcernedly. Not knowing what to do next to get rid of the animal Peter picked up their kettle of hot water and poured it over the hind quarters of the horse. With one almighty roar the poor creature bolted for its life, galloping round and round the field for the duration of the Home Guard shift and keeping as far away as possible from the two madmen who had scorched its rump.

Landgirl Edith (Scarisbrick) Ashcroft

It was not only the menfolk whose services were required during the second world war and most young women also played their part in the defence of our country.

There were four branches of the women's services – the A.T.S. (the army); the W.A.A.F. (the airforce); the Wrens (the navy); and the Land Army, and many women were required to register for munitions work at either Brockhouse in Crossens or at Kirkby as well as enlisting in the A.R.P.

Edith Scarisbrick, who later became my aunt by marrying my mother's youngest brother Harry Ashcroft, worked as a shop assistant with Tickle's grocers in Queens Road and being involved with the provision of foodstuffs was deferred from war service for a time. However, after several deferments the government eventually decided that being a counter assistant at Tickle's was not a good enough reason to avoid active service for her country and she was officially called up and enlisted in the Women's Land Army. She was fortunate in being able to remain living at home whilst working at the farm of Stan Ashcroft by the delph at Hill House, Altcar, where she was joined by another local landgirl, Kitty Sutton.

The two girls worked hard throughout the war years and for part of that time alongside a number of Italian prisoners of war most of whom were billeted at Haydock and who travelled in each day by farm wagon. The busiest periods were hay making and potato picking, and two of the prisoners who must have been very privileged and trusted lived in at the farm. They enjoyed a great deal of freedom and every Sunday morning would walk the lengthy distance down to Our Lady's Church for the morning service and would cause utter embarrassment to the shy young Edith by making a point of seeking her out to wish her good morning and making her feel almost a traitor to be fraternising with the enemy.

Adjoining the fields in which the landgirls worked were billeted the coloured American troops – the G.I.'s – and very often these soldiers would wander across to chat to the girls, doing their best to make dates with them. Both girls, who had boyfriends away in the British Army, were terrified of the G.I.'s following them to Formby so they each invented fictious names hoping to make it difficult for the men to locate them should they try to do so.

Escaping as we did the worst of Hitler's attack made Formby an enviable place to live, and though the village suddenly was awakened from its hibernation by the influx of marching soldiers and airmen parading the streets the real and horrifying dangers which came so close were spared us. We saw the prisoners-of-war with their large black circles on their backs and were reminded of what our own servicemen were facing in the thick of the fighting in the middle-east and far-east as the war raged on, always dreading the telegram bringing news of the loss of yet another of our young men. But gradually the tide began to turn and it was with the utmost relief that victory came in 1945, the servicemen who had survived returned home, and Harrington Barracks became a national service camp until its eventual closure and development into a huge housing estate.

* * * *

Formby has had several royal visits over the years and the first one in living memory was the Golf Club visit by the Prince of Wales, who later briefly became King Edward VIII and then the Duke of Windsor. He arrived in Formby in 1920 and drove past the Blundell Arms to be greeted by the excited flag waving children from all the local schools who had congregated at Cross Green to watch him on his journey down Gores Lane heading for lunch at the Club House followed by a round of golf. At this time he was at the height of his popularity, hailed by the working classes as a champion of the people, and very much removed from the aloof image of royalty, and the cheering crowds flanking the roadside as he passed by left no doubt as to the affection in which he was held. On arrival at the Golf Club he mixed easily with everyone including the servants and greensmen as well as the officials and members. His visit caused great excitement and was a considerable honour for the Club.

Many years later in 1955 the Queen Mother as Colonel in Chief of the King's Regiment visited Harrington Barracks on one of the wettest days in history. The rain made little difference to the throngs of people lining the route she was to take, and her loyal subjects (including myself) endured the deluge for hours to catch a

The Queen Mother's visit to Formby, 1955

Councillor James Rimmer greeting Princess Margaret at Woodvale Aerodrome

glimpse of Her Majesty, looking radiant in a sunshine yellow outfit, as she passed through the village and across the Freshfield Station railway crossing gates en route for the camp.

Princess Margaret flew in to Woodvale Aerodrome in the early 1960's to be greeted by the Chairman of our Council, Jimmy Rimmer, as she made her way to an official function at the Southport Town Hall. Over a quarter of a century later she repeated the journey when she returned to Woodvale on her way to Little Crosby Hall in May 1991. The Queen herself paid a visit to her regiment at Altcar Rifle Range in 1987 arriving first by train in Liverpool and then continuing by car waving to the crowds as she passed.

Prince Charles left the area via Formby after his official ceremony of the opening of the new Southport & Formby District Hospital at Kew, and Princess Diana also passed through on her visit to officially open a new wing of the Birkdale School for the Partially Hearing in 1988. And her brother-in-law, the sporting Duke of York, also flew into Woodvale in 1991 for a round of golf at the Royal Birkdale links. Rather less noble personages, but nevertheless in the celebrity bracket, are the following well-known personalities who have also had connections with Formby.

Percy French, the Irish composer of such melodies as 'Phil the Fluters's Ball' and 'The Mountains of Mourne', who was related to the Rev. Brooke Richardson, the vicar of Holy Trinity Church, and who sadly died whilst on a visit to Formby and was buried in the churchyard at St. Luke's.

A more recent and permanent resident was Beryl Bainbridge, the prolific novelist and contender for the 1990 Booker Prize, whose home in the 1940's and 1950's was in Raven Meols Lane and many of whose novels were inspired by her Formby association including the television screening of one of her works on location in Formby.

During the 1940's the popular husband and wife film star duo of Eileen Erskine and Philip Friend were local residents, Eileen's father being the resident doctor at Shaftesbury House in Raven Meols Lane.

Harold Wilson was a parliamentary candidate when we were within the Ormskirk constituency and in the course of his canvassing made frequent visits, and his successor Robert Kilroy-Silk, now a renowned T.V. personality, lived in Piercefield Road.

At one time Formby was home to the most famous footballers in the land with many of the players from Liverpool and Everton living amongst us. England goalkeeper Ray Clemence, captain Emlyn Hughes, team-mate Phil Neal, Alan Ball, one of the 1966 World Cup heroes, Howard Kendall, Ron Yeats, and countless others whose footballing skills have thrilled spectators around the world all made their homes here and though many have moved on others have taken their place in our midst and Formby remains a popular residential area for the footballing fraternity.

From the world of tennis we have Alan Mills from Lonsdale Road whose interest in the game was nurtured whilst a schoolboy playing at the nets of Holy

Parr's garage (later Turban Motors) and now a second-hand car showroom on the corner of School Lane and Church Road next to the Police Station

Trinity Church Club under the watchful eye of solicitor Gerry Thompson who steered him towards his eventual goal as the top umpire at Wimbledon.

Our Golf Club has welcomed, as well as royalty and the aristocracy, world class players of all nationalities. From the early days of J.H. Lazloe, Alex Herd, Laddie Lucas, Walter Hagen, and Bobby Jones through to the more recent champions such as Lee Trevino and Peter Oosterhouse, Formby has held a fine reputation for its greens and many have been the times when the local youth have rubbed shoulders with the great names of golf as they became caddies during the tournaments.

Wilfred Pickles of radio's 'Have a Go' fame left his mark on Formby through his connection with the building trade. Although a resident of Ainsdale he worked on the building of several properties in Formby including a pair of bungalows in Watchyard Lane.

George Jesse Turner, the 'World in Action' T.V. cameraman, also an Ainsdale resident, is the son of George Turner who took over Parr's Garage next to the Police Station and renamed it Turban Motors. When young George began his career in T.V. his father loved to tantalize his customers by telling them he knew what was coming in the future episodes of the then very new T.V. serial 'Coronation Street'.

Angela Bracewell, the daughter of our dentist, became Bruce Forsyth's 'Beat the Clock' girl at the London Palladium in the 1950's and later married the American actor Stubby Kaye, and another local dancer, Betty Wright, also found fame on the London stage and married actor/comedian Bernard Bresslaw.

From the business world the family of Lord Vestey of the Dewhurst meat empire lived here and the world famous Criddle's treacle was produced at the Bootle factory of the family who lived for many years in Wicks Lane. Criddle's not

George Lowe, brother of farmer Jimmy Lowe, who travelled the world as
chauffeur to Lord Vestey and who died in China following an attack by a rabid dog

only showed philanthropic kindness to their employees by building an estate of
houses for them at Ford, but also expressed their concern for the canine
population of Formby by providing a bowl of water outside their home on the
dusty walk through to the shore.

And, of course, one of Britains's wealthiest men, John Moores, the Littlewood's
football pools supremo, has been a long time resident. Now Sir John Moores, he
reached the heights from very humble beginnings when in 1923 with two fellow
young telegraphists they started as a part time venture from a small office in
Church Street, Liverpool what was to become a national institution. But things did
not come easily and by the end of the first season the scheme had lost £600 and
two of the partners dropped out leaving John Moores to struggle on alone and to
become a millionaire before he was 35.

And so despite Formby's traditional sleepy rural image history shows that we
have had our brush with the rich and famous from time to time who all no doubt
were as favourably impressed with what they found on their visits to Formby as
are the many thousands who chose to come and stay more permanently at a much
later date.

* * * *

We are fortunate in Formby in having an effective and balanced local newspaper.
The 'Formby Times' has been in existence since 1895 and whilst its format has
changed over the years its reporting quality has gone from strength to strength.
Correspondence from local residents has long been a feature, and recent years
have seen the expansion of this aspect of journalism which has made for a lively

The entrance to Little Altcar, sometimes known as Robinson's corner or Lovelady's Farm corner, in 1932. Pierce's Farm, on the right, was demolished to make way for new houses and the Kwik Save supermarket. Altcar Lane now stands on the left (by the signpost) with Hartley's (previously the Lighthouse restaurant) also on the left

and interesting column capable of reflecting the views of Formby people on a diversity of contentious local issues.

The inclusion of many of my own letters and poems have all proved to be an abortive attempt to resist what I, and many others, considered to be unnecessary and undesirable 'progress'. The following pages form a miscellany including some of my poems, most of which met with the wholehearted approval of my fellow sandgrounders but were perhaps less welcomed by some newcomers, and in view of Formby's development had no impact whatsoever on those in authority. However, no matter the outcome, in all cases I felt it to be a series of hopeless causes worth pursuing and only history will show the folly or wisdom of the decisions which have led to the Formby we bequeath to our future generations.

Earlier mention of our roads leads us on to more modern times and their inherent problems. We have seen that Chapel Lane was originally a residential road just like any other. Being situated in the natural centre of Formby its evolvement as the shopping centre was axiomatic and gradually a variety of individuals set up in business to provide the villagers with their needs. Over the years the cottages disappeared to make way for yet more shops until by the 20th century 'The Village' was firmly established. The cobbled road surface eventually gave way to tarmac and by the standards of the day the treelined thoroughfare would have been considered handsomely spacious.

By the end of the 1930's with a population of less than 7,000, and before the mass-production of the motor car, there could have been no thought of what lay ahead or the problems in store.

Pedestrianisation, December 1988
The entrance to Chapel Lane just beyond the School Lane/Halsall Lane roundabout

The 1950's and 1960's saw the development of many housing estates and with them came the first indication of the volume of traffic hitherto unknown on our roads. Formby's growth continued into the 1980's when it seemed we had reached saturation point only to find more and more buildings appearing on any and every spare piece of land. Many of the older and larger properties were being demolished and in their places were coming yet more houses and blocks of flats. We were bursting at the seams and the increase in traffic was creating immense problems on our already overcrowded roads.

The congestion in our Village shopping area was particularly acute and this led to a council decision for pedestrianisation which it was argued could be the answer to the predicament. Many people thought otherwise, but the scheme went ahead and in 1988 pedestrianisation was introduced for an experimental period of six months. Immediate and utter chaos ensued. Formby's roads on all sides suffered arterial thrombosis, the shops suffered economic disaster, and some residents suffered near nervous breakdowns. Amid howls of protest from the public and stormy meetings in Council the whole sorry business was abandoned after just six weeks. Our local newspaper was bombarded with letters of complaint, amongst them my poetic offering:

PEDESTRIANISATION

The traffic whizzes up and down the road,
The bikes, the cars, the lorries with their load,
The noise, the bustle, harassment and rush,
It's got to stop, we can't have all this crush.

The shop-keepers and shoppers don't much mind,
The present busy practice works they find,
It's pretty dodgy trying to get across,
But up to now we've had no human loss.

That's not the point, the planners wisely said,
We can't stop progress and must plan ahead,
This village must be safe and traffic free,
We'll make it better for you all – you'll see!

So on their heads they put their thinking caps,
We'll sort this out 'cause we're such clever chaps,
Pedestrianisation's what you need,
We'll make a vast improvement, they decreed.

And so the barriers came at Three Tuns Lane,
No entry – you must walk down Chapel Lane,
But where's the barrier at the other end?
Has someone really gone right round the bend?

It's slap bang in the middle of the road,
Does this comply with some new Highway Code?
No, we forgot the shops have no back door,
So no one can deliver to their store.

And so the drivers meet a sudden stop,
Outside McDougall's lovely chemist's shop,
Into reverse they quickly move the gears,
And whiz out backwards to three hearty cheers

One day the planners might just get it right,
And the village will be closed from morn till night,
The traffic will be banned and sent away,
To interfere with someone else's day.

Then we will wander round without a care,
And shop in peace if still the shops are there,
While offices, estate agents and banks
Will send the planners their sincerest thanks.

In fairness, however, it must be said that the seriousness of the situation perhaps warranted the experiment if only to prove its ineffectiveness. The traffic is here to stay, and though there has been a shift in the shopping activity the problem is still as pressing as it ever was and remains as one of the biggest dilemmas facing those in civic office.

* * * *

Further development of church land on the War Memorial site against overwhelming public opposition brought yet more dissent when our previously free car park became destined to be a charge park on completion of the superstore. Again the local press was inundated with letters of complaint and again I added my voice to the tirade;

SAFEWAYS

Once we had a car park,
Dead handy for each shop,
Once it cost us nothing
As in and out we'd pop.

Once we had a church here
Concerned about its flock,
Once its door was open
And no one had to knock.

Once we had a village
Full of little shops,
Where everyone knew everyone,
And the church held weekly hops.

Then the great God money
Raised its ugly head,
Then our little village
Knew that it was dead.

We all were conned and brainwashed
Into thinking it was right
That what was just a wasteland
Was a quite disgraceful sight.

This land must be developed
To give us all a store
Packed with lots of goodies
Costing more and more and more.

There'd be jobs for all and sundry
To help us make ends meet
When the other shops had vanished
And just Safeway in the street.

Now we've got our present
Of a shiny super store,
All bright and light and glitzy,
And an ever open door.

And now it costs us nothing
If we only park two hours
And shop inside this palace
That's really truly ours.

But if we want the chemist
Or bank or paper shop
Then we must find a fiver
For just an hour's stop.

So thank you, all our leaders,
For what we now have got,
It's exactly what we wanted
And Formby's best forgot.

Following enormous public pressure Safeway relented and the car park returned to its free status for an unspecified period.

* * * *

The closure of our purpose built Post Office in Brows Lane, with the proliferation of rumours as to its re-location, provoked another barrage of mail to our Formby Times particularly when one of those rumours was for the re-siting to be within the new superstore:

Formby's last Post Office – now a sorting office

OUR POST OFFICE

Where will we go to buy our stamps
And licence for T.V.?
Where will we tax our motor cars?
Where will those pensions be?

Where will the Giros be paid out?
Where will we have to queue
If our Post Office is pensioned off
To make way for something new?

We all have moaned about the size
Our Post Office remained
Whilst half of Formby stood outside
And shivered when it rained.

But though it isn't big enough
Now Formby is a town
Why can't it be extended out
Instead of closing down?

We've all got used to losing bits
Of Formby that we know,
So what's another landmark
We are told has got to go?

And then the final insult
To those who feel betrayed
That we may have to queue inside
The store that Safeway made.

So M.P., Councillors, G.P.O.,
Please listen when we say
Our Post Office built in Brows Lane
Is where it ought to stay.

In the event the Post Office did not follow the rumour and was re-housed in a shop opposite its predecessor in Brows Lane.

* * * *

Since the demise of the Formby Urban District Council and the birth of Sefton local government has in many ways appeared less than satisfactory for Formby. The constant damage to our roads has been one particular area of concern and when a hole appeared in Priesthouse Lane confusion reigned as to who should bear responsibility for it. At first it was attributed to the Water Board. Then to the Gas Board. Then back again to the Water Board, and finally back to the Gas Board. An interesting comment from the Gas Board when they eventually accepted responsibility for the hole that 'now that we are aware of the situation we will be looking into it' was perhaps less than tactful when the residents had all been looking into it for several weeks. The final irony came when the road was unbelievably resurfaced around the hole.

THE HOLE

In the middle of our road we have a hole,
We think it has a most important role,
We've had it here for quite a long long time,
To fill it in would almost seem a crime.

Last week we thought our hole might disappear
When a lorry and some men unloaded gear,
"Oh no", they said, "re-surfacing's our job,
Mending holes is down to Bill and Joe and Bob."

"But how can you do that" we all exclaimed,
"Our hole will hamper all your well planned aims",
"We'll leave that bit and do it later on
When someone else has been and done and gone".

"You're joking", we all cried in unison,
"We're not", they said, and boldly carried on.
Our local councillor will sort this out,
"I'm sorry", said his wife, "he's just gone out".

And so our hole remains so deep and round,
It's great for dumping rubbish folk have found,
The traffic finds it no real detriment,
As driving skills they all experiment.

One day we're going to miss our great big hole,
As down the road we happily all stroll,
How boring it will all turn out to be
When our hole is only just a memory.

* * * *

THE SUPERSTORES

Those poor folk out in Altcar,
Where life has hardly changed,
Must feel like us in Formby
Who sometimes feel deranged,
With traffic pouring past their doors,
Pantechnicons and such,
Delivering all the merchandise
That Tesco needs so much.

It seemed so clear to everyone
That all our present roads
Were not made to accommodate
Such extra heavy loads.

At first our councillors thought so too
And turned down Tesco's plan,
But on appeal they thought again
And then said "Yes you can".

So now we have our second store,
Even bigger than the first,
Right slap bang by the traffic lights
Where hold-ups are the worst.
And they each vie for custom
From Joe Public and his wife,
And leave us wondering what became
Of Formby's village life.

And as the motorists sit and fume
In lengthy traffic lines,
We maybe think of how it was
In gentler, quieter times,
When mothers wheeled their offspring
In stately well-sprung prams,
And never had to worry
About noisy traffic jams.

But that was all long, long ago
And life's moved on a pace,
And Formby's been discovered
As a fashionable place.
And that has made us pay the price
Of being what we were
Because too many liked us then
And all flocked in to share.

So now in 1991,
Like the overflowing brook,
The banks have burst and flooded out
And with it life's blood took,
So that the place which brought the herds
To find the peace they yearn
Has disappeared for ever more,
Never, never to return.

* * * *

OUR SWIMMING POOL

We didn't need a swimming pool
Because we had the sea,
And we didn't need street corners
We had fields galore, you see.

We didn't have a T.V. screen
To stare at day and night,
And the Queens and Embo once a week
Were there for our delight.

And everything was rationed then
When we were all at school,
So we climbed the trees and picked the fruit
And didn't miss a pool.

And when we went to Southport
Or into Liverpool
We didn't care when we came home
That we didn't have a pool
Because we had the space to breath
And the freedom to explore
The countryside and shoreline
Which were ours for ever more.

But we were wrong and progress came
And now the kids at school
Have got no fields to play in
And badly need a pool.

The sea we once could swim in
Is polluted and unclean,
And the fields and trees we played in
Are no longer in the scene.

And even all the old folks
And those who've long left school
Find little in amenities
And wish we had a pool.

So let us stop and muse a while
And imagine foolishly
If just one superstore went bust
And what we all might see,

Inside that mighty labyrinth,
As spacious as a school –
A bowling alley, lecture hall,
And a great big swimming pool.

* * * *

HOLY TRINITY, FORMBY, PARISH MAGAZINE.

Advertisements from 1935

WHY?

"Why is it called The Village?"
The youngster asked Grandad,
"Because it's full of shops, my boy"
He told the little lad.

"Why are some of them closed, Grandad?"
The boy then questioned back,
"Because they can't afford the rents
And business is so slack".

"Why are they building new ones then
If we've got too many now?"
"I just don't know" his Grandad said
As he scratched his furrowed brow.

"Why are there all these offices,
And agents for estates,
And building societies with posh fronts,
And banks with big brass plates?"

"It's The Village, son" Grandad replied,
Feeling weary and ill at ease,
"That's for shops you said" the boy returned,
"Can I have an ice-cream please?"

"I'm sorry, son" the old man said,
"I can't buy you a single one,
They're only sold in packs of ten
Now the ice-cream shop has gone".

"But this is The Village, isn't it?
Or are you telling lies?"
"No, my boy, I'm feeling tired
And there's tears come in my eyes".

"You see, that's how it used to be
When I was just like you,
But times have changed so very much
It's left me muddled too".

"Don't worry, Grandad" said the boy,
"In another fifty years
They'll knock the whole lot down again
And that should stop your tears".

Wilf Wright at Woolton Show
(Photo courtesy of Liverpool Daily Post & Echo)

* * * *

Much of the information contained in my book has to be credited to Mr. Wilf Wright of the famous roses firm. Wilf talked to me on several occasions about the Formby he loved and knew so well. His wealth of knowledge he happily shared with me, and it was with great sorrow that I learnt of his death whilst I was still writing this book and when there was so much I would like to have asked him. His father, Robert, founded the business in 1897 in Halsall Lane on the site now known as The Cloisters, and there seems a certain sadness to now stand in the large car park behind the shops and see only concrete and machines where once grew fields of beauty in the shape of his beloved roses, and to memorise the scented air around his colourful gardens filled with a mass of flowers. Wilf continued the success of his father expanding the business, propagating new varieties, perfecting established strains, and exhibiting at the country's prestigious flower shows where he regularly claimed top prizes. Wilf was one of nature's gentlemen, always ready to give advice on gardening matters, and never too busy to talk. He ensured the continuity of the family business which now passes to his son, Robert, who in turn it is hoped will one day introduce his own young son to the firm.

When the Wright's moved to their present home alongside the brook bank at Altcar Wilf could stand on top of the brook bank and enjoy unrestricted views across the whole of Formby. Slowly those views became hindered by bricks and mortar, but Wilf always said "Aye, but they won't build here as long as I'm around". Let us hope that now he is no longer around his fields of roses will go on blooming for many, many years to come giving pleasure to the people of Formby in the same way they have done for almost 100 years.

* * * *

CONCLUSION

Formby's transition from its rural roots has been a slow process over the centuries when its population remained fairly static with generations of sandgrounders continuing in the steps of their forbears by ploughing, sowing, reaping and mowing in a typical country community. Up to forty years ago life had altered little until those sons of the soil began to forsake their heritage in ever increasing numbers and of necessity scattered to all corners of the world.

The concept of Formby as a village is now clearly anachronistic, and much as many sandgrounders have a desire to cling to that image realism must prevail and we all have to accept that we cannot live in the past. Change is inevitable in all things for without it life would be stagnant and dead.

Halsall Lane corner, then Slaters grocers, later a carpet showroom,
and now The Beacons shopping complex

The attractions we all enjoyed thirty, forty, fifty years ago are memories to be treasured rather than simply losses to be mourned. In the Formby of yesteryear we enjoyed a way of life unparalleled in modern times. The simplicity and joy of our annual galas, and our flower shows, our concerts, our dances, and our whist drives were highlights of those glory years as a village and of a time now gone, and those memories can never be taken away from us.

Modern technology and scientific advancement has transformed life in so many directions and the 20th century has been a century of enormous change, not only to us in Formby, but to all mankind.

We remember the pitchforks and haystacks, the frogspawn and jacksharps, the ditches, fields, trees, and wild flowers, and the freedom of a gentler age; but do we perhaps forget the many families with seven, eight, nine, and ten children living in cramped conditions and with little enough food to go round; the T.B. and diphtheria which were certain death sentences; and the social divisions that created such unfairness? And yet! And yet!

The many advantages of progress cannot be denied, but when we look around our Formby today beneath the apparent affluence is there not a certain degree of discontent or even confusion? With our wealth of local societies and organisations we are a caring town with as congenial an atmosphere as our size will allow but in common with many other small villages our growth has meant the forfeiture of so much.

In the short time since the publication of MY FORMBY we have seen dramatic changes to our landscape particularly in the centre of Formby. The entire block of shops on the corner of School Lane and Halsall Lane has been demolished to be replaced by a development of unseemly dominance effectively reducing our centre to a stereotype of any number of modern small towns. Our Village of small independent shops is already just a memory as the multi-nationals have moved in and the offices thrive alongside them, catering for the needs of the house-hunters and sellers, the finance of big business, and the legal requirements of a prosperous looking town.

Opposite our old Post Office the row of shops which superceded an elegant house of beauty and reduced the site to mediocrity now stand in limbo as the Village fortunes fluctuate and the activity gravitates around the other end of the road. Our purpose built Post Office looks wistfully across to its successor from behind its solidly built and beautifully carved oak doors and sees the face of progress in the cramped corner shop with its plastic facia panel and plywood counter compartments which is now considered adequate to serve an increased population of almost 30,000.

The heartland behind and beyond our War Memorial is transformed. Gone are the Victorian villas to make way for a block of luxury retirement flats. The annual fireworks display and bonfire on the scout field has passed into history – it was only wasteland after all, left to fester and offend the eye convincing a gullible and naïve public of its only value being to the developer.

Then out on our by-pass stands superstore number two, a phoenix risen from the ashes of Woodward's and the temptress of commuter patrons.

On the horizon the old revitalised Power House stands surrounded on all sides by green belt land, itself the subject of doubt and speculation. And we all heave a sign of relief that our pinewoods are under the protection of the National Trust for where might it all end?

* * * *

Brows Lane where it meets Chapel Lane. Holy Trinity School stands on the left
(now a row of shops) and the trees on the right which shielded a large house, The Elms
(later The Priory), have been replaced by a row of shops which includes the new Post Office

Duke Street cottages which stood on the site of Ashhurst Court

Halsall Lane cottages, then the home of Wright's Roses, close to the corner of
Furness Avenue, and now The Cloisters shopping complex

FORMBY TODAY

FOREWORD

The changes described in my previous two books had been a gradual process over many years which had brought Formby from its farming roots to the status of a pleasant town, and by 1992 with the publication of FORMBY REMEMBERED it seemed that Formby's metamorphosis was almost complete and that the greatest upheavals had already taken place, and whatever the future may hold the changes to come would be minor in comparison. How very wrong that assumption would turn out to be as the events of one short decade finally brought to an end the village that was Formby.

THE PINEWOODS

To continue the Formby story makes the final words of FORMBY REMEMBERED ironic indeed, and therefore it is the pinewoods which were to herald a most turbulent decade both environmentally as well as socially.

Like most Formby residents I had always taken our pinewoods for granted. After all, the local landowners, the Formbys and the Weld Blundells, had planted them at the beginning of the 20th century as a coastal defence from the sea and sand and they had served us well and added to the beauty of our shoreline. They were a haven for the unique red squirrel colony and a tourist attraction along one of the country's most attractive coastlines. I had however mistakenly assumed that the National Trust were the sole custodians of all our woodlands, but in fact in 1965 it was English Nature, an unelected government quango, who had taken over the responsibility of the Freshfield woods, known as the Ainsdale National Nature Reserve, and it was this body who in 1996 unbeknown to any of the Formby populace, had massacred thousands upon thousands of healthy trees creating a 'dynamic dunescape' and to further encourage the conservation of natterjack toads and sand lizards as decreed by their European masters. This discovery provoked utter condemnation and anger, and a pressure group, Sefton Coast Watch, was formed which engendered massive public support against the continuation of further planned clear felling which apart from the terrible devastation also threatened the precious red squirrels which were so reliant on the cones for feeding.

The local press was inundated with correspondence throughout the lengthy battle to save our trees accompanied by countless heated public meetings. Up

The massacred Pinewoods, July 1996

Sefton Coast Watch: Barry Griffiths, Joan Rimmer, Jim Hersey (Chairman), Shirley Childs,
Charles Southern, Peter Thornton, Anne Ibbs, Alan Hollway

to this time all meetings had been held in camera with important woodland decisions being taken without the knowledge of any local people, and it was therefore a real breakthrough when Sefton Coast Watch succeeded in gaining access to meetings making for far greater openness of information. At the time of writing despite almost unanimous public and council opposition to any further environmental destruction and an intensified resolve to halt all clear felling and ensure the remaining pinewoods should survive and be properly managed, a question mark still hangs over this most contentious of issues. In view of world wide concern over global warming, coastal erosion and the uncertainties of climate change which has already adversely affected many parts of Britain and the world it would seem only sensible and responsible to exercise caution rather than pursue more deforestation, and this must surely be the fervent hope for the future.

OUR PINEWOODS

(with apologies to The Teddy Bears' Picnic)

If you go down to the woods today
You're in for a big surprise,
If you go down to the woods today
You'd never believe your eyes,
For every tree that ever there was
Has been chopped down for reasons because
The experts say
They got in the way
Of the wild life.

When you go down to the woods today
Prepare for a great big shock,
When you go down to the woods today
A chain saw has run amok,
And not a tree is there to be seen,
Just stumps and mess and what once had been
The natural homes
For lizards and toads
In their hundreds.

So don't go down to the woods today
You'd much better stay in bed,
No don't go down to the woods today
For you'd honestly think you were dead,
Sixty acres of beautiful green
Disappeared in a terrible scene,
Worse than a nightmare
You'd ever seen
In our pinewoods.   (1997)

OUR PINEWOODS (UP-DATE)

(Again apologies to The Teddy Bears' Picnic)

If you go down to the woods today
It still looks a sorry sight,
If you go down to the woods today
You'll see why we had to fight,
Why Sefton Coast Watch battled along
To stop a plan we all thought was wrong,
And save those trees
Still standing so strong
In our pinewoods.

When you go down to the woods today
There's hope in that barren land,
When you go down to the woods today
That grave-yard of stumps and sand
Reminds us all of what was in store
For the frontal woods that shield our shore
From storms and gales
And tidal waves roar
By our pinewoods.

Now hopefully our Fisherman's Path
Is safe from the woodman's axe,
Yes hopefully on Fisherman's Path
The trees will stay by the tracks,
For a change of tack and personnel
Brings consultation and augurs well
For trees and toads
And lizards as well
In our pinewoods.   (2000)

* * * *

THE BAY HORSE

Perhaps a subject of much lesser importance but nevertheless one which touched the hearts of many was the announcement in the summer of 1998 that one of Formby's oldest hostelries, the Bay Horse, was to close for a period of refurbishment which at the same time would also see the end of its name and a change of title to The Toby Carvery at Formby.

The idea was preposterous, but as this was the brewery's national policy it was considered a fait compli and despite loud local protest the deed was done. As I had lived all my life in close proximity to this ancient public house I was incensed that yet another part of our heritage was to be lost for no apparent good reason, and so I began a long and determined correspondence with the brewery, and to my great joy I was eventually invited to a meeting with the hierarchy. As this had been a lone campaign and I would be meeting four representatives of the brewery they kindly extended the invitation to include any one other person of my choice to accompany me, and it was to Major Jim Hersey I turned for moral support. The meeting was amicable and successful and it was agreed that the name BAY HORSE should be reinstated in huge gold letters across the frontage together with an outside hanging sign portraying a bay horse. July 1999 saw the name return and happily the Bay Horse continues to be an attractive part of our community. Sadly, however, the enormous interior modernisation led to the closure of the working men's bar and in turn to the loss of many outdoor community events such as the annual conker competition, the summer barbecues, and the November the fifth fireworks display.

The Bay Horse Barbecue, June 1988

The Bay Horse, January 1996

The Bay Horse Conker Championship, October 1996,
with organiser Peter Wright

The Bay Horse with the extension marquee for TV viewing of the World Cup Football,
July 1998. The roof banner proclaims
"THERE'S ONLY ONE MICHAEL OWEN"

The Bay Horse after refurbishment, March 1999

THE BAY HORSE

Once upon a time long long ago
The Bay Horse was a pub run by old Joe,
It was a pretty seedy little inn
That only those least fussy entered in.

When Joe passed on his daughters then took charge,
The scruffiness continued, by and large,
And World War Two brought forth the flash G.I.s
Who poured inside with disbelieving eyes.

Eventually the pub was smartened up
And a better clientele began to sup,
Refurbishments then started to begin
And we gained a really lovely country inn.

Additions and improvements carried through
Combining old tradition with the new,
A restaurant beside the public bar
Brought patrons flocking in from near and far.

The Bay Horse echoed well our heritage,
Tastefully reminiscent of the age
When life in Formby was so different then
When the Bay was just the place for working men.

But now in one fell swoop we've lost it all,
The character, the charm, the white-washed wall,
In place the gaudy, glitzy, tatty trash
The brewery thinks will generate more cash.

We loved our pub and fought to 'Save the Bay',
We thought a compromise would go half way,
But now betrayal stares us in the face
As through the railings stands a sheer disgrace.

It really is enough to make one weep
That something once so lovely looks so cheap,
Those who've done this should hang their heads in shame,
And give us back the Bay Horse and its name.

Right: The Bay Horse snug bar, c.1970. Bobby Rimmer, George
Mawdsley, Robert (Chick) Rimmer, George White, Joe Armstrong

* * * *

PAVEMENT DISPLAYS

Formby is unique within the borough of Sefton in having a shopping centre which boasts unusually wide pavements which have traditionally always been used by many traders to display their wares. They have never caused a problem and indeed have added to the ambience of the area. All this changed, however, just before Christmas 1992 when a shop in Southport created an obstruction with an outside pavement display and was instructed by Sefton Council under threat of legal action to remove it forthwith. Not only was this shop targeted but the ban on pavement displays was extended to every part of Sefton.

Ray Maddick, one of the affected traders, outside his hardware store on his retirement after 44 years in the business. Happily the shop continues under new ownership.

The decision was ridiculous and caused undue anxiety to several small shopkeepers whose businesses were already struggling against the op-position of new big name superstores whose lavish gifts to the shopping centre had so affected the character of the Village. Following my poetic contribution to the Formby Times and the intervention of the late Councillor Jackie Gibson common sense eventually prevailed and Formby was, quite rightly, excluded from this draconian ruling.

We shouldn't dwell upon the past,
Or yearn for what has been,
We should accept our changing world,
And applaud the present scene.

We must not question what's decreed
By those now in command,
But meekly we must all submit
To what they now demand.

No matter that there's little sense
Or reason to their rules,
They are the wise officialdom,
And we are only fools.

So let them hound the little men,
Sweep tradition clean away,
And mould us into nothingness
By the cruel games they play.

And let the big boys call the tune
And use us as they will,
To pull the strings of those they woo
With gifts for good or ill.

Zebra crossing, traffic lights,
Railings to pen us in,
Paving blocks instead of flags,
And the odd new litter bin.

Then having quite transformed us all,
Wrecked a Village with wanton waste,
They'll dance upon the gravestones
Of those traders they have chased.

And the big shots' tills will jingle
Merry Christmas to you all,
But the others see no shining star,
Just the writing on the wall.

Unbelievably after almost thirteen years of peaceful Village trading history repeated itself in October 2005 when once again council officers, this time accompanied by the police, descended upon the traders demanding the removal of all produce from outside their premises. The normally vibrant Village immediately resembled a grave yard, and just as before the public leapt to the defence of the shopkeepers filling the pages of the local press with letters of outrage at this silly charade, made even more illogical when the newly acquired wine and coffee bars with their frontages littered with street furniture (for which they paid a council rent!) were unaffected and presumably considered not to be the same hazard to pedestrians as the traders' wares. The whole episode was a nonsense. The council looked foolish and the public uproar resulted in a climb down which very quickly restored sanity to the situation with the return of the colourful displays to the 40 foot wide pavements.

However, within weeks of what had appeared a sensible and permanent settlement a lorry arrived unheralded and proceeded to once more remove all advertising boards from the shops' frontages. In anger and frustration some of the more agile traders jumped aboard the lorry, retrieved their boards and replaced them in their rightful places where they still remain at the time of writing. Perhaps the saga is not, after all, over!

* * * *

GREEN BAG SCHEME

In 2002 Sefton Council announced the introduction of a Green Bag Scheme for the re-cycling of garden waste following its initial successful launch in Bootle. Selected areas of Formby were issued with biodegradable green bags and a maximum of five bags would be collected each week separately alongside the normal refuse collections. Unfortunately it would appear that no one had considered the vast difference in the back yards of many Bootle properties compared with the large back gardens of most Formby properties, and utter chaos ensued with green bags overflowing throughout the streets of Formby. The refuse collectors were completely overwhelmed by the sheer volume and were totally unable to cope. Many letters reached the press including the following two poems from myself.

Paddy Kearney outside his Lonsdale Road home [photo: Formby Times]

FIVE GREEN BIN BAGS
(with apologies to Ten Green Bottles)

Five green bin bags piled outside each gate,
Five green bin bags there to congregate,
Until five green bin bags soon numbered twenty-eight
When no lorry trundled round to every gate.

Twenty-eight bin bags full of grass and sticks,
Twenty-eight bin bags just like pick and mix,
Now those twenty-eight bin bags have numbered forty-six
And still no lorry has trundled for the sticks.

Forty-six bin bags breeding by the score,
Forty-six bin bags growing ever more,
Now those forty-six bin bags are up to sixty-four,
Still no lorry trundles round to every door.

Now each road in Formby is a rubbish tip,
And each road in Formby is giving us the pip,
Someone there at Sefton needs to get a grip
Before the rest of Sefton mistakes us for The Tip.

THE GREEN GREEN GRASS OF HOME

The old home town don't look the same
As I step down from the train,
And there to greet me are tons and tons of green bags,
Down the road no bin men and no lorry,
Everywhere looks sad and sorry
As we traipse between the green green bags of home.

And whilst I stand and look around me
Loads of green bags all surround me,
And they seem to be increasing by the second,
And down the road no bin men and no lorry,
Everywhere looks sad and sorry,
Can this really be the jewel in Sefton's crown?

Now I'm awake and I'm not dreaming,
Down the road green waste is streaming,
And I can't believe this really is my Formby,
But in the distance there's a Sefton lorry,
Now we soon won't look so sorry,
'Cause they're here to take the green green grass back home.

The system was eventually regarded a success and plans were made for its extension throughout the entire borough. Regrettably, however, in 2004 following the usual winter suspension and the announcement of its recommencement in early March, Sefton Council encountered difficulties in acquiring a suitable waste site and once again the scheme ran into problems which as late as June of that year had still not been fully resolved. In principle the scheme is admirable and has been welcomed by the public and it is therefore hoped that these troubles will soon be a thing of the past and all will run smoothly.

* * * *

THE COUNCIL OFFICES

Our splendid purpose built Council Offices had been the pride of Formby and the only public building of note, but had been grossly under-used for many years despite their huge potential for full community use.

Whilst Formby had continued to grow our local government needs had not and indeed had been severely eroded. We had seen the loss of our Social Services Department as it moved to Southport, our 1960's public library was far below the national standards for a town of our size, our Citizen's Advice Bureau was housed in a derelict house, and there were no real leisure facilities particularly for the youth of the district. For almost 30 years residents had campaigned for a swimming pool to no avail, yet here stood a centrally located building capable of satisfying all these needs and more. Then suddenly events took a quite unexpected turn with the shock announcement of the sale of the Brows Lane Football Ground by the grandson of the original landowner who no longer lived in Formby and whose interests lay elsewhere. There was great consternation as the Club faced possible extinction, and property developers showed keen interest in the site. For quite some time speculation raged about its future until the summer of 2000 and the surprise intervention of one of Formby's wealthiest families, the Moores of Littlewood's Pools fame, who bought the Ground and presented it to Sefton Council as a gift for leisure purposes. It was a truly magnanimous gesture. Instead of it remaining as the Football Ground it was decided that it should be earmarked for the swimming pool, and the Football Ground would be relocated across the Formby By-Pass alongside the river Alt hopefully making the football club's future secure.

Demolition of the Formby Council Offices, April 2003 [photo: Formby Times]

At long last it seemed the pool was in sight, but then quite inexplicably in the autumn of 2000 the local councillors introduced a proviso that unless our Council Offices were sold for development there would be no pool. There was instant public outrage. Never in all the years of campaigning had there been a hint of such a condition until this moment and the whole community rose in anger. Public meetings were held, a hastily organised petition showed enormous opposition to such an unpopular move, and sound and reasoned arguments were put forward for the sale of alternative public assets. Once more our benefactors stepped in with yet another unbelievably generous donation of £3 million to Sefton Council making the sale completely unnecessary, but despite all this the wishes of the people were ignored, the democratic process was a sham, and the Formby community witnessed probably the shabbiest of deals in its history. Like all other towns of comparable size it is not at all unreasonable that Formby should expect both a pool and a civic building, and it seems beyond all comprehension that any other authority in the land would ever consider trading a Town Hall for a pool, but this was Sefton and we are Formby and this was the most ingenious of all red herrings. To the shame of our council we lost our protest and we lost our Council Offices, and in their place now stands an unseemly and appallingly over-sized nondescript four storey block of 85 apartments which every year will swell the Sefton treasury as no public building ever could. This issue caused more local outrage than any other and left the community with a real sense of betrayal. The local press was bombarded with letters of protest and when the final act of civic vandalism took place in April 2003 a further barrage of correspondence battered its pages. The following are just two of those letters representative of the many the first one being my own contribution and the second reproduced in full with the kind permission of the writer, Alan Niker of College Avenue, Formby.

The site of the newly demolished Council Offices, April 2003

"Endless correspondence has appeared in this newspaper about the undemocratic sale of our Council Offices and no issue ever caused such outrage. The terrible sadness I now feel as the bulldozers moved in is, I know, shared by many so I make no apology for this final comment on a part of our history which I consider utterly shameful.

This demolition should never have taken place. The land and building belonged to us, the Formby People, not to Sefton Council, having been bought and paid for through the rates of my generation's parents and grandparents, and neither they nor we bear any responsibility for their deliberate neglect.

They were our finest asset with huge community potential. It is a well known fact that wise planning for the future requires a sound knowledge and understanding of the past and sadly none of our councillors appeared to know or care enough about Formby's past or have any real vision for the future. Their total disregard of massive public opinion and repeated claims of being unable to wield any sort of power over local issues only frustrated those they represented and seemed the weakest of excuses.

There was absolutely no need whatsoever for this dreadful act of civic vandalism and if those councillors are remembered for anything at all in the future it will surely be for this. The whole episode has been disgraceful and speaks volumes about local democracy which, like our Council Offices, lies in ruins."

"Despite the wishes and the needs of the local population we have this week been treated to the disgraceful sight of Formby Council Offices being demolished, not in the name of progress, but to further Sefton's rather obvious plan to turn the whole of Formby into a Council Tax farm. The revenue from the sale of the site and the prospect of another eighty plus Council Tax payers was obviously too difficult to resist, and our elected councillors totally ineffective in reflecting local priorities.

In order that our loss may not be forgotten I would suggest that Sefton Council spend some of their revenue upon a memorial to the building which reflects the part of their planning department and of our councillors. A bronze statue of a braying jackass mounted by the figure of a builder with a sledgehammer in one hand and a cash bag in the other would be appropriate. It could have the inscription (with apologies to War Memorials) "Their Shame Liveth For Evermore".

Our thanks are due to local petitioners who proposed practical solutions which would have retained a fine building, and who proved that there are at least some people left who have the needs and interests of this community at heart.
Alan Niker

As a final comment it is probably the biggest irony that our former Council Offices in Moorhouse's Building, Church Road still stand, albeit in the guise of a fish and chip shop, whilst the new superbly custom built replacement, deemed so necessary in 1927 by the men of vision who ran our council, and which would have stood forever, has been smashed to the ground.

The luxury apartments are now completed and have been named Hillary Court in honour of the man who established Britain's first lifeboat station here in Formby in 1776. However it would seem he did not. According to the well researched and authoritative book 'Britain's First Lifeboat Station' by R. & B. Yorke that particular honour goes to William Hutchinson and not to William Hillary who was responsible for the station on the Isle of Man – an unfortunate mistake but perhaps not of such vital importance when most local people have already christened the apartments The Council Flats.

Hillary Court, 2006, replacing Formby Council Offices

Once again letters flooded in to our local press and again I have chosen Alan Niker's contribution which is reproduced in full with his kind permission:

"I see from your pages that our Green Bag service had been suspended because Sefton were having difficulty in gaining planning consent for a rubbish dump.

How can this be? Perhaps they should have consulted McCarthy & Stone who have experienced no difficulty in dumping a load of architectural rubbish on the site of the old Council Offices. Their new development is without doubt an appallingly nondescript mish-mash of styles which is totally over-sized for the site and out of character with the environment. It seems to be an unhappy mixture of Hacienda, Georgian, and Mock Tudor with elements of Walton Jail which should exist only in an architect's nightmare and not in a prominent position in our town.

The site-hut which was once used as a Sales Office had more architectural merit, and now that this and the fencing has been removed even more of the eyesore has been revealed. Trees have even been chopped down which once mercifully screened the side elevation and the logs sold on the traffic island by one enterprising Philistine.

To think we may now have to stop our cars outside this edifice at the proposed pedestrian crossing on Freshfield Road (a corporate bung to Sefton courtesy of the developers) adds insult to injury when we consider the aesthetic merits and the great potential of what used to occupy the site.

This is surely yet another manifestation of the "smash 'em down and squeeze 'em in" philosophy of Sefton planning department which aims to increase numbers of high rate council tax payers at the expense of our environment and quality of life.

On a positive note, the crossing will be useful for the hordes of newly fleeced senior citizens who have bought apartments to access the Village with its charity shops and new swimming pool.

Are the developers planning any sort of opening ceremony? I would suggest that they invite Sefton planning department who could point out areas of outstanding design with their white sticks. Speeches by our local councillors would be next to tell everybody of their valuable part in the exercise, and then any new residents who were still awake could join in party games such as "Pass the Brown Envelope" and "Pin the Policy on the Donkey". What an event it could be!   Alan Niker"

We are now four years on from this disgraceful episode and the long awaited pool, which so unwittingly and unfairly became the subject of such controversy, is in the course of construction. But even here unforeseen problems and prolonged delays continue to dog its progress as rumours abound regarding the extent of the promised facilities.

Meanwhile the public wait and wonder with the recent knowledge that, in the interests of economy, two of Sefton's existing leisure centres have been closed, just as Formby's nears completion.

* * * *

PARISH COUNCIL

The events over many years have given Formby every reason to feel discontented with its position in local government and when a campaign was launched for Formby to have its own parish council it met with some interest and a degree of enthusiasm coming as it did hot on the heels of several contentious local issues which had so enraged the community, the final straw being the loss of our Council Offices, and so in the emotion of the moment many signed up to the petition. It was only later when the full implication of another tier of local government and its lack of power became known that the prospect looked far less appealing and a counter campaign attempted to point out the futility of such an unnecessary and costly concept. Eventually and at considerable public expense a referendum was held in which there was much confusion and also much apathy with the result that on a small majority of only 2% from a very low poll in which only 25% voted yes and a huge 75% voted no or abstained, Formby found itself with a parish council to be constituted on 1st April 2004 (perhaps appropriately the same date exactly 30 years before on which Sefton was created) and yet another tax was added to our already burgeoning local taxes. Elections were held to appoint an incredulous 15 new councillors (Formby has just 6 borough councillors) but from the entire Formby electorate only 13 persons were attracted to stand. On election day itself Formby achieved the dubious honour of holding an all time U.K. record for the lowest ever turn-out (4.26%) and we now await whatever benefits of what many consider this ill-conceived venture may or may not bring.

* * * *

THE POWER HOUSE

In FORMBY REMEMBERED I had mentioned the uncertain future of the Power House standing at the south end of Formby alongside the railway line and surrounded by green belt land. In its heyday it had provided work for many when the Liverpool to Southport railway line had become the first in the country to be electrified in 1904.

Since those early pioneering days of progression from steam when the Power House had revolutionised the railways it had been an essential hive of industry, but by the 1930s railway power had become centralised thus rendering the building redundant.

Its use was transferred to other various business ventures until its final closure in the 1980s whence it had stood empty and vandalised and was often the site

The Power House [photo: Formby Times]

of illicit gypsy encampments. In the 1990's, despite its green belt status, developers had shown an interest in the land but had been unsuccessful in gaining the necessary planning permission, whilst all the time the Power House was becoming more and more of a problem and an eye sore as vandalism escalated.

In 2003 a local businessman acquired an option on the site for possible housing development should the green belt ruling be relaxed, and a year later with Liverpool, lying only 14 miles away, having gained the Capital of Culture Award for 2008, ambitious suggestions for a cultural centre on the site were being mooted. So once again the future for the Power House and its land still lies shrouded in doubt, but what is very certain is that change is inevitable for one of the last remaining open spaces in Formby.

* * * *

EDUCATION

The building boom of the 1960s had seen the arrival of hundreds of young families to fill the vast housing estates of affordable properties springing up all over the district, and it soon became apparent that the four original junior schools and the one senior school were totally inadequate to cope with the massive influx. With Formby topping the national birth rate it was crucial that new educational facilities were to be met and so commenced the schools building programme which saw the emergence of seven new schools – Park Road Primary (now Raven Meols Community Centre), Formby County Primary (now the Pinefield centre), Redgate Primary, Freshfield County Primary, Woodlands Primary, St. Jerome's Primary, and Range High School. The existing schools were also to undergo large

The main classroom at Holy Trinity School c.1950. The front row includes, left to right: John Rimmer, Pat Thomas, Gillian Lloyd, Tony Metcalfe, Barry Rawlins

extensions, with the demolition and re-siting of two of the originals, Holy Trinity and Our Lady's, in Lonsdale Road and Bull Cop respectively.

Now forty years on from this youthful invasion times have changed and those youngsters have grown and flown. Property prices have escalated and retirement apartments have proliferated resulting in the redundancy of schools. Park Road Primary and Formby County Primary have been long gone, but now the axe is to fall on one of Formby's oldest church schools, Holy Trinity, the original school having been established in 1901 and demolished in 1966 after continuing to function alongside its new replacement school which had opened its doors in January 1962. This being my old school it is a great sadness that such a once thriving and happy school with its long history should be lost in preference to one of the newer establishments, but regrettably it may well not be the last as falling numbers dictate the future in an area with an ageing population.

* * * *

Our Lady's School prior to demolition, 1986.

Kensington Court [which replaced Our Lady's School]

Our Lady's school meals staff
with caretaker Bobby Rimmer at
the new school in Bull Cop
(1970s)

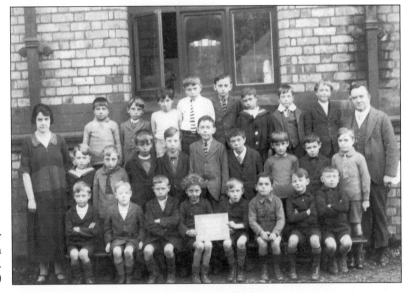

Class of boys at Our
Lady's School with
headmaster Mr.
'Buggy' Ryan (c.1927)

Below: Class of children at St. Peter's School with headmaster Russell Brown (1950s)

DUKE STREET PARK

Between the two world wars many new roads and houses began to develop on the mass of fields and open spaces in this small farming village. One of Formby's most respected residents, Dr. Arthur Barry Sykes, our family G.P., could see the prospect looming of housing development on the field opposite his house, Ashhurst, on Duke Street, and so in 1930, not wanting to be overlooked, he bought the field from the owner, Jonathan Formby, and the tenant farmer, Ephraim Walker, left his Duke Street farm for a period of farming in Aughton before later returning to Marsh Brows Farm, Formby. Dr. Sykes presented Walker's field as a gift to Formby Urban District Council to be used as a public park for the people of Formby in perpetuity.

At the opening ceremony in July 1935 the park was simply a large expanse of green which later acquired a most picturesque thatched pavilion alongside a bowling green and a small pitch and putt area (much later to become the children's play area). Public toilets were situated at both ends of the Park.

During the 1970s the thatch of the pavilion suffered a series of arson attacks which sadly culminated in almost total destruction of the pavilion and it was decided to replace it with a concrete building which, unlike the thatch, would withstand the mindless vandalism so frequently wreaked upon it.

The Park became the venue for victory celebrations in 1945 when world war two ended and the whole village turned out for a huge bonfire and fireworks to mark this joyous occasion.

Probably the most prestigious period for Duke Street Park was that following the second world war when the renowned Formby Horticultural and Agricultural Show (the Flower Show) reached its peak. However, times change and as Formby continued to grow the show began to decline until it eventually transferred its location to the Gild Hall on Church Road where it still continues in a very much reduced form.

When the Formby Show relocated to the Gild Hall, and with memories of the long lost Formby Gala, a new and popular different event emerged at the instigation of local couple Peter and Jennifer Wright who launched their annual Gala weekend to raise funds for Diabetes charities following the diagnosis of their five year old son with the illness.

Carried out on a truly grand scale, the two day event includes a huge car boot sale, professional fairground rides, and a host of other attractions and side shows which to date still brings visitors flocking to the Park each July to enjoy the carnival atmosphere on offer.

Continuing the importance of the Park in community life, August 2006 saw the first Churches Together Family Fun Day which brought such delight to the Park in so many imaginative ways as the sun shone down so brilliantly on children, parents and grandparents who revelled in an entirely free day of unbridled joy with face painting, hair spraying, bouncy castle, throwing the sponge, making bird nesting boxes, craft work of all kinds, music and free food and drink for all. Its success led to the decision to repeat the occasion in following years together with a silent prayer for weather to bless the day. And so looking back over 75 years to when the benevolent Dr. Sykes, himself a talented footballer for the local team, made his purchase of a farmer's field for the use of the community in which he lived and worked, could he ever have realised the potential for his gift and of the many diverse ways in which it would be used? His main concern had been to protect the privacy of his beloved Ashhurst, but in ensuring that aim he also secured the future of a very precious plot which has been so central to Formby and its people, and for that we all owe him enormous thanks.

Therefore, mindful of his love of football he would no doubt have been delighted when in 1959 the wonderful Jim Rourke arrived on the scene with his young son, Frank, to kick a football around the park. Other boys joined in and from that simple act was born the Formby Junior Sports Club which still thrives today as the largest club of its kind on Merseyside with over 750 members and 78 teams and now with Frank in charge following the death of his father in 2006 at the age of 93 having continued to be actively involved almost until the end of his life. As the numbers escalated 'Rourkie's League' as it became known, moved to the Deansgate Lane Playing Fields in 1979 and can boast several members to have become professional footballers as well as the children of some of the most famous names in the game such as Howard Kendall, John Toshack, Kenny Dalglish, Phil Neal, Alan Hansen, Steve McMahon, David Fairclough, Neil Ruddock and Steve Staunton. So successful is the club that it is worth recording some of its landmarks over the last five decades:

1959   Jim Rourke founded Formby Junior Sports Club

1961   The First Inter Club Cup final held at Brows Lane Ground and attended by 900 people

1961   Chess Section started

1973   A few Representative Teams enter local league

1977   Jim Rourke receives M.B.E. for services to Youth

Jim Rourke in the mid 1980s

Jim and Frank Rourke, runners-up in the North West Big Difference Awards 2003. The pair were short-listed with the likes of Everton F.C., Marks & Spencer, and Barclays Bank

1979   Clubhouse opened at Deansgate Lane

1984   Representative teams at all ages enter local leagues

1990   Inter Club Section lowers age to eleven

1999   Girls football section starts

2000   Mini-Soccer introduced and the club lowers age to join to reception age group (four years old)

2001   Extra pitches at Deansgate Lane allowing all Inter Club games to be played on one site and extra car parking spaces

2001   Membership exceeds 750 for the first time

2002   F.J.S.C. receives Charter Standard Status from the Football Assoc.

2005   F.J.S.C. receives the Charter Standard Development Award from the Football Association

Jim Rourke receiving a football shirt to mark his 91st birthday

2006   Inter Club football teams from Reception (four years old) through to Year
        12 (seventeen years old) for the first time

* * * *

CONCLUSION

Whilst the character of Formby had gradually succumbed to the events of several decades of change and drifted far from its rural roots, the Village area, though also subject to change, had still remained an attractive heartland until 1999 when even our Village, once so picturesque, was scarred by the acquisition of a set of traffic lights in its centre accompanied by the ugliest of metal railings – all so very unnecessary when a simple zebra crossing would have more than sufficed – and in one ill-advised action our unique and lovely Village was reduced to mundanity.

Most of the old established small shops had long since vanished and the proliferation of charity shops had filled once empty outlets, whilst estate agents, travel agents, and banks all rubbed shoulders with the multi-nationals as the wine bars and restaurants multiplied. The atmosphere was in a state of flux and although there are still a limited number of delightful small shops they diminish with the years.

Thankfully the large horse chestnut trees still bloom each year and the wide pavements provide colourful displays and continue to welcome the annual art exhibition making it still a pleasant centre, but today's residents can have no conception of how enormous has been the change over the last fifty years.

Since the coming of the railway in 1848 when Formby's population was below 1,000, to the 7,000 it reached with the second world war, on through the 1950s to 10,000, and ever upwards with the building explosion of the 1960s, 1970s, and 1980s, and continuing throughout the 1990s towards 30,000 and on into a new century when housing development progressed unabated with recent years seeing the demolition of almost every large house which came on the market to accommodate the multiple apartments to take their place.

Formby Fields was probably the last example of the old Formby with its muddy footpath and quaint cottage amidst the trees, but in 2003 the heart was ripped out of it and in that leafy backwater now stands an extended replica cottage alongside two gigantic detached houses so closely packed into the tiny confines of the lane and hemmed in by the now almost obligatory metal railings. To the old Formby residents the transformation is hideously obscene but to the newer ones it has been greeted with euphoria to now have a perfect surface or which to walk.

It is impossible for any of us to have envisaged such seismic change, and of course change will continue, but whatever the future holds it is sure to be more acceptable to the present community who are far less parochial and can never experience the same degree of nostalgia as the sandgrounder.

However, it would be wrong to consider all to be doom and gloom as new innovations have revitalised our community in ways unimagined. Perhaps the most notable event came in 1994 with the celebration of the Police Station centenary, followed the next year by a week long celebration of the 50th anniversary of the end of the second world war. The following year, 1996, saw the first of the now annual Dickensian Day in which I was privileged to be one of the small handful who helped community policeman Dougie Knight with his brainchild and which has gone from strength to strength to attract thousands to visit us each Christmas and marvel at the carnival atmosphere in our Village whilst also boosting the local economy. The new millennium also saw a week of community events culminating in a grand fete in the grounds of the newly restored Formby Hall. And so the growth of Formby has not been the end of a community as well it might have been, but rather a renaissance as new residents have integrated to form a new and different community.

However, there can be no doubt that MY FORMBY has gone forever and is now just a memory to the few and a mystery to the many. It is perfectly natural and right to look back and to not forget our roots and heritage, but it as also healthy to look forward with hope for the future. We are all privileged to call this ancient Viking village our home and we all have a responsibility to care for it, preserve the best of what we have left, and ensure that future generations are able to share at least some of the pleasures that were ours. Only time will tell whether we succeed or fail, and that, of course, will be a whole new story.

Michael Rawlinson outside his butcher's shop (Charters) on the last day of trading in October 1997

"Lynwood" and "The Gowrey", Church Road, now replaced by a block of 14 flats

"The Gowrey Apartments" which replaced the two houses

Formby Hall, July 1990, prior to its restoration by new owner Mike McComb.

The newly restored Formby Hall, 2000

NEW FORMBY POEMS

THE SIMPLE LIFE

A simple cottage in a lane,
A water butt to catch the rain,
A patch of land to grow the food
To satisfy each family's brood.

A roof of thatch comprised of straw,
Rag rugs upon the earthen floor,
A door knocked up of slats of wood,
A cow close by to chew the cud.

An open fire to heat and feed,
With just enough for each one's need,
Some ducks and hens supplying eggs,
A wash tub and some dolly pegs.

A self-sufficient simple life,
A working man, a homely wife,
Lots of children running round
All helping cultivate the ground.

This was the way of Formby folk
Whose northern accents softly spoke
Of country ways shared by them all
When a Squire lived at Formby Hall.

These memories of those days of old
Are stories great grand parents told
To children sitting at their knee
To hand down through the family.

Those children now themselves are old,
And their grandchildren now are told
The tales of how life was before
When homes were thatched with earthen floor.

VILLAGE INNS

In days when menfolk laboured long
For precious small reward,
The village inn was all they had
And all they could afford.

From toiling on the farms and fields
Or fishing in the sea
Their wages earned them just enough
To keep their family.

The Lifeboat Inn, Birkey Lane

No extra cash to splash around,
Just coppers for their ale
And an ounce or two of baccy
When they'd meet and swap a tale.

And this was all the leisure time
These simple folk enjoyed,
Their lives just spent between their homes
And where they were employed.

The Lifeboat Inn in Birkey Lane
Was one such hostelry
Where Mary Neil dispensed the goods
And hospitality.

And further over in Green Lane
There stood the Formby Arms,
Ideally placed for all those men
Who worked the Squire's farms.

And yet another tiny inn
Was nestled in Moss Side
Where many weary labourers
Would quench their thirst inside.

No longer is the village inn
The only recompense
For working men who dawn to dusk
Slaved for those hard earned pence.

Now working men collect their wives
And dress up smart and fine
And drive to some expensive pub
For dinner and for wine.

OUR TRAVELLERS

Our lives were charmed by visitors
From varying walks of life
Who hawked their wares from door to door
Or came to grind a knife.

Our favourite was the onion man
Who always took the chance
To cross the channel every year
And visit us from France.

The rag and bone man also came
Quite often through the year
Exchanging gold fish or balloons
For what he gathered here.

And 'Annie Fish' who weighed her fish
On tiny little scales,
And sometimes lent out ready cash
Between her other sales.

The pot man with his basket high,
Well balanced on his pate,
Visiting every welcome door
To sell a cup or plate.

Also cans of paraffin
Supplied by Mr. Peek
Who did the rounds of all of us
The same day every week.

But gradually our village changed
And all these tradesfolk stopped
As we became suburbia
And our village bubble popped.

THE ONION MAN

The onion man, the onion man,
Who came each year from France,
The onion man, the onion man,
The children sang and danced.

Togged out in his stripey jersey,
His beret on his head,
Strings of onions around his neck
To keep us all well fed.

Onions festooned around his bike,
And ringing loud his bell,
He pedalled up and down our lanes
His luscious veg to sell.

With sunny smile and Gallic charm
Year in year out he came,
And we looked forward to his trips
Though we never knew his name.

But slowly as the years passed by
Our village changed and grew,
And our onion man got older
As all of us must do.

Until these changes brought an end
To those trips across the sea
Of the onion man we'd grown to love
From far off Brittany.

FORMBY'S BOMBS

The target for the German planes
Was Liverpool's docks, not Formby's lanes,
Their bombs, however, missed the spot
As one dark night we got the lot.

Just fourteen miles north of their aim
The bombs rained down to start the flames
And quickly through the woods they spread
As Nazi planes flew overhead.

A blazing stretch of pinewoods lit
The night-time sky as they were hit,
Those German pilots truly thought
They'd wrecked that vital north-west port.

But that night they had got it wrong
And Liverpool Docks stood firm and strong,
But then the planes returned again
And got another Formby lane.

Bull Cop and what's now Gardner Road
Were battered with another load,
Also Carrs Crescent, Chapel Lane,
And Graburn Road and Old Mill Lane.

But we escaped the worst onslaught
As on and on this war was fought,
And we became a welcome host
As Britain's cities suffered most.

We opened up our rural doors,
Had people sleeping on our floors,
Made lifelong friends in times of woe
Of those who had nowhere to go.

Now all this lies in history,
To children just a mystery,
But this was real and they should know
Just how it was so long ago.

And the only way that this can be
Is from the likes of you and me
Who lived throughout that great mayhem,
And hand our memories down to them.

* * * *

In 1994 plans for a private golf club at the newly developed south end of Formby had been rejected by Sefton Council on sound environmental grounds. However, the company concerned appealed against the decision, but following an expensive court case the decision was upheld by the Secretary of State and the developers lost their appeal. The site was subsequently bought by Sefton Council and is now a local nature reserve.

OVER DEVELOPMENT

In nineteen-fifty-nine it all began,
The start of Formby's great ambitious plan,
Kirkby, Speke, and Skem took overspill
Whilst here the private builders built at will.

And so Park Road and Briscoe let the way,
A fine estate where once grew Sutton's hay,

St. Peter's College, College Avenue, previously a training college for Roman Catholic priests, and then taken over by the Leonard Cheshire Foundation and renamed Freshfields. It was demolished in 1989 and replaced by smaller units.

Bishop's Court, a private boys' school in Wrigleys Lane, now replaced by York Close and Canterbury Close.

Hurstwood, on the corner of Victoria Road (unadopted) and Gores Lane, orginally a private house which was taken over by the local authority as pensioner's bed sits, then demolished and replaced with new retirement accommodation.

And slowly all the others followed on
Till most of all our greenery was gone.

The Formby folk looked on quite mystified
Saying little, though a few were misty-eyed,
How could we argue with the powers that be?
You just can't win against authority.

Years later, and in quiet reverie,
We recalled the scenes locked in our memory,
Beneath the houses elegant and new
We saw the farms and fields and cattle too.

And as those faded images smiled back
Marsh marigolds we gathered by the stack,
And watercress from ditches growing wild
We picked with the wild flowers as a child.

Those passing years have turned us old and grey,
Our village quite unrecognised today,
And new residents who filled our fields and dykes
Speak out, much louder than we country types.

They seek to keep their blessed Formby plot,
Established on the land they now have got,
That land we Sandgrounders allowed to die
As bricks and mortar rose from earth to sky.

"Enough's enough!" they beg with heartfelt plea,
Concerned about this mad depravity,
"We've seen it all before" the old folk cry,
"It's your turn now to stop and question why".

* * * *

Sefton is a very diverse borough and it was this diversity which had often been the cause of discontent amongst some of its members which in 1997 resulted in Southport raising the question of breaking away to form a new authority which would include Formby. As attractive as the idea may have appeared it was never seriously pursued but it did inspire the following poem.

BOOTLE OR SOUTHPORT?

Well over twenty years ago
Ted Heath devised a plan,
And our M.P., then Graham Page,
Became his hatchet man.

He helped to engineer the change
Which lumped us all as one,
From Southport down to Bootle docks,
We all became Sefton.

We none of us had any choice,
Despite us saying no
The powers that be knew what was best,
And so we had to go.

We'd always had twelve councillors
On Formby U.D.C.
In Sefton we had only six,
Outnumbered totally.

And so the downward trend began,
Swamped by the mighty two,
The big boys from the north and south
All told us what to do.

Our local taxes went sky high
'Cause we were affluent
And we could subsidise the rest,
Our wealth was heaven sent.

We watched as every inch of space
Was sold for building land
To swell the borough treasury
For all the things they'd planned.

As Bootle got the swimming pools
And leisure centres too,
Repeatedly we all were told
"There's nothing down for you".

Our little Village shops closed down,
The charities moved in
As two new super stores were passed
Despite the local din.

And those who passed these wondrous plans
Lived miles and miles away,
Knew nothing and cared even less
For what we had to say.

But now how different all things are,
We're flavour of the day,
With Bootle terrified we'll leave,
And Southport that we'll stay.

And what of us – what do we want?
It isn't hard to say,
We only want what we deserve
For what our taxes pay.

But most of all we want a say
In Formby's local scene,
And not to be dictated to
As we have always been.

* * * *

FORMBY POLICE CENTENARY

Our policemen had a birthday,
Their station reached a stage
When they must have a party
To mark this special age.

One hundred years of service
Through peacetime and through war,
Taking care of all of us
Behind their big blue door.

So P.C. Knight decided,
He'd get us all involved
In a week of celebration
And some problems maybe solve.

Through winter into springtime
He beavered with his plans,
Arranging lots of functions,
And making lots of fans.

He visited the classrooms
Of all the Formby schools,
And went into each Village shop
To tell them all the rules.

The kids would paint a poster,
The shops would all dress up,
Their windows look Victorian
And maybe win a cup.

He'd open up the station
And let us see the cell
Where once they locked the prisoners
In the time of Sergeant Bell.

The policemen would wear uniforms
From Queen Victoria's time,
And we would see examples
Of how they fight the crime.

We'd see again the horses
Which once were stabled here,
With the mounties in their finery
And other fancy gear.

The police dogs would be brought here
To demonstrate their skill,
And on show in the station
We'd see weapons that can kill.

There'd be an old folks' concert,
The Police Band would perform,
Then we'd get to Saturday
And take the place by storm.

The Village would be vibrant,
The chestnuts in full bloom,
The sun be brightly shining,
No sign of any gloom.

And that's the way it happened,
That glorious day in May
When dancers, singers, shoppers
Chased all our cares away.

So a very happy birthday
To those lovely lads in blue,
And thank you P.C. Dougie Knight,
We owe it all to you.

P.C.s Mike Bell and Dougie Knight

John Tyrer, aged 101, in the doorway of the police station and the only person to have lived in Formby when the police station was built in 1894.

Argomeols Clog Dancers, May 1994

The mounted policemen, May 1994

Above: P.C. Dougie Knight;
Joan Rimmer; Traffic Warden
Joan Costello and
P.C. Mike Bell

Below Left: Town Crier,
P.C. Steve Baker

Below Right:
Mrs. Josie Goulbourne,
Mrs. Anne Williams,
P.C. Dave Budworth,

FIFTY YEARS

How quickly fifty years have passed
Since we were kids at school,
Collecting shrapnel in the fields,
And acting out the fool.

We watched the searchlights in the sky
And saw the Liverpool blitz,
A city battered by the bombs
And almost blown to bits.

But we were far too young to know
The horror of it all
As marching troops arrived at camp
And we heard the bugle call.

Our pounding feet in time with theirs,
All marching on parade,
The darkness of the shelters
Where we hid throughout each raid.

The wailing of the sirens
As the German planes came near,
The bombs which caused such mayhem,
Followed by the glad 'all clear'.

The blackout and the ration books,
No sweets and no ice-cream,
The coloured troops with chewing gum
To us were like a dream.

For kids this was normality,
The only life we knew,
But our mothers longed for victory
And for our Dads to come home too.

Now looking back down all those years
Such memories still remain
Of when we lit the bonfires
And the lights came on again.

A peace we take for granted
Which was won at dreadful cost
To the young men of our nation
And those kids whose Dads were lost.

So we must not forget that price
A generation paid,
And cherish well our freedom
In the land those heroes made.

OUR VE CELEBRATIONS

Our VE celebrations
Of nineteen-forty-five
Had nothing on the weekend
Of nineteen-ninety-five.

For fifty years of peacetime
And joy for victory
The whole of Formby whooped it up
For everyone to see.

The childrens' concert set it off
With drama, poems, and songs
To teach our youngsters history
Of triumph over wrongs.

The Forties dance was in the mood
As oldies jived and sang,
Remembering war-time dances
With the Barracks army gang.

Then Saturday saw the grand parade,
The Village packed with throngs
As cameras clicked and videos whirred
To patriotic songs.

A sea of red and white and blue
Beneath the chestnut trees,
Resplendent with their candles,
Without a hint of breeze.

The sun shone down relentlessly
From morning until night,
The dancers danced, the bandsmen played,
And we sang with all our might.

The jugglers and the barber shop,
The unicycle boy,
The 'Guess Your Formby' picture quiz
To bring nostalgic joy.

To round it off on Saturday night
The Police Band thrilled us all
With St. Jerome's to help them out,
We really had a ball.

On Sunday all the faiths combined
Remembering the brave
In ever grateful thankfulness
For the sacrifice they gave.

And then at night the pensioners
Who'd lived throughout the war
Enjoyed a well earned party
Like they'd never had before.

On Monday came the climax
Of the Victory Concert Show,
A kaleidoscope of talent
Telling how the war did go.

Five hundred happy people
Inside the great marquee
Saw something quite spectacular
From fun to poignancy.

And all this did not happen
Without ambitious plans
And lots and lots of real hard work
By lots and lots of hands.

So to the British Legion
And the cast of every show
And all the back-room helpers
Enormous thanks must go.

But the man who had the vision
And saw it all come right
Was our community policeman,
P.C. Douglas Allen Knight.

So from all the Formby people,
Young, old, and in between,
We thank him for the best four days
That Formby's ever seen.

* * * *

Grand Parade,
Saturday, 6th May 1995

Holy Trinity Scouts

Mayor and Mayoress of
Sefton (Cllr. Norman
and Mrs. Jones) with the
Mayor of Gdansk,
May 6th 1995

Above: Grand Parade Jeep

Above:
Gladys Bevan, Joan Parkinson, Joan Rimmer

Above: Standard Bearer Cyril Goulbourne

Above: Audrey Wright, P.C. Dougie Knight
and Val Knight

Above: Evacuee Anne Aindow, G.I. Anne Byrne

Above: Compere David Davies, Lord Lieutenant of Merseyside Alan Waterworth, and British
Legion President Norman Farrell, Victory Concert, Monday 8th May 1995

Above: Audience at the Children's Concert with the Mayor of Sefton, Councillor and Mrs. Norman Jones, Friday 5th May, 1995

Above and Below: Childrens Concert

Carmen Miranda a.k.a.
P.C. Dougie Knight

Left and Above:
Grand Parade,
Saturday 6th May 1995

The Barbershop Singers, Saturday, 6th May 1995

American troops,
Victory Concert,
Monday,
8th May 1995

The Jean Berel
Dancers,
Victory Concert,
Monday,
8th May 1995

Local history quiz,
Saturday,
6th May 1995

Parade from the British Legion to Holy Trinity church,
Thanksgiving Service, Sunday 7th May 1995

Right: The Bishop of
Warrington,
Rev. Christopher Quine,
Mrs. Pam Lawson
and Mrs. Eddy Jones

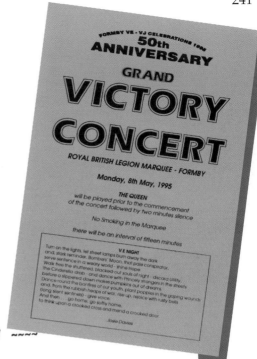

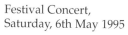

Festival Concert,
Saturday, 6th May 1995

Above: Civic guests including
Sir Malcolm Thornton, M.P. and
Lady Rosemary Thornton, and
Col. Mary Creagh

Thanksgiving Parade,
Air Cadets

Thanksgiving Parade,
St. John's Ambulance

Left: Thanksgiving
Parade,
Army Cadets

Below: Senior
Citizens' Party,
Friday 5th
May 1995

Victory Concert –
Evacuees

Victory Concert –
Landgirls

Festival Parade,
Saturday 6th May 1995

Fire engine in the
Festival Parade,
Saturday 6th May
1995

The Bay Horse
tractor in the
Festival Parade,
Saturday 6th
May 1995

"Tank" decorated
by New Road
residents in the
Festival Parade,
Saturday
6th May 1995

OUR DICKENSIAN DAY

The sound of carols filled the air,
Fine voices raised on high,
The strains of brass accompanying
As all the folk passed by.

The swish of ladies sweeping skirts,
Black toppers for the men,
And urchin boys with grimy face,
Just like it was back then.

Charles Dickens walked amongst us all
Twirling his regal cane,
While handbells rang in harmony
Uncaring of the rain.

The Southport Swords great morris team
With bells a-jingling loud
Competed with the clogging girls
Attracting all the crowd.

The festive stalls down Chapel Lane
Brought back a former age
As hosts of people all flocked in
To turn back history's page.

The butcher's roasts, the boy scouts' soup,
The baker's pies and puds,
The girl with tangerines and nuts,
The children came in floods.

Two noble horses, big and strong,
Dragged Santa on his sleigh
To wave and shout and ho, ho, ho,
Prepared for Christmas Day.

And as the evening darkness fell
The happy festive throng
All gathered round the Christmas tree
And raised their voice in song.

And as the day had first begun
It ended just the same
To celebrate our Saviour's birth
And praise his holy name.

DICKENSIAN DAY
(Photos by Ron Ellis)

Left: Compere Roger Kelly, 2005

Above: Judy Hitchcock, Paddy Dyson and Sally Williams on RDA stall, 2005

Help The Aged –
Best Dressed Window 2004

DICKENSIAN DAY

Dickensian Day, 14th December 1996, Bob and Hilda Cannon and Dave Campbell

Eric Acland and Freda Granagan,
Delahunty's, 14th December 1996
which closed September 2005

P.C. Dougie Knight and Eirlis Armstrong, the
first Dickensian Day, 14th December 1996

DICKENSIAN DAY

Maghull Parish Handbell Ringers

One Man Band - Dan Budimir

The big Rock Climbing Wall

DICKENSIAN DAY

Above: Argomeols Clog Dancers

Sue Farquharson on
Clatterbridge Cancer Care stall

DICKENSIAN DAY

Above:
The Barrel Organ

Left:
Southport Model
Engineering
steam railway

Left:
Compere David Davies,
local M.P. Claire Curtis-
Thomas. and Dickensian Day
Committee Member Stacey
Garland, 2006

DICKENSIAN DAY

OUR FOOTBALL GROUND

For very nearly eighty years
We've had a football ground
Superbly centred in Brows Lane
Where football skills abound.

Throughout the years the pitch has seen
Some very famous names
Who graced the hallowed turf in style
In marvellous football games.

But that was all long long ago
When our great football team
Were heroes to the villagers
Who through the gates would stream.

And all this was made possible
When Jonathan Formby
Allowed his land for football use
In perpetuity.

Now his descendants own the land,
In exile from their roots,
Uninterested in Formby life,
The ground, or football boots.

And sadly, so it seems to us,
No one could care a toss
About the old man's solemn pledge
Or what will be our loss.

And though we've always played the game,
We find it very hard
That when we think we ought to win
We're shown that bright red card.

Happily through the generosity of the Moores family (the Freshfield Foundation) who purchased the ground the crisis was averted and the Club re-located to near the River Alt.

* * * *

THE FRESHFIELD ROUNDABOUT GARAGE

Way back in nineteen-thirty-eight
Our by-pass was laid down
To speed the route from Liverpool
To Southport's seaside town.

And with it came the service needs
For petrol, oil, and air,
Which led to Isaac Buckley's plan
To build his garage there.

The Freshfield Roundabout Garage
Strategically was placed
To fill the Ford and Morris tanks
As the by-pass road they paced.

Until the German Luftwaffe,
One dreadful war-time night,
Let fly a high explosive bomb
On the Freshfield Garage site.

Amazingly no one was killed,
The Garage, though, was gone,
But one day it would be re-built
And life would carry on.

And that was how it all worked out,
Another Garage grew,
Expanding with the passing years
As Formby expanded too.

Through the days of Freddy Allen,
With petrol at four-and-six,
To the escalating prices
That modern times would fix.

Now the Garage comes full circle,
Demolished once again,
This time by high powered business men,
And not a German plane.

And risen from the dust and bricks
A grand oasis came
To satisfy the every need
The motorist could name.

Light years from that Freshfield Garage,
Once Isaac Buckley's dream,
Stands the futuristic vision
Of a petrol company's team.

* * * *

In 1999 government plans threatened the reduction of our full time fire service to part time. Overwhelming public and council opposition eventually saw the proposal dropped.

OUR FIRE SERVICE

My Dad was once a fireman
Back in nineteen-forty-six,
But that was not his proper job
From eight a.m. till six.

You see, we had no full time crew,
But only volunteers,
Who were on call if fires occurred
In those past post-war years.

And in each volunteer's house
A warning bell was placed,
Which belted out a piercing ring
When emergency was faced.

In case the men were not at home
The air-raid siren wailed,
And men would leave their work or club
And to the station trailed.

Some came on bikes or tractors then,
Or ran with racing legs
To the station by the factory
Where they packed the crates of eggs.

And each man got a call out fee,
The princely sum – five bob,
Their training was one night a week
When they'd finished their main job.

Then Formby grew and the station moved,
We got our full-time crew,
Professional fire fighters now,
Expert at what they do.

Full fire protection round the clock,
Paid by our Council tax,
The same as every other town,
But now faced with the axe.

And though it's not quite like my Dad,
They plan no night time shift,
Once more our men will be on call –
But just Formby – get my drift?

Yes, again WE'RE being targeted
To lose what bit we've got
To save some dosh to benefit
Another Sefton pot.

Enough's enough, our firemen stay
Through day time and through night,
We need them and we pay for them,
Their service is our right.

* * * *

TWO MINUTES – FORMBY,
11th *November 2002*

They gave their all that we might live,
Young men in the prime of life,
The living Hell of two World Wars,
Unimagined battling strife.

Never forget their sacrifice,
If only one day each year,
When we keep two minutes silence,
Grateful for all we hold dear.

So on the dot of eleven
The bustling Village fell still,
Bowed heads remembered the fallen
In the sunshine's autumn chill.

One minute into the silence
A girl and a man strolled by,
Ignoring the silence around them
And those with a tear in their eye.

She was a girl in her twenties,
He was about forty-five,
Selfishly uncomprehending,
No thanks that they both were alive.

For those names on our War Memorial
All paid the ultimate cost,
Not one returned to his village,
Much more than two minutes they lost.

And whether the Somme or the Desert,
We'll never repay the debt
To those who gave us our peace time,
Which is why we must never forget.

* * * *

OUR LOCAL ELECTIONS

Election time is coming round
And that means we should vote
And put in power someone we think
Will listen and take note
Of all the things which matter most
To us who pay the tax
Which every year gets more and more
So here then are some facts.

Let's start with our flooded road ways,
Leaves blocking all the drains,
No gangs of men to sweep them up
Or tidy up the lanes,
Those roads with neat grass verges too
Just look a dreadful sight
When some cowboy on his mower
Flings rubbish left and right.

The newly mown grass verge, Priesthouse Lane/Kenyons Lane corner, August 2004

We needed a zebra crossing
To traverse Chapel Lane,
Just a simple zebra crossing
In keeping with the Lane,
Instead we got great traffic lights
And ugly railings too,
And forty-thousand smackeroos
Went sailing down the loo.

Then the Council Offices shock
To sell the whole bang lot
Against the public's wishes for
The best asset we'd got,
Such blinkered views and arrogance
Spurned thousands here that care
Who proffered good alternatives
Which all of us could share.

Next came the promised swimming pool
And traffic problems too,
No consultation for the route
With plans just bulldozed through,
And though the pool's been funded by
The Moores Foundation clan
We've still to raise a whopping sum
To manage Sefton's plan.

And lastly the Parish Council,
A worrying debate,
With fears of more bureaucracy
To simply duplicate
Another tier of government
Without a guarantee
That anything will really change
In the services we see.

And all these things have come about
'Cause those we voted in
Care more for party politics
Than the place they all live in,
And how that's ever going to change
Is difficult to say
But fresh new blood would be a start
When we vote on polling day.

* * * *

FORMBY FIELDS

Once there was a cottage
In a shady leafy lane,
Beside a dusty footpath
Turned muddy with the rain.

An ancient sylvan idyll
With every kind of tree,
The home of birds and squirrels
A joy for all to see.

A ditch along the footpath
Drained excess rain away,
And children fished for jacksharps
In times of yesterday.

But that was all so long ago
Before the mushroom farm
When Formby was a village
Enchanting in its charm.

The cottage days were numbered
When the owner sadly died,
No more the well kept gardens,
No more the countryside.

Now Frog Lane's gone forever
In the madness of the age
Where progress is the master
And railings are the rage.

A spanking brand new footpath,
So soulless and so bland,
The pride of our officialdom,
To them superbly grand.

And only bricks and mortar
Now dominate the lane
Where once a dusty footpath
Turned muddy with the rain.

* * * *

ALL THE SAME
(Tune: Amazing Grace)

Churches Together in Formby is an active ecumenical group which encourages church unity within our community. The following poem was sung as a hymn at the combined service in Our Lady of Compassion Church in Holy Week 1994.

We all are individuals,
We've all a different name,
We all have varying kinds of faith,
And yet we're all the same.

We all believe in just one God
And that his son became
A human like the rest of us
To show us we're the same.

And as he led his ministry
He cured the blind and lame,
And showed his deepest love for us
So we could be the same.

We know he died upon the cross
To save from sin and shame
A people so divided
Who could be all the same.

And with his resurrection
His triumph we proclaim
That black or white or rich or poor
To him we're all the same.

And through the gospels we have learned
The reasons why he came
And why we ought to follow him
And try to be the same.

So joining all together
United in our aim
He'll bind us ever closer for
He knows we're all the same.

Anglican Bishop of Liverpool David Sheppard with the Roman Catholic Deacons from Our Lady's Church, Rev. Fred Cook and his wife, Theresa, and Rev. Paul Collins and his wife, Mary, at Holy Trinity Redgate Church, March 1995

Representatives of 'CHURCHES TOGETHER IN FORMBY' with the Bishop of Warrington, Good Friday Service in Formby Village, 1998

THE SEFTON MAYOR

Once Formby had a chairman,
And Bootle had a mayor,
And so did sunny Southport,
Each with a Town Hall there.

And then we all were Sefton
With just one civic head,
And all these little boroughs
Joined a bigger one instead.

So we became united
With a comprehensive mayor
Representing all of us
And mingling everywhere.

A brand new chain of office
Was needed to define
The new created M.B.C.
In appropriate design.

This splendid badge of office
Made of silver and of gold
Enhanced the mayoral finery
Of those who office hold.

And now our mayor resplendent
In his flowing robes and chain
Looks a fitting representative
To greet the royal train.

For we've had royal visits
And civic dignatories galore
Bringing kudos to our borough
And glory to our shore.

And the Lord Mayor of the borough
Could be you or could be me
If we became elected
To serve the community.

So be a local councillor,
A pretty thankless job,
Always in the firing line
And at the mercy of the mob.

But if you somehow do survive
And stick it out for years
You one day might become Lord Mayor
And well deserve those cheers.

* * * *

In March 1996 the entire country was shocked at the tragedy of Dunblane, and though the following poem has no connection whatever with Formby I am including it as a personal indulgence as I was so moved by the events that I would like to include it as a reminder that, just like Hillsborough, Dunblane touched the hearts of us all and will never be forgotten.

DUNBLANE

The crispness of the winter's day,
The laughing children's sound,
The crunch of footsteps off to school
Upon the snow clad ground.

All ushered in the school hall gym,
These five-year-olds skip round,
Bright eager faces thrilled to see
The magic snow clad ground.

Each new experience of play
This P.E. class they'd found,
In safety from the ice outside
Upon the snow clad ground.

Excitement in their innocence
Crushed by an evil sound
As through the door burst wickedness,
In from the snow clad ground.

A messenger from Hades came,
Who Lucifer had crowned,
And slaughtered all those innocents
Who'd loved that snow clad ground.

In mad deranged insanity
The murderous gun shots sound
As sixteen tiny hearts are stilled
Beside that snow clad ground.

Unspeakable depravity
That left a nation drowned
Beneath the tears of disbelief
All round that snow clad ground.

The whole land weeps in shock and shame,
A minute's silence bound
The hearts and minds of all the world
Who saw that blood soaked ground.

And sixteen families' lives are wrecked,
No greater grief is found,
Those tiny souls now rest in heaven,
Not 'neath the snow clad ground.

My final poem is a tribute to Muriel Sibley whose death in 1993 was a great loss to Formby. Her generosity and encouragement was instrumental in starting me on my journey into print with the combination of her drawings and my poems, and I shall always be grateful to her.

* * * *

MURIEL SIBLEY (2)

She came in nineteen-forty-nine
With her husband and son, Paul,
To a place she'd never heard of
And didn't know at all.

From the top of Formby Station bridge
She saw banks of daffodils
And the pinewoods standing to the west
Shielding our sandy hills.

And she knew in that first moment
That she loved us right away,
And never stopped that love affair
Until her dying day.

She found their dream home in Brows Lane
And her adventure then began
Exploring all our lanes and fields
And how the ditches ran.

She talked to all the old folk
And learnt about our past,
And delved into the history books
And local facts amassed.

She saw our landscape changing
As the building firms appeared,
But she got there first and captured it
Before it disappeared.

She cycled round our village
Recording every scene,
The farms, the shops, the shore, the life,
Over every inch she'd been.

Through the fifties and the sixties
When our village blew apart
She quietly kept on painting
Producing brilliant works of art.

Her art shows and her slide shows
Of a gracious lady's skills
Created untold interest
Illustrating planners' ills.

And so she still continued
Almost until the last,
Giving pleasure in abundance
With her pictures of the past.

And all this lifelong talent
She used solely just for us,
No thought of personal gain or wealth,
No outward show or fuss.

And now she's sadly left us
With a massive gaping hole
That never, ever can be filled
By any other soul.

But she's also left us memories
And a priceless treasure chest
Of the finest record in the land
Of a place she loved the best.

Muriel Sibley with Joan Rimmer in January 1993 at her final art exhibition in Holy Trinity Hall.
She died the following October, aged 80.

CHANGE AT HALSALL LANE/SCHOOL LANE

Before demolition

After demolition

After reconstruction

'Freshfields' Leonard Cheshire Home Garden Party, 1981

'Much Ado About Nothing' at The Leonard Cheshire Home

The Big Toddle in the Park 2006 (Churches Together)
Mayor of Sefton Tommy Mann with Mayoress Jean Lilley

(Photos by Ron Ellis)

Kath Williams, stallholder at Formby Theatre Club's Christmas Fair at the Luncheon Club

Formby Village – new doctors surgery, 2006

(Photos by Ron Ellis)

Brows Lane with the shops which replaced the first Holy Trinity School

The corner of The Village and Elbow Lane showing the restaurant which
replaced Charter's Butchers

(Photos by Ron Ellis)

Formby Village with the shops which replaced the last two remaining cottages

Marks & Spencer, November 2005 (moved to Cloisters site in March 2007).
Holy Trinity Church is in the background

(Photos by Ron Ellis)

Tony Higginson (Manager) and Jon Russell (Deputy Manager)
outside Pritchard's Books, January 2007

SKETCHES OF OLD FORMBY BY ERIC B. GERRARD

The Homesteader run by Mr. & Mrs. Nimmo
(now The Beacons development)

The Old School House in School Lane
(now the Halil Balti Indian restaurant)

Vistalawn at the corner of Gore's Lane and
Old Town Lane (now a doctor's surgery)

Postscript

The success of the GREEN BAG SCHEME became a pointer towards the government's ever expanding mission for waste recycling and the decision was made to replace all Sefton's plastic bags with wheelie bins.

It was a decision supposedly made as the result of a questionnaire to the public which few seem to recall ever seeing. However, the plans were announced to take effect from June 2007 amidst concerns of those unable to handle the larger bins or those with limited access to the rear of their properties.

Most people are aware of the importance of recycling, and in Formby have been praised for their efforts, but strong opposition has been shown towards the wheelie bins on sound financial, hygienic and even environmental grounds which even at this late stage deserve serious consideration before the plan is implemented if only for the sake of the adverse visual impact of such bins which in many cases will adorn the frontages of homes.

The present system has worked efficiently and well to overall satisfaction and, with the provision of extra plastic bags, could continue to do so at far less cost than that proposed.

THE POWERHOUSE

The degenerate state of the Powerhouse was eventually resolved when legal orders were issued for a mammoth clean-up of the site involving major structural and demolition work by the owners, Ovenden Investments Limited, based in the Cayman Islands.

The plan would appear to indicate future residential development to be an ever more likely prospect and therefore the end of the site's greenbelt status.

Photographs by Natasha Robson

* * * *

FORMBY POOL

An announcement was finally made that the long awaited Swimming Pool was to open on Saturday January 27th 2007, three years behind its scheduled date and over thirty years since its original inception. It was made clear that the Pool, which will also contain a gymnasium and a café, is not a Sefton Leisure Centre but is under the care and administration of the Formby Pool Trust.

Photos by Ron Ellis

FORMBY POOL
February 2007

* * * *

CHURCHES TOGETHER IN FORMBY

Churches Together in Formby held possibly its most ambitious community event in Formby Village at 11am on Saturday December 16th 2006 when the greatest story ever told came to life in the form of a Nativity Play with a cast of over a hundred.

A 45ft. articulated lorry formed the inn and stable at the Elbow Lane end and the action took place along the length of the Village which had been closed to traffic.

The dialogue had been pre-recorded and all actors mimed to the soundtrack, making every word audible to the throngs of people lining both sides of Chapel Lane.

Sheep, horses, goats, a donkey called William and a beautiful two month old baby added realism to the spectacle with the stunning appearance of the Angel Gabriel on the overhead balcony of Grant's Wine Bar! Quite superb and a most fitting start to Christmas 2006 and yet another example of the great community spirit that prevails in Formby.

Photos courtesy Formby Times